Hilary of Poitiers:
A Study in Theological Method

European University Studies
Europäische Hochschulschriften
Publications Universitaires Européennes

Series XXIII

Theology

Reihe XXIII   Série XXIII

Theologie
Théologie

Vol./Band 108

PETER LANG
Bern · Frankfurt am Main · Las Vegas

G. M. Newlands

Hilary of Poitiers:
A Study in Theological Method

PETER LANG
Bern · Frankfurt am Main · Las Vegas

©Peter Lang Ltd., Berne (Switzerland) 1978
Successor of Herbert Lang & Co. Ltd., Berne

ISBN 3-261-03133-6

Printed by Fotokop Wilhelm Weihert KG, Darmstadt

To my Father and my Mother

CONTENTS

PREFACE

Saint Hilary of Poitiers is perhaps the most neglected of the great
Patristic theologians. He played a major role in the theological and
political conflicts of the fourth century. Later his writings were to
be admired and quoted by such diverse thinkers as Peter Lombard, Luther
and Barth. Yet there has been, at least until very recently, remarkably
little detailed analysis of the biblical interpretation which provides
the central strand of his theological method.

Hilary's early work on St. Matthew's Gospel is almost the first
extant commentary in the Latin West. The first section of this book
contains an analysis of the literary form of the work, including for
the first time a survey of the development of the commentary as a
literary form. In succeeding chapters the development of Hilary's
exegesis in his later writings, in the De Trinitate and the treatise
on the Psalms is examined, with particular attention to the interplay
of hermeneutical and more strictly theological concerns, of exegetical
technique and Christological debate. Beginning from the traditional
Western exegetical techniques in the work on St. Matthew, Hilary
developed, with the aid of the doctrinal concentration in the De
Trinitate, a greater versatility in the use of new techniques, some from
the eastern tradition, the latest stages being exemplified in the work
on the Psalms.

The concluding section attempts, on the basis of the particular
example of Hilary's work, a critical evaluation of the role of patristic
material in the ongoing work of contemporary theology, in this case with
reference to the still intractable problem of the precise uses of the
Bible and of biblical exegesis in theology.

The volume contains detailed discussions of both historical and theological issues, and deals with questions of both patristic and modern theology. This reflects the author's belief that theology, though it certainly has its own distinctive concerns and questions, is better pursued in dialogue with other disciplines than in a supposedly isolated realm of pure theological thought. At the same time, it has been well said that historical research alone will produce, and indeed ought to produce, nothing but history, and that theological considerations have to be imported by those who wish to do theology: history is in any event capable of innumerable different interpretations, and it is unwise to offer historical judgments on 'the meaning of history'. This means that though some of the material in this study will be primarily of interest to the specialist student of the history and literature of the fourth century Latin West, the overall purpose of the work is to explore basic theological issues which continue to be in question, though the forms of the disputes and their cultural contexts vary widely. This combination of concerns may be at once of course a source of illumination and a snare and delusion. The strangeness of the less familiar context in the past may lead us to sharpen our critical perspectives in tackling the problems of the present, or it may lead to confusing anachronisms of various sorts. In addition, there is no reason to suppose that all or even many of the features of one period are to be discovered, far less reproduced or repristinated in another period.

In dealing with issues which involve cultural traditions widely separated in time and raise questions of history, philosophy and theology, one is all too conscious that mistakes are likely to be made and that there are always new avenues opening up which ought to be explored. One

hopes to make some sort of contribution to the continuing scholarly process: granted that there may be no definitive solutions it seems reasonable to expect of scholarship a cumulative process of the acquisition of
knowledge. But there comes a time when it seems wise to seek the benefit
of public criticism before returning to further exploration of the issues.

This is a study of influences, sources and techniques. It is neither
an assessment of Hilary's theology as a whole nor a portrait of the bishop
as an historical figure. The principal architect of the victory of the
Western Church over Arianism and the courageous defender of the claims of
Church over Emperor remains firmly in the background: though it may be
hoped that some at least of the intellectual springs of the action of the
public figure are brought to light. We shall not attempt, either, to cover
all of Hilary's literary or even his exegetical work equally; the specific
lines of our enquiry will lead us to pay more attention to the commentary
on St. Matthew than to the work on the Trinity and on the Psalms.

It would of course be perfectly possible to discuss the role of the
Bible in theology today without reference to patristic study, especially
in such a detailed form. But quite apart from the value of the inter-
disciplinary dialogue indicated above, if we are to understand the complex
heritage of the Christian tradition as a whole, it is desirable that there
should be the maximum possible mutual understanding and comprehension
between students of the more classical sort of patristic study and students
of modern theology.

This book attempts to make a modest contribution towards that task of
understanding. It arose out of a doctoral dissertation submitted in
Edinburgh in 1970 and based on work done in the universities of Heidelberg,
Paris, Zurich and Cambridge. For guidance on the original submission I

would like to thank Professor T.F. Torrance and Mr.D.F. Wright. In the
intervening period I have come to look at the issues from a rather different perspective. In the pursuit of my studies I have been indebted, for
much encouragement and many kindnesses, to a large number of people. Only
a few can be mentioned here. To my Edinburgh teachers in classics and
divinity, and to my long-suffering colleagues and students in Glasgow and
Cambridge I am deeply grateful. To Professors Alec Cheyne and Hans von
Campenhausen in particular my debt will always be immense. Sincere thanks
are due too to the Trustees of the Bethune-Baker Fund in the University of
Cambridge, especially to Professor Geoffrey Lampe, and to the British
Academy for the generous contributions towards costs which have made possible the publication of this book. Lastly, my thanks are due to my
wife, who has lived patiently with Hilary for a decade, and to Mr. and
Mrs. Gerald Hedge, for their transformation of an impossible typescript
into a readable text.

Cambridge
1978

List of Abbreviations

(excluding some standard abbreviations
listed in L & S, LSJ, RGG, etc.)

BZNW	Beihefte zur Zeitschrift für neutestamentliche Wissenschaft.
CC	Corpus Christianorum.
C. Const.	Contra Constantium Imperatorem (Hilary).
CHLGEMP	Cambridge History of Later Greek and Early Mediaeval Philosophy.
Comm.	Commentary.
CSEL	Corpus Scriptorum Ecclesiasticorum Latinorum.
CUA	Catholic University of America (Washington).
DDC	De Doctrina Christiana (Augustine).
De Syn.	De Synodis (Hilary).
De Trin.	De Trinitate (Hilary).
EE	Evangelische Evangelienauslegung (Ebeling).
EKL	Evangelisches Kirchenlexikon.
Et. Aug.	Études Augustiniennes.
GCS	Die griechischen christlichen Schriftsteller der ersten drei Jahrhunderte.
GS	Grundfragen Systematischer Theologie (Pannenberg).
HTR	Harvard Theological Review.
In Matt./ In Mt.	In Matthaeum (Hilary).
In Ps.	In Psalmos (Hilary).
JSS	Journal of Semitic Studies.
JTS	Journal of Theological Studies.
L & S	Lewis and Short. A Latin Dictionary.

LSJ	Liddell and Scott. A Greek-English Lexicon, revised by Sir Henry Jones.
NPNF	A Select Library of Nicene and Post-Nicene Fathers of the Christian Church.
PG	Patrologia Graeca (Migne).
PL	Patrologia Latina (Migne).
PRE	Realencyklopädie für protestantische Theologie und Kirche.
PWK	Pauly-Wissowa-Kroll. Realencyklopädie der Klassischen Altertumswissenschaft.
RAC	Reallexikon für Antike und Christentum.
RGG	Die Religion in Geschichte und Gegenwart (3rd edition).
RSR	Revue des Sciences Religieuses.
SBBAW	Sitzungsberichte der Bayerischen Akademie der Wissenschaften.
SC	Sources Chrétiennes.
St. Patr.	Studia Patristica.
TLL	Thesaurus Linguae Latinae.
TLZ	Theologische Literaturzeitung.
TTK	Tidsskrift for Theologie og Kirke.
TU	Texte und Untersuchungen.
Vet. Chr.	Vetera Christianorum.
WA	Weimarer Ausgabe.
WCC	World Council of Churches.
WS	Wiener Studien.
ZThK	Zeitschrift für Theologie und Kirche.

1.   Introductory: Hilary and the

hermeneutical problem

Hilary of Poitiers's first extant work is his commentary on St. Matthew's gospel, and all his later theological work is intimately connected, even in the so-called 'historical' works, with the interpretation of scripture.

Throughout the history of theology, and particularly in the patristic period, there has been, with some notable exceptions, a constant interconnection and mutual influence between the process of the exegesis of scripture, the results of that process, and the systematic development of theology. The de facto presence of and even the need for some degree of interconnection are not a matter of serious dispute today.

In the past, however, and at no time more acutely than in the present, there have of course, been great differences of opinion and practice concerning the nature of these interconnections.[1]

To explore these interconnections in a theologian of the early church will in itself provide no solution to the problem in the present. If we analyse that theologian simply in the light of modern discussion, the result may well tell us little that we did not already know. If we seek to analyse the connections in their historical context, then we may reach some new understanding of that period, which though bearing the marks of our own age may provide a new piece of evidence by enabling us to view related problems in a different cultural tradition. But this will still contribute little to our contemporary theological concerns unless we can make comparative theological assessments of the different contexts, while still recog-

1. cf. the reports on 'Scripture and Tradition' of the group on biblical hermeneutics and patristics in 'New Directions in Faith and Order, Bristol 1967' (WCC, 1968), and Louvain 1971. (N.B. Where not given in the text, details of bibliographical references may be found in the Bibliography.)

nising the significance for the method we choose to follow of the historical differences.

The more precise purpose of this study is to take Hilary as a major patristic theologian and to examine matters relevant to the use and place of the Bible in his work, that is to say the nature, background and development of the exegetical process itself, its place in his thought as a whole, and the interconnections between theology and exegesis in detail, in terms both of method and conclusions.

We shall then consider briefly the value of information gained from this type of study for the assessment of contemporary theological problems, in the field chosen here, of the interrelation of exegesis and theology.[2]

The progress of work on Hilary's exegesis to date

The choice of Hilary as our subject complicates this study in one important respect. Compared with, for example, the amount of published material relevant to matters of exegesis and theology in Luther, the work already done on Hilary is still in its infancy, and at the present rate of progress it will be several centuries before many of the issues discussed below can be regarded as established with a comparable degree of certainty. But this does not rule out our present exercise, granted its provisional and limited character. We can only begin from the prevailing state of affairs.

2. The sharp dichotomy between historical and systematic theology which has characterised much research in this century appears to me to have been to the advantage of neither branch of study.

Previous studies, some of which will be discussed later, consist of
(1) attempts to establish the dating and context of the exegetical works,
(2) textual studies, still very incomplete, (3) analysis of basic theological themes and the tracing of their historical background - in which the
diversity of speculation indicates the paucity of solid evidence, (4) analysis of passages dealing with the different levels of meaning in scripture
(especially for the Tractatus in Psalmos: which we shall refer to as In
Ps) (5) for the De Trinitate (hereafter De Trin.) apart from study of the
theology, some work on the role of biblical quotations in the argument and
in the anti-Arian controversy, and (6) some recent investigations, partly
simultaneous with this study, of the theological background of the commentary in Matthaeum (hereafter In Mt.).

Considered more precisely, previous study may be grouped under
(a) text and (b) interpretation.

(a) The MSS tradition for Hilary is exceptionally old and good. The
best discussion is that of Zingerle in his Praefatio to the In Psalmos
(CSEL 22). A useful report on the most important of the MSS, D 182 Basil-
icanus (c. 510) was given by A. Wilmart in the Festschrift for E.K. Rand,
pp. 293ff, 'L' Odyssee du manuscrit de San Pietro qui referme les oeuvres
de Saint Hilaire'. The gist of Zingerle's discussion is reproduced by
Gastaldi, pp. x-xii. A scientific account of the text of the In Matthaeum
and De Trinitate must await the editions of Doignon (SC) and Hanslik (CSEL)
respectively. The text of the Tractatus Mysteriorum is ably discussed by
Brisson (SC) pp. 61-70.[3] Printed editions begin with that of Leonard
Pachel, Milan 1489. Improvements and commentary were added by the Paris

3. cf. too the list of MSS in P.L. 9 219-20.

edition of 1510, by Erasmus in 1523, and by a series of editions (listed with descriptions in Migne) up to 1789, of which the best, by the Maurists (1693 and 1730) was the basis of the Migne text of 1844. Zingerle produced a critical edition of the Psalms in 1896 (CSEL/22) and Feder of some of the historical fragments in 1916 (CSEL 65). The Tractatus Mysteriorum was edited excellently by Brisson in 1947 (SC). New editions of the De Trinitate (Hanslik-CSEL) and of the In Matthaeum (Doignon) are in preparation.

(b) The first modern student of Hilary's exegesis was Richard Simon, in his 'Histoire critique du Vieux Testament (Paris 1680)' 439-59 and 'Histoire critique des principeaux commentateurs du Nouveau Testament 'Rotterdam 1693) pp.125ff.

On the Psalms, Simon follows Erasmus in seeing the widespread influence of Origen and deploring this. 'Cette methode n'est pas exacte: outre que sous pretexte de donner un sens spirituel en va trop avant, et l'on donne ses imaginations pour les spiritualities'. On the exegesis of the New Testament, he noted that the De Trinitate pays more attention to the literal sense of the text than the In Matthaeum. For him the commentary on Romans by Hilary the Deacon (Ambrosiaster) is also by Hilary of Poitiers.

The fundamental monograph of J.H. Reinkens, (Schaffhausen 1864) superseded all previous work, and long provided, along with Loofs' article in PRE[3] (largely dependent on it) the best introduction. At the same time Diestel added some insight on the In Psalmos in his excellent 'Geschichte des AT in der christlichen Kirche' (1869) pp.74-80, as did E.W. Watson rather later in the excellent introduction to his translation of the De Trin. and three of the psalms (NPNF 1898) cf. pp.xl-xliv.

3.   cf. too the list of MSS in P.L.9, 219-20.

After a long gap much light has been thrown upon the exegetical situation recently, for the De Trinitate by P. Loffler (1958) (esp. p. 85ff) and by Martinez Sierra (1964), for the In Matthaeum by M. Simonetti (1964), W. Wille (1968) and above all by J. Doignon (1971), and for the In Psalmos by Nestor Gastaldi (1969).[4] Hilary's theology as a whole is well analysed by C.F.A. Borchardt (1966) and, briefly but excellently, by C. Kannengiesser (1969).

Diestel's work superseded that of such predecessors as Rosenmüller and Schrockh (Hist. Eccles. 12. 252f) and often follows Simon: cf. 78n. on the In Ps. 'Die Auslegung eilt gern von dem rein exegetischen Tenor zu dogmatisierende Paranese. Er verrath sich als Schüler des Origenes, doch ohne dessen Geist. Bemüht er sich bisweilen, den Unterschied der Testamente hervortreten zu lassen, so bleibt doch der eigentliche Offenbarungsinhalt in beiden derselbe.' Simon we recall followed Erasmus. This example may serve for hundreds to illustrate the striking tendency to repetition, not seldom vain repetition, which characterises the history of Hilariusforschung and is not unlike the formulaic epithets which in heroic verse link the present with the mist of time - pius Aeneas: imitator Hilarius etc.

The Background to Hilary's work

Before turning to an analysis of the structure of the text, we shall set them briefly in their context of Hilary's own life and background. The details of Hilary's biography have been described often enough. We repeat only the salient facts for our present purpose.[5]

4. cf. note on p.140.
5. cf. Loofs, Borchardt, Wille etc.

Hilary was born in Limonum, later Pictavi and today, Poitiers, some time during the second decade of the fourth century.[6] The high standard of education reflected in his works indicates that he came from a prosperous family. His parents were probably not Christian,[7] and the date of his baptism, like the date of his episcopal consecration, remains unknown. It is not known where he went to school, but the nearest and most likely place for him to have acquired the sound classical education which he possessed would at that time have been Bordeaux.[8] At the synod of Arles (353) he appears to have played no major role, and this would suggest that, if already a bishop, he had not long been consecrated at that time.[9]

In the same year (353) Constantius came to power in the West and began to support the Arians, thus bringing to a head the conflict between Arian and anti-Arian parties in the Latin church. Two years later Constantius brought together the synod of Milan, which exiled the old leaders of the Nicene party and so brought Hilary to the head of the Nicene cause. Now with other bishops in Gaul, Hilary dissociated himself officially from Saturninus of Arles, Ursacius and Valens.[10] Saturninus then presided over a synod at Beziers (356) which condemned again Athanasius, only Hilary and one other bishop dissenting.[11] This was enough to set in train the

6. cf. Jerome, Comm. in Gal. 2.3. 'Gallus ipse et Pictavis natus'.
7. cf. esp. the account of his conversion highly stylised, in De Trin. 1.1-14.'
8. cf. below p.78f.
9. This is also the force of the aliquantisper of the famous sentence from De Synodis 91. Regeneratus pridem et in episcopatu aliquantisper manens, fidem Nicaenum numquam nisi exsulaturus audivi.
10. c. Const.2. (PL 10,579D)
11. Ibid, (PL 10,579A)

emperor's banishment of Hilary, (the precise details and official grounds of which are unknown).[12]

Most of Hilary's literary work dates from the period after his banishment. Before then however, he had written the first part at least of the historical work 'Adversus Valentem et Ursacium'. He had also written the commentary In Matthaeum. The detailed evidence for the dating of this work will be discussed below. Though he probably knew something of the Arian controversy at the time of writing, he was clearly not as acutely concerned with it as he was to be later in the De Trinitate.[13] No reference to exile appears in the work. As we shall see in detail in a later section, the influence of Origen and of Greek exegesis is much less direct than in the later In Psalmos and even the De Trinitate. The lack of mention of the exile, coupled with the comparatively mild influence of Greek exegesis and of the Arian controversy suggests a date after 353, when the controversy began to be discussed widely, but before the events of 355.

Exile produced the challenge and stimulation from eastern theology which was to make Hilary a major theologian. Here he wrote the De Trinitate, the separate books being spread over a considerable period, beginning from 356/7. Here too came the De Synodis, in which he attempted to link the eastern 'homoiousian' and the western 'homoousians' against the 'homoeans'. Slightly later he produced the 'Ad Constantium' in which he sought to defend his position and bring the emperor round to the true faith, and the 'Contra Constantium', in which he attacks the emperor as the Antichrist.

12. cf. Wille 13 and 237f.
13. cf. below p.

8

The precise reason for the end of the exile is not clear,[14] but Hilary
was back in Gaul around the turn of the year 360-361.[15] The fall of Constantius and the rise of Julian cleared the way for fresh efforts against
the Arians. To this period belong the 'Ad praefectum Sallustium sive contra Dioscurum' and the two tracts directed, without success, against the
Homoean Auxentius of Milan.

Hilary returned in his last years to the predominantly exegetical
concerns of his first work. To this period belongs the 'Tractatus super
psalmos', extended meditations, which as we shall see, were probably first
delivered in church and later put together to be read. Towards the end of
the meditation on the Psalms he also produced his 'Liber Mysteriorum', an
allegorical meditation on Genesis in the manner of the work on the psalms.[16]

Apart from these, Hilary also wrote hymns, though not all of those in
his name are authentic.[17] He may have written further exegetical works
and even compiled a book of liturgies,[18] but the evidence for such works
is only fragmentary. The exact date of his death remains unknown, but it
was at the end of 367 or the beginning of 368.[19]

14. He may have returned without permission cf. c. Const.11, 'fugere
     mihi sub Nerone licuit'.
15. Wille makes the very reasonable suggestion of 361-2 for the former
     and 364-5 for the latter.
16. cf. below and the excellent introduction by Brisson.
17. The best text is that of Bulst.
18. cf. the discussion of Wille op.cit. p.16f.
19. According to Jerome (Chron. CCS 47,245) and Gregory of Tours (hist.
     Franc. 1.39) who is probably dependent on him, Hilary died in the
     fourth year of the reign of Valentinian and Valens. For the details
     cf. Borchardt op.cit. 183; cf. too now A.J. Goemans' article 'La date
     de la Mort de saint Hilaire' in 'Hilaire et son temps' 107-11
     G. prefers 1 Nov. 367 but provides no fresh evidence.

Exegesis was done by Hilary in three connected but clearly distinguishable contexts. These only correspond to the early, middle and late periods into which both his fortunes as a churchman and his literary career may be usefully divided. The considerable connection between the periods reflects the fact that probably not much more than a decade separates his earliest and latest extant works.

The first of these periods, represented by the commentary on St. Matthew, involves continuous exposition, commentary and theological interpretation of the gospel narrative in groups of verses, corresponding roughly in appearance, if not in method, to a modern exercise in exegesis and biblical theology. It is the first extant commentary on a complete book of the Bible from the western Church.

The second period, represented by the De Trinitate, involves the use of argument from and exegesis of the Bible in the exposition of doctrine, corresponding roughly to modern systematic theology. It has been shown that much of the exegesis is done in direct refutation of Arian argument from scripture.

The third period, represented by the tractatus on the Psalms, involves the exposition of scripture in a devotional context, for the moral and scriptural edification of Hilary's congregations, and would correspond to some modern devotional commentaries. It has long been known that Hilary is here indebted to Origen on the Psalms: to the details of this debt we shall return.

Other writings of Hilary, especially the Tractatus Mysteriorum, will be mentioned on occasion, but are not of primary importance for this study.

It will be convenient to conduct our study of Hilary in three main sections corresponding to those outlined above, with a further section on comparison and assessment of results.

The commentary on St. Matthew is the first nearly complete extant commentary on a complete book of the Bible in the western Church. The sources of the work are far from clear.[20] Was it purely accident that Hilary chose this particular form as a vehicle for his exegesis, and if not, why not? Did the medium itself make any distinctive contribution to the development of his exegesis? It is astonishing to discover that despite a flood of literature on the interpretation of scriptures sacred and profane in the ancient world, there exists, it would appear, not a single investigation of the history of the literary form of the commentary as such. In order to assess the significance of the role played by the commentary form in Hilary's exegetical method, we shall attempt to fill in something of this historical lacuna. It is not however suggested, as an important group of patristic scholars long believed,[21] that the form can provide the 'key' to the nature of the process of interpretation by itself.

20. The exact sources of the In Matthaeum remains unclear. A search of exegesis on the gospel reveals no direct borrowing by Hilary. Echoes of the western tradition of Tert. and Novatian, of Cyprian and Irenaeus have long been noted, but detailed evidence is lacking. The proposals of Wille, and the possible assistance of the literary structure in providing clues we shall consider below.

21. The real founders of this school were Fr. Overbeck (cf. Über die Anfange der patristischen Literatur (1882) and H. Jordan 'Geschichte der altchristlichen Literatur' (Leipzig 1911), but its influence in patristic studies is far from dead. The limitations of the approach are well brought out in the conclusion of his dissertation 'Die Paulinische Predigt',(1910) by the youthful R. Bultmann, who though forced to conclude that similarity in form must indicate 'Ähnlichkeit in Geist', characteristically prefaces this by the comment that 'Wir wollen uns zum Schluss nicht verhehlen, dass der Eindruck der Verschiedenheit grosser ist als der Ähnlichkeit'. Provided that the method is restricted to the analysis of the technical structures, without thereby forgetting other and often more important factors on the development of a theologian's thought, much useful information may however be gained.

As with many literary documents, there is an important sense in which the 'content' is the 'form'[22] and closer inspection will reveal the existence too of powerful influence from philosophical, theological and historical as well as literary traditions in the final shaping. The content of the In Matthaeum is itself quite remarkable. It has long been observed that the gospel narrative is explained almost entirely in terms of the contrast between the law and the gospel, between faith and unfaith, the disciples and the scribes, the Gentiles and the Jews, the Church and the Synagogue. At the same time, in this particular period, examination of the literary structure may be a valuable source of new information on the exegetical activity as a whole.

In the all important middle period between the early and late works of strictly exegetical character, the pattern of interconnections changes. This means that the exegesis of the late period cannot be understood adequately except in the light of the exile in Asia Minor and the intense exegetical activity of the De Trinitate. The work of the early period, as will be shown below, contains few direct traces of the 'Alexandrian' tradition of exegesis, while that of the tractatus on the Psalms is steeped in that tradition, with its carefully worked out rules of interpretation. The same influence is traceable to some extent in the De Trinitate: but here the decisive factor is the stress on more strictly dogmatic considerations, both in the course of the exegetical process and in the application of its results. The roots of this movement we shall examine at some length.

22. cf. R. Jolles, Einfache Formen passim. (Jolles' point is well
    illustrated in the context of New Testament Formgeschichte by
    E. Jüngel, Paulus and Jesus, 3, p.291f).

The exegesis of the late period, principally in the tractatus on the Psalms, (a work made up from homilies spoken in church) will be considered mainly in terms of its relation to the Alexandrian tradition to which it owes much, but from which it also differs in important respects.

The force of the literary genre

2.   Text and Commentary in the historical

background to Hilary's exegesis

Text and Commentary in the historical background

to Hilary's exegesis

Though countless books have been written on the interpretation of
scripture in general in the patristic period, and even the detailed inter-
relations between interpreters are comparatively well established, very
little work indeed has been done, as already mentioned, on the history of
the commentary as such.[1] Because of the importance of the subject for this
and similar studies, we must now attempt to reconstruct a sketch of the
relevent factors. In doing so, we must obviously seek to avoid reduplic-
ation of findings in the history of interpretation and of discussions of
Hilary's sources which are already available, but we shall include selected
aspects of interpretational practice which have a bearing on the development of the commentary form or upon Hilary's own interpretation of scripture both in his commentary and in his other exegetical works, in view of
the still problematic nature of his sources, and also of our critical
analysis of his methods.

The question 'what is a commentary?' is not, on the face of it, difficult to answer. In describing those extant works which in ancient and in
modern times have been regarded as commentaries (a form which has been

1. On the commentary form as such cf, J. Geffcken 'Zur Entstehung und zum
Wesen des griechischen Wissenschaftlichen Kommentars', Hermes 67
(1932) 397-412, and the arts, on Hypomnemata (very weak) and Scholien
in PWK. I am also indebted for advice on this area to Prof. W. den Boer
Leiden and Prof. A. Dihle, Köln. The evidence for the history of the
commentary has never been assembled in detail.
For the standard discussions of Hilary's sources cf. Reinkens, Loofs,
Watson, Wille, Borchardt, Gastaldi, Kannengiesser and Doignon.

described by different words at different times)[2] we may say that a commentary is an independent literary work which provides a continuous scholarly exposition of a given written text, the continuity distinguishing the commentary from e.g. the scholion.

When however we ask for a fuller description of the form of the commentary in the sense of a detailed literary structure with recognised standard characteristics, (as in the case of the dialogue, the written homily, the 18th century novel) problems arise. For the evidence is that up to the time of the great Byzantine commentaries and with some few exceptions, the commentary need have no essential form whatever beyond the minimal description.[3]

2.　Typical of modern definitions is that of Heinrici (art. Hermeneutik in PRE 7, 741) 'Während Glossen und Scholien ein Hilfsmittel fur das Verständnis des Einzelnen sind, stellt sich der Kommentar die Aufgabe, das Ganze zu erklären, also das Einzelne als Teil einer literarischen Einheit und das Ganze als in sich zusammenhangendes literarischen Produkt verständlich zu machen'.

3.　The salient facts of the ancient usage may be found in L.S.J. Hypomnema is used of Aristarchus' commentaries to Homer (sch. 11 2.420 al), and these are contrasted with his syngrammata or full treatises. This usage corresponds exactly with Galen's classification of Hippocrates' work (15.424 cf. 16.532.543) and with the sense of explanatory notes at Sch. Ar. Av. 1242. (other uses, as a reminder, mention in a speech etc. need not detain us here). Tomos, used of Origen's work by Jerome, is late also (D.L.6.15) and P. Mich (cf. Birt, Buchwesen, p.27f) (2nd Cert) AD Scholia were short notes (cf. below) Diegeseis were short paraphrases of narratives, and not remnants of commentaries (cf PL Rep. 392 d, Grafenhan 3.47, and R. Pfeiffer in SBBAW 1934. 10f) on the diegeseis to Callimachus. Hyldahl, discussing the hypomnemata of Hegesippus (St. Theol.14 (1960)70f), comments that hypomnemata were essentially incomplete, rough notes considered of little value: (77 op. cit): his judgement echoes that of Koepke De Hyp. Graec. 1842, 1.3 'Nullam artem adhibebant scriptores in componendis hypomnematis'. On the other hand, there were probably different types of H.D.L. 4.1.5. speaks of hypomnematikous dialogous and hypomnematon cf. too the exx. in LSJ clearly there was no single precise meaning for the word H. or single designation for commentaries. Hypomenmata was soon taken over into Latin cf. Cic ad Fam. 16.21.8 multum mihi enim eripitur operae in exscribendis hypomnematis (quoted by Bousset 296 nl)
　　　　　　　　　　　　　　　　　　　　　　　　　　　(contd.)

In practice, the commentary tends to approximate to the nearest literary genre which deals with the same subject matter at the same time:
hence the oft repeated observation that the commentary is often difficult
to distinguish from the homily, scholion, treatise, etc. This means that
the tracing of the history of the commentary is a complex process involving constant comparison with related genres and defying rigid differentiation. We must look at the use of texts in general and at the relation of the shape of the commentary to the content of the texts.

The problem is complicated by the fact that the commentary was not
regarded generally in antiquity as a form worth preserving for its own
sake, and so existing commentaries were constantly 'cannibalised', ex-
cerpted and so altered that the original structures were speedily rendered
unrecognisable. The 'source' left today consists largely of a multitude
of names of commentators and a smaller collection of fragments bearing
scant resemblance to the works from which they were once taken.

Why this neglect? A major reason is that there were here no classical models to be preserved and imitated. There grew up indeed the types
of the grammatical commentary, which provided a continuous series of
scholion-like comments, and the philosophical commentaries of Alexandria,
the sections of which were almost monographs in their own right. But the
models themselves, e.g. Didymos, canonised the habit of excerpting earlier

3. (contd.)
   Commentarius in classical Latin never refers to a commentary in the
   sense in which it is used in this study (cf. PWK IV 1.726-59 and
   F. Borner De Commentariis in Hermes 81 (1953) p.210f. But cf. later
   e.g. Isid, Orig. Lib. 6.85 'Nam quidquid breviter componitur com-
   mentarius dicitur, quid vero elongatur, expositio.'
   See also A. Buck and O. Herding, Der Kommentar in der Renaissance
   Deutsche Forschungsgemeinschaft. Kommission für Humanismusforschung.
   Mitteilung I. Bonn-Bad Godesberg 1975, for which I am indebted to
   Prof. Waszink.

works and were in turn so used. It is not till after Origen that we find a standard pattern, that of Origen himself, used generally in the East, and after Ambrose in the West, and here too, as we shall see, qualifications must be made.

An examination of the extant material indicates, as one might be led to expect in the nature of the case, that the main reasons for the writing of commentary were first that a written text had achieved a considerable, often quasi-legal significance for a community, and secondly, that the meaning of the text was no longer self-evident.[4] Thus the earliest known commentaries were in Egypt on the Book of the Dead, in Greece on Homer, on Plato, Aristotle and the rhetoricians (disregarding the scholia on the poets) and in Italy on the Twelve Tables. The text is usually regarded as verbally inspired in religious commentary, and this may explain in part why Old Testament commentaries occur first in late Judaism and in the Church in the second century. Finally, it is in education, at an intermediate perhaps even more than at an advanced level, that commentaries are needed: hence the frequent connection between the presence of an educational institution, sacred or secular, and the use of this genre.

All these factors go some way towards explaining the fact that the commentary appears first in Christian literature in the middle of the second century and suddenly becomes abundant in the second half of the fourth. The nature of the Christian public, the lack of texts of the Bible with which the commentaries would often have to be read, and the needs of the day, in practical, often ethical concerns, in worship, in

4. On the role of inspired texts, cf. Leipoldt-Morenz, Heilige Schriften, 1953, and G. Lanczkowski, H.S. 1956.

preaching and in controversy rendered other literary forms more attractive. After its first brief appearance in the west, the commentary was
swiftly overshadowed, and its later popularity must to some extent at least
be accounted for by the influx of Latin translations of Greek works.

Some further mention of the relation of the commentary to other media
may here be made. As already noted, the most immediately related form is
that of the scholion, which originated in and reflects grammar rather than
rhetoric in the educational process, but may include some philosophical
observations (thus Porphyrion's scholion-commentary on Horace is in its
present form, and probably was also in its origin, predominantly grammatical, whereas Servius' scholia on Virgil have more philosophical
comment). In terms of MSS production, scholia may be interspersed with,
added as marginalia/or separated from the text proper, but commentaries
are normally independent, do not repeat the text and may be read without
it, though this is not always the case. The scholia draw their continuity if any from the text, but the commentary has its own continuity,
though of course, it too may contain scholia.[5]

5. On scholia cf. too the art 'Scholien' in PRE[3] 17.732f. For MSS prod-
    uction cf. Zuntz In Byzantium 1938 (13) and 1939 (14). He comments,
    13.552, 'Wir dürfen als regal ableiten: der antike Kommentar, auch
    der im kommatischen Scholienstil wird als Sonderbuch, unabhängig vom
    erklärten Text überliefert.' But here too there are exceptions.
    Z, too, concludes that hypomnemata were on the whole only by-products
    of oral teaching: and that 'Bei den Kommentatoren fiel der Begriff
    der individuellen Verfasserschaft fast vollständig' (op. cit. 560).
    There were also economic reasons for not combining text and comment-
    ary even in the scholia cf 'Scholien' in PWK, S.V. 'Die Praktische
    Verbindung von Text zu Randkommentar gehört erst einer viel späteren
    Zeit, etwa dem 3/4 Jahrhundert, als der Pergamentkodex allgemein an
    die Stelle der kostspieligeren Papyrusrolle trat.' But all books
    were in fact costly to produce (cf. Birt, Das antike Buchwesen) and
    not widely available e.g. for the use of Christian communities.

Elements too from the homily, the sermon, the diatribe, oration, historical epitome in various forms (but not the commentary in its classical sense!) anything which involves exegesis may be present. For example, since the homily and the diatribe deal with the explanation of written texts, introducing a paraenetic accent, a commentary may be built up from a series of homilies, as in Philo's commentary on Genesis, and the difference may be more of accent than of formal distinction. Again, there are different types of commentary, homily etc. and variations in structure within a single commentary.

What of the content of the commentary? It is clear that the history of the commentary is closely bound up, as already mentioned, with the history of interpretation of texts, and so particularly with that figural or allegorical method of interpretation which served to reveal a hidden meaning in texts, and which was to be so significant for the exegesis of the Bible.

It is often said that the development of commentary on Homer runs parallel with the development of the use of allegory in interpretation, but it is now evident that the latter was a comparatively late development, as far as commentaries were concerned.[6] Despite the mutilated character of the remains, it is clear that the earliest commentators concentrated on grammatical, historical and philosophical topics. The history of allegorical interpretation, on the other hand, goes back to the presocratic interpretation of Homer in the lyric poets, and later was practised in philosophy and in rhetoric alike (cf. too Plato's myths) before being taken

6.   On the relation of allegory and commentary cf. now PWK supp., IV 16f. art. 'Allegorische Dichtererklärung' Wehrli 25f and Gräfenhan IV, 254. A typical critique of the allegorists is made by Cicero DND 2. 335.

up by the commentators (cf. Buffière, Pepin etc.)[7]

The historical development of the commentary outside the Graeco-Roman world remains, it would appear, unexplored, and cannot concern us here.[8] The beginnings of commentary in the Greek world have been traced to Herodotus' use of the second book of Hecataeus, but in this period the lines of distinction cannot be drawn with a useful degree of precision. The main stream for practical purposes comes in the commentaries to Homer: of these, however, there remain only scholia, and all evidence for the original structures has gone. The pattern of the best of these works, that of Aristarchus, consists of grammatical/lexical comment of a kind that was to be reproduced in Hellenistic commentaries, which ranged from marginalia to extensive independent treatises, but are alike in treating the words and phrases examined as unconnected entities. This applies too to the scholasts' remains of commentaries to Pindar, the tragedians, comic poets and orations down to the time of the schools of Alexandria and Pergamon.[9]

---

7. On the interpretation in general of Homer by Plato and his school cf. S. Weinstock, Die Platonischen Homerkritik, Philologus 82 (1927) cf. 121f.

8. Some perfunctory mention of commentary on the Book of the Dead is made by H. Schneider, 'Aegypten'.

9. cf. the fragments edited by A. Ludwich, Aristarch's homerische Textkritik, Leipsig 1884-5, and for the Scholia, H. Erbse's edition. For Pindar A.B. Drachmann, Scholia vetera in Pindari carmina, Teubner 1903, which probably contains remains of commentary, and for Didymus on Demosthenes, the best preserved, M. Schmidt. Didymi Chalcenteri fragmenta: Leipzig, 1854 and the edition of Diels/Schubart, Teubner 1914. Typical of the fragments, which no longer refer to consecutive lines is no.16 (D/S p. 41).   (contd.)

A very different type of commentary appears in the interpretation of Homer and others in the schools of the Platonist and slightly later of the Aristotelian traditions. These dealt with aspects of the topic under consideration in what was really a philosophical treatise, and set a pattern for 'scientific' commentary in general; again however, the surviving debris tells us little of the details of the original form. But their existence created precedents which were to be followed in a great flood.[10]

A very late (contemporary with Hilary's work) but complete example of this type is provided by Chalcidius' commentary on the Timaeus: here the Latin translation is followed by an extensive philosophical commentary which sticks closely to the text, is clear and precise, and avoids allegory and all extraneous material.[11] Similar Latin adaptation of Greek

---

9. (contd.) περίστοιχοι. Δημοσθένης ἐν τῷ πρὸς Νικόστρατον (LIII. 15) περὶ τῶν Ἀρεθούστου ἀνδραπόδων· φυτευτηρία ἐλαίων περιστοί-χους καλεῖ ἃς Φιλόχορος [FHG 139,Fr.62] στοιχάδας προσηγόρευσε.

Süsemihl, II, 1-27 lists hundreds of Alexandrian grammatical commentators of whose work scarcely a shred remains.

10. cf.Geffcken op.cit.402 'In der Tat, wissenschaftliche Kommentar im eigenlichsten Sinne is eine Schöpfung der Platoniker. Heraklitus Ponticus erklärt den Heraklit, Krantor später den Platonischen Timaeus.' But of these only reports remain (cf.Wehrli, op.cit.) Christ 769f lists lost commentaries to Aristotle. W. Norvin edited the fragments of Olympiodorus on the Timaeus (Teubner 1913) but these, offering glosses of varying length and of a mainly grammatical nature, reveal little of the original. On Poseidonius, whom Switalski showed to be the source for Chalcidius, Gronau in his standard work 'Poseidonius' could only write 'Das grundlegende Werk, in dem er eine eclectische Vereinigung von Pythagoras, Platon, Stoa and zT auch Aristotles vernahm, scheint ein kommentar zum platonischen Timaios gewesen zu sein'.

11. In the same genre cf.Proclus' commentary on the Parmenides (ed. V. Cousin 1961) and on the Timaeus (tr. and ed. A.J. Festugiere 1966) in which the main points of difficulty are dealt with in a scholarly
(contd.)

forms may be seen in Macrobius' work on the Somnium Scipionis and
Marius Victorinus' commentary to Cicero (which is however, a grammatical/
historical rather than a philosophical commentary).[12]

The considerable scholia-remains of Alexandrian commentary add little
to our picture of the literary structure. Philo,[13] an important link in
the literary transmission, follows in his biblical works the pattern of

11. (contd.)
    manner without exhortation etc, and without any attempt at a re-
    interpretation of the work as a continuous whole, and Porphyry's
    Quaestiones Homericae (ed. G. Schraeder, Leipzig 1880) which again
    seek to resolve specific difficulties in interpretation (cf. on
    D.H. Dorrie in Zetemata 20, München 1959). The last in the class-
    ical tradition, Boethius' commentary on Porphyry (CSEL 1906) is
    really an independent philosophical essay in its own right.

12. For Marius Victorinus cf. Cicero, opera ed. Orelli and Halm Vol.5,
    Turin 1833, MV seeks to explain the Rhetorica for students in short
    lexical/historical notes cf. p.479 line 23 'Hypothesis, id est,
    quaestio circa personam propriam'. Use is made of the rhetorical
    categories of division, a feature we shall see again in Hilary cf
    p.9 133 'diximus rationem rei gerendi ordinem necessarium'. The
    same procedure is followed in biblical exegesis cf. PL8 1146f, ep.
    ad Gal. To 1.1 ordo in principio sententiae hic est, etc. Again
    there is little allegorising and the tone is matter of fact. On
    the Cicero interpretation Suringar noted that 'non est igitur oratio
    integra, sed auctor quasi ad marginem notavit Ciceronis verba quasi
    explicaturus esset et his suam deinceps explicationem subiunxit'
    (p.150), and 100 years later Benz seeing the same feature in the
    biblical exegesis notes independently 'Methodisch ist auffallend
    dass V. nicht mit der allegorischen u. typologischen exegese arbeitet,
    sondern mit der aristotelischen Schulmethode der wörtlichen Exegese'.
    Not the difference between sacred and secular interpretation, but
    between different types of the use of figural interpretation, char-
    acterises the development of commentary. (We may note too in PL 8
    1139 the argument for the acceptance of the homo ousion haec si vera
    sunt, accipite homo ousion and 1164 to 2.14 ipsa enim fides sola
    iustificat, justificationem dat et sanctificationem cf. below, cf. too
    Halm, Rhet, Lat, Min. pp.152ff, 422f, and Gräfenhan op.cit. IV, 90f.
    There is also an edition of Marius Victorinus, Commentarii in
    Apostulum,   Teubner 1972.

13. For Philo cf. below.

the philosophical commentary, even though his Genesis commentary was in all probability build up from homilies. Paraenetic material was a common element in the Alexandrian philosophical commentary, and his predecessor Aristiboulos appears to have been no exception in his work to this general pattern.

Philo is of course an important link too in the transmission of interpretation, in his use of allegory. Though, as already mentioned, most commentators were not allegorists, it is in connection with commentary on the Iliad that the Stoics, learning from the Platonists (rather than the Aristotelians who in general disapproved and were in turn espoused by the Epicureans against the Stoics) first developed allegorical interpretation in the context of commentary. From these controversies the use of allegory and figural expression in general was to follow two distinguishable lines, the one running through Philo, Barnabas, Irenaeus and Origen to the tradition of Christian exegesis in general, the other through the Hellenistic and then the Latin schools of rhetoric, to be reunited at different times, notably in Augustine but also, as we shall see, in Hilary, in different ways. These branches used allegory and other forms of figural interpretation in rather different connections with other contexts, the former tending to blend Stoic and Platonic concepts, the latter Stoic and Aristotelian, though never of course, with complete purity of tradition. This nuance was to be of not a little significance for the future, and particularly, as we shall see, for Hilary.

We have seen how Latin letters took over the philosophical and grammatical commentaries of the Greeks. This was the pattern at all stages, with the possible exception of the Latin legal commentary,[14] which

may, beginning from the commentary or scholia on the Twelve Tables, be a

native growth. The fragmentary remains of the early literary grammatical

work, particularly of Asconius, Cornutus and Philargyrius, suggest simple

grammatical scholia.[15] The most important group apart from the philosoph-

ical commentaries already considered is composed of the commentaries to

Virgil. The works of Donatus (often revised) and Servius were longer than

those of their predecessors, probably commenting on each line but still

scholion-like, i.e. without a continuity in the exposition itself.[16]

14. For reports on the lost work on the Twelve Tables cf. Suringar 13f.
    Classical legal commentaries took the same form as non-legal comment-
    aries (Schulz p.185) Gaius' Institutes were at first called comment-
    arii, (cf. Wieacker p.187,) but these have nothing in common with com-
    mentaries in Hilary, being more like greatly expanded scholia. The
    methods of interpretation varies. cf. Kübler, Insts. introd. p.117
    "Meist geht die Erklärung von der Etymologie des Wortes aus, oft gibt
    sie durch eine Paraphrase den Sinn an."

15. On Asconius cf. the ed. of Th. Stangl in Ciceronum orationum Scholast-
    icae (1912) and of Giamatano 1967. Asconius' method is that of Marius
    Victorinus, who is dependent on him in his work on Cicero. For frag-
    ments of the others cf. Keil Gramm. Lat V., comment by F. Lampert in
    Bursian's Jahrbuch 251 for 1936, 107f, and Gräfenhan IV 276f, Suringar
    45f, lists the names of the main writers. Philargyrius was edited
    by Hagen in Appendix Servianae. The order of much of this work is
    reflected by the comment in Spartian. Ant. Gel. 5 that many grammar-
    ians put questions in their commentaries 'velut agni balant, porcelli
    grummiunt'! (Quoted by Gräf. IV.278n).

16. On Donatus and Servius cf. Thomas, Travis, Funaioli and Jones. On
    Fulgentius cf. Stroux. For Servius' caution with regard to allegory
    cf. to Aen. 1.292 'alii volunt hos Romanos intelligi (in historical
    characters portrayed in disguise by Virgil): vera tamen oratio haec.
    cf. on Aen. 7.303 sunt propria verba quae nulla ratione mutantur (Thomas
    compares Quint. 10 1.817) Jones finds that Servius uses allegory not
    to refer to a type of interpretation but to 'the figure which arises
    from a succession of metaphors' (i.e. the rhetorical tradition) and
    divides these into four categories: historical, moral, physical,
    euhemeristic and 'ex ritu romano': this division cannot detain us
    here, except to note that no significant affinities in form and inter-
    pretation with Hilary can be shown: the rhetorical tradition is not
    sufficient in itself to explain Hilary's methods.

It is only really with the arrival of the Byzantine standardised commentary form that a continuity of exposition and concept in a tight literary structure appears. There is then in the Latin non-theological tradition a considerable familiarity with the scholion tradition and, in the fourth century, with the philosophical commentary, the literary form depending on the nature of the subject matter itself. With one minor
partial exception,/which as we will consider below, no significant affinities with Hilary's commentary can be detected: apparent similarities derive more from the common source in Latin rhetoric than from relations between the commentaries themselves.

We have yet to consider the tradition of biblical commentary and interpretation in the Church. In the Old Testament, there is of course, much exegesis of earlier parts of the biblical tradition, but no use is made of the commentary for this purpose. It is not till the 2nd century B.C. that traces of the form are found, both in Hellenistic and Rabbinic Judaism. The first source for the former is Aristoboulos, whose allegorical interpretation of the Torah is not however a full commentary.[17] Infinitely more significant was the work of his pupil Philo. We recall that Philo's commentaries were probably built up from the series of homilies, such as were held in the Hellenistic synagogue: these in turn were influenced by the general Cynic/Stoic homily of late Hellenistic popular

17. On the background to Philo cf. Walter's edition of the Aristoboulos fragments: they probably consisted in form of aporiai kai luseis (Walter 124f). The letter of Aristeas (cf.Michaelis in RGG sv. Aristeasbrief) may be a source of the glorification of the LXX, later so striking in Hilary. E. Stein in 'Die allegorische Exegese des Philo aus Alexandrien' (BZNW 51.1929) has noted Stoic influence on Aristeas, in the use of 'tropologein' for in allegorical interpretation, and in the presence of figural equivalents e.g. Egypt as a symbol of the body, many of which recur in Philo.

ethics. It is then inaccurate to suggest, as has been done, that the
commentary was a Hellenising literary adaptation of the originally Hebraic
material from the preaching activity of the Church. Both streams of homily
and commentary, grew up together in the common context of Hellenistic
culture.[18]

Philo used different types of commentary for the exegesis of different passages, and different varieties of allegory. In terms of form and
structure, Origen shows nothing that is not already in Philo, who was also
a main source of inspiration for the Gnostic commentators. It was to be
of great significance for Latin Christian literature that the direct influence of Philo was limited until Ambrose took up his techniques with the

18. In his Quaestiones in Genesim Philo's interpretation varies between
    speculation with only the remotest connection with the text e.g. on Gen.
    4.9f (p.41 Markus) and exaggerated adherence to the literal text, out
    of which then a deeper meaning must be produced in order to make
    sense e.g. Gen 18.10 (p.293 Markus). Much use is made of explanation
    of etymological detail e.g. καρποφορία καλεῖται ὁ Ευφράτης κ.τ.λ.

    (p.194 Markus); the frequent questions in the text e.g. Gen 2.15 p.
    205 Markus, recall Hippolytus (but not Hilary!). Adler finds three
    main types of structure - short explanation of a word, explanation
    with biblical citations, expanded explanation, to which may be added
    a combination of 2 and 3 and long complex series of citations. He
    concludes (72) that the style of the work is devotional rather than
    scholarly. On the homiletic element cf.Thyen 7-11. Siegfried (196-7)
    notes the Stoic division into physical and ethical allegory. For
    Philo's influence on the Gnostics cf Sagnard p.598f, 622f, on Ambrose
    Siegfried 371, and on Hilary 398. (The explanation of Edom in Ps. 137
    - probably indirect). On Philo's interpretation in general cf.Goppelt,
    Typos, p.48f. Heinisch ch.7, 69f and Hanson p.37f. The central point
    is well summarised by Ebeling EE100 ' Im Unterschied zur Homeralleg-
    orese ist das besondere der alexandrinische Allegorese (Philo) das
    nicht nur der postulierte Inhalt. "sondern der Auslegungsvorgang als
    solcher eine grundsatzliche religionsgeschichtlicher Bedeutung hat.
    Sie wird aus einer formalen zu einer existentiellen, aus einer ration-
    alen zu einer mystischen methode. Das prägt das alexandrinische
    Verständnis von Offenbarung'.

enthusiasm of the discoverer. The indirect influence of Philo, and especially of his theological understanding of scripture as a verbally inspired medium in which nothing is accidental or superfluous, and all may reveal the secrets of God, was all pervasive.

Though the beginnings of Rabbinic Jewish commentary may also be traced back to the 2nd century B.C., the earliest recognisable fragments are from the first century A.D. The influence of this stream of Gentile Christianity in the first three centuries A.D. was minimal: it is only with the influence in Hebrew on Jerome that Rabbinic influence becomes a possible real factor, though here again, the structure is that of the Philonic/Origenist tradition.[19]

For Jewish Christianity the only remaining evidence is for the commentaries of Symmachus the so-called Ebionite: this allows little to be said of the structure of the work, and increasing suspicion of the orthodoxy of this stream ensured that its influence was to be negligible. Symmachus' work, if indeed a commentary, appears to have pursued a purely theological aim, namely that of distinguishing of true and false pericopes in a gospel, probably that of St. Matthew.[20]

19. cf. F. Maas, Von der Ursprung der rabbinischen Schriftauslegung, ZThK52 (1955) 129-61, and for Jerome's knowledge and use of Hebrew cf. J. Barr in JSS, Jan 1968 ff. cf. too H.A. Wolfson, Philo.

20. On Symmachus, text and interpretation, cf. H.J. Schoeps, Theologie des Judenchristentums, pp.366ff. Eusebius 6.17 refers to a commentary (Hypomnemata) on St. Matthew's gospel. These may have been worked into the Kerugma Petri., and would have been interpretation of logia from an ebionite version of the gospel. The Fragments suggest short unconnected scholia, usually beginning 'tout estin ...' As Schoeps has it (379) "Es muss also einstweilen bei der Vermutung bleiben."

Also of little wider influence is the Qumran commentary tradition.
Of particular interest for the history of the commentary structure is the
Habakkuk commentary, which combines a highly developed, unified interpretation on a line by line basis with great concision, and in this respect anticipates Hilary's style. The basic purpose of the interpretation is not that of scholarship as in the Rabbinic commentaries or in
the philosophical tradition, but of comforting the writer's congregation
and exhorting them to stand firm in the final hour, a message based on
the claim of the writer to a special prophetic illumination.[21]

It is a remarkable fact that there are no biblical commentaries,
for some of the reasons set out above, before those of the Gnostics, with
the possible exception of Symmachus who also sought to impose a 'special
interpretation' on the texts: though many of the fruits of the exegetical tradition of the time were to be incorporated in commentaries when
these appeared.

Papias and Hegesippus have been thought to have written commentaries,
but this description is probably inaccurate. The books of the New Testament were still being made and spread, read and accepted: these appear
to have played little part in the development of principles of interpretation, but served rather to confirm from select references the validity
of procedures already established. The scriptures of the Old Testament
were used more as a source of the demonstration of the fulfilment of

21.   cf. the excellent analysis by Elliger. The work is extremely con-
      densed, the 64 lines of text being divided into 35 parts, each with
      an exposition generally of 3/4 lines.
      The exposition is determined by the author's own overall interpret-
      ation, in which the original accent of a text in its context is much
      altered. As in Hilary's In Matthaeum, extraneous material is care-
      fully avoided for the sake of continuity and brevity.

prophecy than as continuous literary works in themselves. Contact between the Christian communities and the Hellenistic literary world was still limited, and contact with the Rabbinic tradition was broken off, as we saw, just when commentary writing began to flourish there.[22]

Thus it happened that the first Christian commentaries were produced by the Gnostics, who were in the relevant cases in closer contact with the literary world, were interested in applying a particular line of interpretation consistently to the New Testament, were less interested in the traditional use of the Old Testament as a source of proof texts, and shared Philo's doctrine of the mystical inspiration of scripture which was to lead Marcion to stress the idea of the canon of holy scripture.

The first hint of Gnostic commentary has been seen in the letter of Ptolemy to Flora, but here the commentary form is not explicit. Fragments and information on others including Basileides allow no firm conclusion. But Heracleon wrote at least one commentary, on St. John's gospel, which is thus the earliest extant commentary in ancient Christian literature.[23]

Origen speaks of Heracleon's work as _hypomnemata_, and for him it is too succinct. It may be that he commented only upon those verses for which he wished to introduce a special interpretation, but the large fragments of Jn[4] suggests a comprehensive, practically verse by verse

---

22. On Papias cf. Jordan op. cit. 377f and on Hegesippus Hyldahl op. cit. passim. On the role of the New Testament in the hermeneutical tradition cf. Ebeling EE p.101f, and for the interpretation of scripture in the NT Hanson 65f, Ellis, 'Paul's use of the Old Testament', Dodd, According to the scriptures, etc.

23. Attribution of commentary to Ptolemy is made by Iren A.H. 1.85. On the letter cf. Sagnard 615f, Eusebius HE IV 716f speaks of Basileides 'exegetika eis to evangelion (Windisch, Das Ev. des Basileides, 5).

treatment. Heracleon avoids all grammatical, historical and other
issues, concentrating on theological exposition, often in the form of
explanatory paraphrase. Unlike Philo he offers no homiletic material,
concentrating on exposition. He makes much use of allegory, often centred
on the figure of Christ, as in the episode of the Samaritan woman; as is
usual in the period, no explanation of the figural interpretation is
given, but the equivalents are simply stated.[24]

The next commentator who played a crucial role in the development of
genre in the West, is Hippolytus. Hippolytus was however deeply indebted,
as was the whole western tradition, to Irenaeus. Whether or not Irenaeus'
exegetical works once included commentaries - and this is not clear - his
use of the Bible in theology and his principles of interpretation, much

24. For the fragments of Heracleon cf. Stählin's edition (TU6.3) and
    Volker, Quellen 63-87. In the fragments, which may be fairly well
    preserved, the expositions are usually on a line by line basis, and
    concern single words. The interpretation is a 'pneumatic' one which
    takes little account of the original context cf. to Jn 2.19; ten triten
    (phsei) ten pneumatiken hemeran etc. It is difficult in the absence
    of the original complete context to generalise on the form Preuschen
    speaks of "knappgefasste Glossen" (82) but Origen may have made
    drastic cuts. V. Löwenich (Johannesverständnis 92) suggests that
    where Origen doesn't mention H's exposition he probably agreed with
    it: on occasion he describes H's version as 'ouk apithanos'.
    Origen himself refers to hypomnenata (cf. Fr 4 'en hois kataleloipen
    Hypomnematois' Simonetti (Eracleone et Origene) agreed that these
    were probably very short. Janssens notes the lack of extra biblical
    citations, but these might have been cut by Origen. Heracleon too
    stresses the Church (the Samaritan woman in Fr[4]) and for him as for
    Origen the middle point of the exegesis is Christ, however understood.
    Carola Barth, p.54, has noted allegorical interpretation 1) where
    the honour of the saviour seems at risk, 2) where words are obscured
    and odd 3) where there are contradictions, 4) where the words are of
    a key theological nature and 5) where, etymology suggests allegory
    i.e. the Stoic/Philonic method. 'Ein Interesse, das Leben das
    Erlosers historisch zu erfassen, besteht nicht'. cf. too Sagnard
    306-20 and 451-79, also Heinrici, Die Val. Gnosis.

of which bore Philo's influence, but which had its own theological character, were to be an important influence, direct or indirect in the western Church, and many echoes of Irenaeus are to be found in Hilary: the
importance of the scriptures the inspired nature of the text, the reflect--
ion in it of the history of salvation.[25]

Hippolytus shows no advance on Heracleon in structure, but there is
a unifying factor in much of his interpretation, the history of the populus
Dei from the Old Israel to the New, to the disadvantage of the Jews, which
anticipates Hilary's use of the motif.[26]

---

25. Much early exegesis is carried on in controversy with heretics, and
    Irenaeus' is no exception. Scripture is of the greatest importance.
    Flessemann op.cit.196 concludes that for I, 'Scripture can be rightly
    understood only by tradition, but also, interpretation of scripture
    constitutes tradition'. Many of the accents familiar from Hilary are
    present. cf.A.H. 4.18 (HII p.201) of scripture Nihil enim otiosum
    nec sine signo nec sine argumento apud eum.
    The interpreter must note the context (so 1.8.1; 1.19.1, (HI p.175)
    5.13.2 (HII p.356) etc. cited by Hoh). Scripture has its own
    perspicuitas A.H. 2.27.2; (HI p.343) 2.28.3 (HI p.352) etc. Yet, as
    Brox (p.78) notes, I. says that Jesus himself had spoken only in
    parables and riddles; against this Tert., (De Res. Mort. 33) polem-
    ises, and Hilary clearly is aware of the passage in Tert. (cf.below
    p.43 31). Irenaeus himself borrows much from Barnabas, including his
    scriptural quotations on occasion (Benoit p.185). For him all
    scripture has a spiritual significance A.H. 2.28.3, and there is much
    use of types (cf. AH 4.10.4 (HII p.351) where the exodus is a type of
    the people of God). For 'Cognito veritatis context cf.IG 7 Frags
    p.1246 (HII p.493). The date of the Latin translation remains un-
    clear. It was used by Augustine in 421 (Lundstrom). Lundstrom's
    last conclusion (New Studies) was 'not more than 100 years after
    300'. Examination of the Latin and Greek versions produces no pos-
    itive evidence for direct use by Hilary, but the similarity of many
    interpretational principles and the theological affinities suggest
    a connection.
    AH - page references are to the edition of W.W. Harvey, 2 vols.,
    Cambridge, 1857.

26. Hippolytus' commentary has little formal structure. Sometimes he
    uses the second person singular in bursts of exhortation. Often the
    exposition is introduced by a question, e.g. on Dan.13.3 (GCS 1 1897,
    p.20) dei oun epizetein to aition. The main points of the narrative
    are selected for comment and theological interpretation. The Song of
    (contd.)

32

After his death, doubts as to his orthodoxy led to the neglect of his work. The Christian community in Rome went over to the Latin language and new works were produced for new purposes: with the reintroduction of commentaries in the 4th century, it was to Origen rather than to Hippolytus that writers were to turn for inspiration. In this period too fall numerous exegetical activities from which commentators may have learned, but which cannot detain us here - the enormous anti-gnostic exegetical interest in Genesis, notable in Theophilus and in Justin's Dialogue, the lost work of the mysterious Rhodon, Candidus and Apion, and the work of Malito of Sardis.[27]

Of commentary production in Egypt before Origen, we know nothing. Nag Hammudi has yielded no commentaries. Clement of Alexandria wrote homilies, perhaps even in series, and glosses, and his interpretation

26. (contd.)
Songs is interpreted in terms of the resurrection hope. The fragments are all in a revised condition, so that it is difficult to speculate on literary structure but the addresses in the second person suggest close links with the homily (as Hamel, 15f) Hippolytus appears to have been entirely independent of Origen cf. Danielou Message 237 'Mais nous ne trouvons chez Hippolyte aucune trace d'exegese alexandrine'. This does not preclude the use of allegory however, cf. Schol. in Dan. PG10 673C quattuor regna allegorice significat, etc. The fragments on St. Matthew (ch.24.15f in GCS 1/2 1887) show no parallels in substance with Hilary on Matthew. cf.too Bonwetsch TU 16.2 1897 59f for the work on Daniel and in general the arts. on H. in Schmidt-Stählin 1331-46 and Christ 2.1105f.

27. On the exegesis of Genesis cf. G. Armstrong, Die Genesis in der alten Kirche, on Rhoden art. s.v. in PRE3, and on Candidus and Apion Altaner 148 and Redepenning 378. Melito speaks of a typos aletheias, but his exact influence on later exegetical work is hard to determine precisely. It appears unlikely, that e.g. Hilary was influenced directly by him: already Eusebius of Caesarea regarded him with reserve (H.E. 4.26).

prepared the way for his famous pupil:[28] but the commentary proper
appears first with Origen.

Origen never gives reasons for the writings of commentaries: we
may point to the presence of the grammatical and philosophical commentaries of the school tradition, and above all to the influence of Philo.
Apart from the biblical commentaries the contra Celsum has many of the
features of the philosophical commentary. He is said to have written
homilies, commentaries and scholia, the remains of which are notoriously
difficult to distinguish. In structure his work combines the methods of
the grammatical and the philosophical commentators, in interpretation he
sets Philo's rules in a Christian framework and imports the Platonic
trichotomist schema of body, soul and spirit (in theory, but not always
in practice) for the articulation of the revelation of its secrets by
scripture: the details of the latter will concern us below in considering his influence on various stages of Hilary's work.[29]

28. The references to Clement's 'hypotyposes' tell us nothing of the
    original (on these cf. Zahn, Forschung zur Gesch. d. NT/Kanon 3.136).
    Clement's exegesis too is developed in controversy with opponents, whom
    he seeks to refute by floods of scriptural citation (cf, Kutter 13f).
    He uses the methods of Stoic polemic and even Valentinus' allegory,
    turning it back on him (Kutter 91f) in this anticipating Origen (cf.
    str. 5. passim). For him the whole of scripture is parabolic (Str.
    6.15. 126). The law may be understood in 4 ways (Str. 1. 28.136)
    to historikon, to nomothetikon, to hierourgikon, to logikon anticip-
    ating the later 4 fold sense of scripture. Like Irenaeus he makes
    much use of Barnabas. E. Schwartz (2 Predigten p.31) notes that C.
    on occasion uses allegory not as huponoia but as in Quint. 8.6.44.
    an instance of the meeting of the two strands mentioned above.

29. For the division of Origen's work cf, Jerome, Praef. Hom. Ezech.
    (PLG 25.586A) 'Originis opuscula in omnem scripturam triplicia.
    Primum eius opus excerpta, quae Graece scholia nuncupantur, in quibus
    ea, quae sibi videbantur obscura atque habere aliquid difficultatis,
    summatim breviterque perstrinxit: secundum homileticum genus; tertium
    quod ipse inscripsit tomoi.' The scholia are today all lost (cf,
    Zuntz 554).

(contd.)

In the Greek world Origen's interpretational principles, though
not always his precise literary structure were, as is well known, to be
followed by friend and foe alike. Of this tradition, only Eusebius of
Caesarea can be shown to have had a direct influence on Hilary. Though
the 'Antiochenes' sought to stress the grammatical-historical element
against the 'spiritualising' of the 'Alexandrians', the structure, in
line by line commentary in the manner of Origen, remained the same, and
this pattern continued in the Greek tradition into Byzantine times.[30]

29. (contd.)
The difference between commentary and homily is at most of accent
only (compare the commentary on Mt. (PG 13.829f) with the homilies
on Lk (GCS 9) or on the Psalms (PG 12 1053f) cf.too Klostermann,
Formen, partly because of the much larger scale and expansive style,
the structure of the commentary does not play the important role of
the structure in Hilary or e.g. in Qumran. The details of Origen's
interpretation we shall reconsider below. Origen unlike Hilary,
deals with practically every word in the text cf.on Mt. 13.36f
(PG 13.829f). Like Hilary he differentiates between parable and
similitudes (PG 13.843) justifying this by reference to scripture
(Mk. 4.30). He too is concerned with the centrality of Christ in
scripture cf.PG 13.859 'instituta sunt ad perfecte intelligendum
evangelium et omnem de Jesu Christi factis et dictis mensum (ergon
kai logon) cf.Hom 2 in Ps 36 (PG 12). Jesus Christus veritas est
(cf.on veritas and Marcionite influence below!) and yet as Molland
puts it 'there are certain thoughts of the NT for which Clement and
Origen have no understanding, viz the Pauline thought of Christ as
the end of the law'. This is inter alia due to the influence of
Philo. In commenting on John Origen probably had Philo before him
(Forster 30). On Origen's use of allegory cf.too Pepin, 461f,
Harl 155f, Danielou, Message, 156f. Doignon , Hilaire de Poitiers
avant l'Exil', 545f offers a complete table of comparisons between
Origen and Hilary on St. Matthew.

30. For Eusebius and Hilary cf.the sect. on the In Psalmos below. The
Connection with Athanasius remains unclear: Athan.in Mt (Frags P.G.27.
1362-87) offered, it seems, fuller commentary than Hilary, and the
few resemblences in phraseology between the two e.g. Jesus as rex et
sacerdos/Basileus kai hiereus, may be coincidence. Altaner (altlat,
Übersetzung) thought that Hilary possibly knew some of Athan's writing.
The Vita Antonii was tr. by Evagrius Pontus in c.370. None of the
other commentators of this period show connections with Hilary, nor
does their work advance the development of the commentary. For the
(contd.)

In the West, by the time the Church turned to the Latin language the great battle with the Gnostics was practically over: none of the Gnostics wrote Latin commentaries, and so none were written to refute them. The problems of the day in Rome and in Africa were tackled in other literary forms. Exegesis in Tertullian, Cyprian and Novatian is in the context of sermon, homily or tractate, always applied to some practical purpose rather than in scholarly explanation as such. Though their methods of interpretation were to influence commentators including Hilary in different forms of his exegesis, to the structure they contributed nothing. Apart from the direct connection with the De Oratione, Tertullian's understanding of figural interpretation and the key to the

30. (contd.)
     Greek Mt comms cf. Reuss (esp. Theodore of Heraclea, p.55f) and
     Theodore of Mopsuestia (96f cf. too Greer). On theoria cf. Vaccari
     in Biblica I 1920 3-36. As might be expected, Hilary's practices
     are often paralleled without any connection being present. Thus
     like him Diodore of Tarsus orders his themes according to the titles
     of the psalms (Maries p.60), and Basil makes much use of the theme
     of humilitas and the need for silence in speaking of God (cf. Vischer
     p.105f), borrowing on occasion straight from Philo without using
     Origen (Bousset p.392). Opposition to Origen did not necessarily
     mean renunciation of his methods: cf Methodius of Olympus' use of
     anagoge and tropologia in De Lepra 1.4 (Bonwetsch, M. of O.)
     Weight of biblical quotation was no guarentee of biblically orient-
     ated theology: cf the floods of citations in the Pss commentary of
     Asterius the Sophist (ed. Richard) - this may indicate the presence
     of concordances. On the use of parable in the Alexandrian school
     cf. Kerrigan 210f (Cyril). On Origen's exegetical legacy see too the
     splendid study by R.A. Greer, Captain of our Salvation.
     (Despite the stress in the De. Trin. upon the literal rather than
     the allegorical, direct evidence of the influence of anti-Origenist
     exegesis on Hilary is lacking, but cf. p.254 below on Eusebius of
     Emesa.)

illumination of the gospels, were, as we shall see further below, important for Hilary's interpretation.[31]

31. Examination of all references to St. Matthew in Tert. produces no
literal quotations. Again, Tert. never applied his exegetical use
of figural interpretation and of the rhetorical tradition in general
to the construction of a commentary. But his works are full of
material clearly echoed by Hilary. Quite apart from surface
resemblances (navis-ecclesia Pud 13.20 Res 6.6 cf. Hil In Mt 12.31,
umbrae futurarum Marc. 5.19.9. etc) the same principles are stated,
esp in De Res. Mort. which Hilary clearly knew cf.33. It is not
true that our Lord spoke all things in parables: he spoke some things
plainly, and must be taken to have meant what he said. In any given
parable text (33.5) Christ will interpret for us, or the evangelist
will do so or the parable will be self-interpreting. On the whole
the interpretation in De Res. Mort is not however allegorical; it
does not object to allegory as such, but only when e.g. the resurrection of the flesh is to be interpreted spiritually (cf. CC 1957).
In the De Oratione, which Hilary also knew and which is T's nearest
approach to commentary, he divides the 'sermones Domini' into
parabolae, exempla, cf.too Pud. 17 'pauca multis, dubia certis,
obscura manifestis adumbrantur'. Scorp. 9 'Verba non sono solo
sapiunt, sed et sensu, nec auribus tantummodo audienda sunt et
mentibus' Pud. 9 'Non ex parabolis materias commentamut, sed ex
materiis parabolas interpretamur (cf.Hil. non sermoni res etc.)
Marc 4.4 (cf. 3.16) hoc est corpus meum. figura autem non fuisset,
nisi veritatis esset corpus' on which Auerbach (Figura 550) aptly
comments that, for Tert. 'Figura ist etwas wirkliches, geschichtliches
welches etwas anderes, ebenfalls wirkliches und geschichtliches
darstellt und ankundigt'. Scripture is interpreted according to the
regula fidei cf Marc 3.24 'quomodo allegorica interpretatio eius
spiritaliter competat', but it is going much too far to say (Karpp.
196) that 'bei der Schriftauslegung brauchte Tertullian die
Glaubensregel nicht anders als der römische Jurist seine regula iuris'.
His concern was rather to avoid the speculation of e.g. Marcion, for
whom all was 'per allegorias et figuras et aenigmatum nebulas
obumbrata' as he saw it (Marc 4.25) For him, Res in litteris tenentur,
ut litterae in rebus leguntur (Res. 20) Atque ita corporalia
defendentur corporalibus destinata,id est non spiritalia, quia non
figurata.' The tensions reflected in these quotations reflect in my
view, very closely those of the In Matthaeum. For Tert. cf.on
rhetoric Welter, on legal terms Beck (exaggerated), and in general,
Karpp, Hanson in JTS 1961, D'Ales esp. 242ff, Zimmermann 8ff, Barnes
and Sider.
Tert. was also of course a channel of the Stoic tradition cf. De An.20,
Seneca saepe noster etc. The general influence of Tert. is well set
out by Doignon op. cit p.221f, 263f, 520f.

The influence of the exegesis of Cyprian[32] and Novatian[33] is less
direct, concerning only occasional passages.

Of other western writers, Tyconius appears to have had no influence
on the commentary form itself or upon Hilary in particular, despite his
importance for Augustine. Of Rheticius of Autun and Fortunatianus of
Aquileia only their names remain, though they testify to some Latin commentary in Gaul before Hilary; possibly they were influenced by Origen,
of whom something, impossible to state precisely, must have been known
even in Gaul in the early fourth century: though again the lack of
testimony, and the evident surprise which Rufinus' translation produced
suggest that this influence was indirect. Iuvencus, Commodianus add
nothing to our purpose.[34]

32. It is not impossible that Hilary had read Cyprian on the Lords Prayer
    (CSEL 3.1.2 and ed. Reveillard). cf.1.11 'evangelica praecepta'
    echoed in In Mt. but the form of the works are different. Cyprian's
    work is no close knit commentary in the manner of the In Mt. Its
    content is heavily dependent on Tert De Oratione, in thought if not
    in words, and this was probably known to Hilary himself. (Cyprian
    rearranged the order of Tertullian's paragraphs cf.the analysis of
    O'Donnell, diss. CUA 1960). Cyprian too took over many of the loci
    communes of the rhetorical tradition (cf.Quacquarelli) Koch thought
    that he knew a Latin tr. of Irenaeus (Cypr. Unt. 475) but this was
    demolished by Lundstrom op.cit. Examination of the refs. to St.
    Matthew in the Testimonia etc. show no connection with Hilary. Goetz'
    work showed that his works, though exciting for modern historians
    speedily passed into neglect before being revived in the late 4th
    century. His influence on Hilary, will have been in theological
    rather than technical interpretational issues. On his exegesis cf.
    D'Ales 33-75; Fahey, esp. 612ff. There is no appreciable advance on
    Tertullian. cf,Doignon pp.211ff.

33. On C. as a theologian cf.too M. Wiles in JEH 1.4 (1963) 140ff. On
    the influence of Novatian cf below p.116. Simonetti (Ilario e
    Novatiano) stresses Novatian's strong dependence on Tertullian.

34. Wohlenberg's text, whether or not by Fortunatianus (very probably not)
    bears no resemblance to Hilary's work. (cf,Jordan p.400). Tyconius'
    rules appear to have been unknown to Hilary. Like Hilary, Tyconius
    has a single theme: 'Nihil est enim quid praeter ecclesiam describat'
                                                      (contd.)

We must note however the commentaries in Latin in Victorinus, at Pettau on the fringe of the Roman world. From the remains of his rather disorganised work, it seems possible that Victorinus, influenced by both Origen and Hippolytus, was more at home in Greek than in Latin, and that his use of Latin is something of a geographical accident: nevertheless, his is the very first extant Latin commentary.[35]

The only other evidence for Latin commentary is the frequent mention of _Aliqui_ etc. in the In Matthaeum itself. If these writers had been widely popular in Gaul, we might perhaps have expected Hilary to deal with them in more detail than he did, but this question must remain open.[36]

After Hilary, in the West commentary continued in the tradition of Origen, as seen in Ambrosiaster, Ambrose and Jerome, but with the theological accent of the western tradition not entirely lost. In the work of Augustine all was taken and transformed, and a basis was set up which was to be definitive in the West for a thousand years and indeed, though the Reformation brought changes in historical understanding, up to the rise of

---

34. (contd.)
    ch.23 Hahn, but this is pursued with less theological perception than in the In Matthaeum. 'In jeden Kapital wird etwa dasselbe gesagt!' (Hahn 20). Iuvencus (CSEL 24) and Commodianus (CSEL 15) assist us not at all, though the latter's Carmen Apologeticum echoes Hilary's concern with the transfer of the inheritance of the Jews to the Gentiles.

35. The commentary on the Apocalypse (CSEL 49 ed. Haussleiter) is short, and consists of short glosses, dealing with the text almost verse by verse (as far as can be seen from the remains). The larger unity and unifying interpretation of Hilary is not present. It may be as Jerome suggests (De Vir III, 74) that Origen was a main source for Vict. Occasional echoes, ratio veritatis (in De Fabr. Mundi) types, ordo dictorum, etc. are not enough to confirm a significant influence upon Hilary, to whom he is much inferior in every respect as an exegete and theologian. But cf. Doignon, 201f.
    On Vict. cf. Haussleiter in PRE[3] sv.

36. Aliqui etc. cf. below.

the historical-critical method in the eighteenth century. In the East, Origen's structures and, even in reaction against it, much of his theological framework of interpretation, held the field and in many respects, hold it today, though here too for a short period, Augustine in Greek translation, still played a role, though a very minor one.[37] Hilary's role in the future, though overshadowed by Ambrose and Augustine, was as we shall see to provide theological foundations for interpretation rather than technical structures for commentary or even schemata for interpretational rules.[38]

The place of Hilary in this tradition, his debt and his contribution to the tradition in terms of structure and interpretation, will best be seen in the light of the detailed analysis of his own work in the following sections. But already, from the factors indicated in the text and cited in more detail in the notes, a preliminary picture begins to

37. Zeno of Verona (PL 27.1) clearly borrows from the In PSS and possibly from the In Mt. with modification: e.g. at 27.418 'vanis typus est synagogae'. Ambrosiaster (CSEL 50 and PL 17 45-508) shows a large advance qua exegetical detail upon Hilary, offering long and scholarly notes (probably under the stimulus of Origen in structure, but western in its Pauline emphases), almost verse by verse and word by word (cf.17.489 on Tim). Ambrose (cf.Comm. in Luc. CSEL 62) works in the tradition of Origen though he clearly knows Hilary's in Pss. (Seibel lists reminiscence.) Jerome blends both the eastern tradition with the Latin grammarians using e.g. Asper, Donatus and Marius Victorinus (Penna), as Hilary had done: he knew Hilary's work well (cf.EP. 5.2. on copying 2 books of Hilary for Rufinus at Treves). On Augustine's reference to and echoes of Hilary in individual exegesis cf.Comeau 40f. While Hilary had worked with a twofold meaning in scripture, Ambrose reverted to Origen's threefold division (into historia, mores, mysterium in his In Lk. (PL 15.1603 C and 1792 B etc - Burghardt) while Augustine developed a fourfold sense (in two quite different versions) De Gen. ad Lit. and De Gen. opus imperfectum), which was to be the basis of mediaeval interpretation in the West. On Augustine in Greek translation cf Altaner's essays, now collected in his 'Kleine patristische Schriften', Berlin 1968.

38. cf.below pp.221ff.

emerge. With the special exception of Victorinus of Pettau, it is possible that the first extant nearly complete western Latin biblical commentary, the In Matthaeum, was also one of the first to be written. The techniques of commentary and also many of the characteristic interpretational principles are given: Hilary has added the theological conception of the unity of the work in the service of which he then uses the techniques available to spell out this unity, demonstrating the internal connections. The techniques themselves however have functions and historical associations which in turn affect the final interpretation. This process we must now attempt to 'unpack' for the In Matthaeum, beginning from the gospel texts and seeking to distinguish the inter-related layers of interpretation. The particular role of the commentary form in achieving continuity and consistency of interpretation, and the difference caused by the direct and indirect influence of the tradition of Origen, will be seen by comparing the results obtained for the early and the late periods. At the same time, we shall have to take into account the influence on the entire process of factors arising not from the tradition but from the intellectual concerns of the cultural situation in which the writing was done.

The Law and the Gospel

3.   The Early Period

The commentary on St. Matthew

The early period: the commentary of

St. Matthew

Introduction

We have mentioned that all Hilary's extant works were written within
a decade, when the author was already a mature stylist and theologian. The
exact dates have not been established, but the approximate datings are clear:
the In Matt. was probably written in 353-5, the De Trin. in 356-7, the In
Ps after 361, and the Tractatus Mysteriorum towards the end of the work on
the psalms.[1] The exact sources for the In Matthaeum are, as we have seen,
very difficult to establish, its precise influence no less so, and the
public for which it was written, is never referred to in the work itself.[2]
The prologue which might have provided much information has long been lost[3]
and other sources for Hilary are late and notoriously unreliable.[4]

1. As M. Buttell, The Rhetoric of Hilary of Poitiers, 171. Dates: On
   internal evidence (the lack of mention of the Greek text and of explicit reference to the Arian controversy, the less direct influence
   of Origen in interpretation, the traditional western features of the
   exegesis), the In Matthaeum is dated before the exile, which followed
   the synod of Beziers in 356. The De Trinitate was written largely
   during the exile (though Hilary may have begun it before his exile and
   may have finished it on his return): cf Borchardt 40-2, and Doignon
   165f, where the debate is summarised. The In Psalmos cannot be dated
   more precisely than somewhere between his return from exile and his
   death, which came at the end of 367 or the beginning of 368. That the
   Tractatus Mysteriorum was written towards the end of the In Psalmos
   is deduced from the In Psalmos itself (references to the work as still
   to be done in Ps CXXXVIII and as completed in CXLVI cf. Brisson 13n2).

2. cf. Loofs op.cit. 59ff cf. below.

3. This prologue clearly existed. It is almost certainly mentioned at
   1.2 (diximus), and by Cassiodorus, De Inc. 7.24: cf. Jeanotte in
   Bibl. Zeitschr. for 1912 op.cit.

4. Basic to the lives is that of Venantius Fortunatus (PL 88) (cf.
   535-600 - cf.art. sv in PRE3), which is, as Loofs put it 'fast ohne
   jeden Wert'. Fortunatus used Sulpicius Severus as his main source.
                                             (contd.)

What are the general characteristics of the work? Perhaps the most striking is the extremely close knit and concise structure. Whatever latent influences we may detect, it is clear from the first that the commentary has a very different character from that of the minute scholarly investigations of the large commentaries of the Alexandrian tradition, of the close attention to historical and philological detail of e.g. Jerome, of the psychological realism of Chrysostom - and it is not a 'learned' work, like the commentary of Hippolytus. Even the wealth of scriptural quotation characteristic of most early Christian literature is almost entirely absent, indeed all extra-contextual reference seems to have been avoided with deliberate care.[5]

For whom was the commentary written? It uses few apologetic motifs, it assumes belief and indeed considerable familiarity with the Bible and the Christian faith on the part of its readers.[6] It is not primarily of a homiletic nature, and though individual portions of it may have been

4. (contd.)
How far local legend at Poitiers where Fortunatus became bishop at the end of his life, may be reflected in the Life, is impossible to say.

5. In Mt. 5.1 (PL 9.943A) referring to Cyprian and Tertullian 'De orationis autem sacramento necessitate nos commentandi Cyprianus vir sanctae memoriae liberavit'. Quamquam et Tertullianus hinc volumen aptissimum scripserit: sed consequens error hominis, detraxit scriptis probabilibus auctoritatem.

6. cf. the detailed references to the book of Kings in 1.2 (PL 9.920), or to the problems for the faithful after baptism at 3.1 (PL 9.928C) 'tentatur igitur statim post baptismus Dominus, tentatione sua indicans in sanctificatis nobis maxime diaboli tentamenta grassari: quia ei est magis exoptata de sanctis', and many similar passages.

used in sermons, it is clearly not constructed out of a series of homilies.[7]

Whether it was intended for private use as an aid to diocesan clergy in
the preparation of sermons, for clergy or laity, for Gaul or for the
Church at large, is never indicated. There are no local and no direct
contemporary references whatever.[8]

It soon becomes clear that for the purpose of his commentary (and we
may take this to reflect both Hilary's own understanding of the text and
his understanding of the evangelist's intention) the entire text of the
gospel is to be understood in terms of the relationship between law and
gospel. This may also be expressed in terms of a contrast between the law
and faith (faith sometimes complemented by bona opera caritatis), between
the Jews and the Gentiles or the church and the synagogue, and by the types
of the apostles and the preaching of the need for faith.[9] This theme is

7. cf. the homilies of Chrysostom of Zeno of Verona, Hilary never sues
   'vos' but always 'nos', does not always end on a homiletic point,
   shows no traces of sermonic introduction, ascription, etc. (contrast
   the In Psalmos below) and is clearly constructing in terms of a
   continuous narrative.

8. The references to Cyprian might suggest that this work is intended
   for a congregation in a didactic, non-learned context, as the treat-
   ments by both Tertullian and Cyprian suggest that their work was
   intended. This would be supported further by the exhortational
   material (present in nearly all early Christian literature). But this
   remains only an indication, not a proof.

9. cf. In. Mt. 4.22 (PL 9.939C) (Quicumque dimiserit uxorem suam, det illi
   repudiem etc. Nam cum lex libertatem dandi repudii ex libelli auctoritate tribuisset, nunc marito fides evangelica non solum voluntatem
   pacis indixit verum etiam reatum coactae in adulterium uxoris imposuit,
   si alio ex discessionis necessitate nubenda sit.) Also (PL 9.963) on
   John the Baptist 'Usque in eum enim lex et prophetae sunt; et, nisi
   lege finita, in fidem evangelicam eorum nemo concederet,' and numerous
   others at 5.6; 8.4; 9.2; 12.6; 14.11; 19.10; 20.4; 20.9; etc.

understood by means of the illumination of the interior significantia of the text.[10] The text is itself a witness to the history of God's actions in transferring salvation from the Jews to the Gentiles, from the inheritance of faith. The pivot of this movement is Jesus Christ, the sinless Son of God who in faith reverses the effect of the sins of Adam through the law.[11] Apart from a few references to angels and demons, and, in the first chapter only, a discussion of Mary's virginity, of the brothers of Jesus and an explanation of Dt 25.6, and later a gloss on 'Rachel' and one on 'Hosanna', the commentary contains NO OTHER THEMES![12] Such a strict economy in subject matter would appear to be unique among ancient commentaries (with the possible exception of the special case of Tyconius). A survey of all ancient commentaries on St. Matthew shows a comparable concision and unity of material elsewhere only in the (incomplete) fifth century scholia of Arnobius the younger (MPL 53) (Indeed an examination of the relevant texts shows no evidence of direct connection with any single patristic exegete of St. Matthew).[13]

10. cf.2.2 (PL 9.924C) In Johanne locus praedicatio, vestitus cibus est contuendus: atque ita, ut meminerimus gestorum veritatem non idciro corrumpi, si gerendis rebus interioris intelligentiae ratio subjecta est' etc.

11. cf.3.5 (PL 9.930) where Christ prevails over the temptations to which Adam succumbed, and 8.5-7 (PL 9.960-1) ending 'postremo reditu in domum propriam iter in paradisum credentibus esse redhibendum, ex quo Adam parens universorum peccati labi dissolutus excesserat.

12. cf.ch 1.; 4.17; and 21.3.

13. Some evidence for this conclusion has been given in ch. 1 above (sv Irenaeus, note, etc.) A sample of the situation in the commentaries, especially those on St. Matthew, might be set out as follows:
1. The Western Church. Hippolytus - no connection with the fragments on Mt. 24f can be shown. Unlike Hippol. Hilary makes no mention of the eikon of the emperor. For Hipplytus the sabbath signifies the end of mankind, for Hilary, otium bonorum operum etc. The fig tree
(contd.)

Interior significantia of Jesus Christ as vere Deus, vere homo, lex

fides - inevitably discussion of the commentary has focussed on Hilary's

relation to the Alexandrian tradition and to Origen, to the Arian contro-

versy, and on his Paulinism. Our own first concern however, is an examin-

ation of the commentary structure as such, seen against the background of

the previous chapter, in order to find out what affects if any, this

structure has had on his exegesis. We shall examine the relation of the

biblical text to the exposition, to see how the text was treated by and

appeared to Hilary as he began its exegesis. How far, if at all, was the

text already seen as a characteristically fourth century document by

Hilary before he began his further interpretation of it? At a later stage,

we shall then attempt to distinguish in the wider interpretation of the

text those catagories which derived originally from the literary tradition

and those which derive from particular theological and philosophical

traditions.

13. (contd.)
     for Hippolytus is like any other tree. Novatian, references to Mt.
     in the De Trin show no parallels but in the western tradition there
     are references to 'scripture' 'coelestis', 'deus per scripturas
     ostenditur' etc. Tertullian's references to the gospel of St. Mt.
     appear to have no similarity to those of Hilary, likewise with Cyprian,
     except for the single reference to 'evangelica praecepta'.
     2. The East. Origen (GCS 10) is very different, e.g. in his treatment
     of the episode of the loaves and fishes; none of the familiar equiv-
     alents navis=ecclesia, pueri=gentes, mater=lex, ficus=synagoga, occur
     in Origen on St. Matthew, Athanasius (MPG 27) has only one parallel,
     to 1.1 where Hilary, Jesus Christ is referred to as rex et sacerdos
     cf Athan, kai hiereus kai basileus ho Christos etugchanen which poss-
     ibly comes from a common source in credal formulation.
     Theodore of Heracles (Reuss p.55f) Theodore of Mopsuestia (Reuss
     p.96f) and Apollinarius of Laodicea (Reuss) are very different both
     in general scope and particular use of figural expressions. Likewise
     Theophilus of Alexandria (Reuss p.150) and Cyril of Alexandria
     MPG 72). A completely different treatment is provided by John
     Chrysostom (MPG 57,58).

a) The formal structure of the commentary.[14]

In writing the commentary on St. Matthew in Gaul around 353-5, why did Hilary choose this particular gospel for exposition and this particular literary form? No direct answer is given in the text. It may be that he had preached a series of sermons on the text of the gospel, but there is no trace of these in the commentary.[15] Hilary describes his work as a book, and cross references reveal that it was intended to be read through as a continuous work.[16] Paraphrases in the text would allow the work to be read with or without the text of the gospel to hand.[17] Gaul was at this time the scene of a magnificent late flowering of the Latin language, yet with the exception of certain technical terms which we shall consider below, the work shows no affinity with any distinctly Gallic literary genre. Its language is elegant but not elaborate.[18]

14. It should be stressed that these divisions , convenient for exposition, in no sense represent exclusive and virtually independent categories.

15. Earliest evidence for a lectio continua in Gaul is from the mid-fifth century (Gennadius of Marseilles in De Script. Eccles. 79 (MPL 58)). On liturgy in Gaul cf. Jungmann 1. 37f. But sermons in series on texts are common before this, cf Chrysostom's homilies on Genesis (cf. A. Niebergall in Leiturgia II, (1955) 181-353) and arts. 'Perikopen' and 'Geschichte der christliche Predigt' in PRE3.

16. Esp. 19.11 (MPL 9. 1027B) 'sed in primordio libri (2.2) sub vestitu Johannis, in camelo gentes significari admonuimus' cf, too below.

17. cf. ch. 21 (PL 9.1034C) Duo discipuli ad vicum mittuntur, etc.

18. A characteristic piece is to be found at 21.1 (PL 9.1035B) 'Pullum veri idem Dominus ascendit, novellum contumacem, durum; atque haec omnia gentilis ignorantiae vitiae dominantur, et tot animae ferocitates vectio Deo factae sunt (reading the lectio difficilior with the Migne text).

We have seen that Hilary was not the first to write commentary in Latin,[19] and that he himself sought to correct previous misinterpretation.[20] Yet the general custom in the West has been to expound the biblical text in the form of homilies, or when developing a particular theme to use the looser form of a tractate.[21] There is, it seems to me, a close connection between the choice of the commentary form and Hilary's understanding of the nature and purpose of the text itself. The concise, strictly inter-related nature of the exposition corresponds to his conviction of the con-tinuity and single purpose of the gospel narrative itself - a purpose which we shall examine later in detail[22] - namely the history of the action of God in transferring the inheritance of faith through Jesus Christ from the old people of God to the new. He admits, partly in deference to a literalist tradition in the West, that the text has a valid literal and open meaning[23] (the relation of this to the theological concept of an

---

19. On Rheticius and others cf section 2 above.

20. cf.12.18 (PL 9.990A) In futurum vero omnem fidei perversitatem coarguit, eorum scilicet qui...in diversa hereseos studis efferbuer-unt. cf.31.3 (PL 9.1066D) Sed eorum omnis hic sensus est etc. In this connection it is worth bearing in mind that much of Gaul was opened to mission really only in the first half of the 4th century. cf Frend in 'Mullus', Festschrift Klauser, 128 'It was not till a generation after Constantine that a native Latin Christianity owing, as Hilary of Poitiers suggests, little to the east, began to make its presence felt in Southern Gaul.' cf.too 4.19 quid enim a pluribus in hoc capite sensum est. 1.3. plures irreligiosi et a spiritali doctrina admodum alieni 31.2 aliquorum opinio est. cf.too 26.5 on heretical opinions.

21. cf.sect. 2 above on the homilies and tractate of Iren., Tertullian and Cyprian.

22. On the unity of the text cf below.

23. 7.1 (PL 9.954B) Nihil enim veritati detrahit, imitationem veritas consecuta cf 10.1 (PL 9.966B) Paria in dictis atque in factis signif-icationum momenta consistunt (though the stress here is on the future significance of the words).

'externa claritas' we shall have to explore): but beyond this there is as in most Patristic exegesis, an inner meaning in the movement of the history of faith, which can be understood through the Spirit of God, which can be understood by paying attention to the hidden continuities and significant points within the narrative itself.[24]

We must now analyse these technical means by which Hilary extracts his interpretation, as a consistent whole and in its constituent parts, from the text of the gospel, and assess the consequences for his exposition involved in the procedure followed, i.e. look at the resultant state of the basic data. We shall then go on to consider the wider contexts in which the interpretation is developed.

The text of the gospel and of the commentary is divided up in the Migne text into a number of sections - 33 in the authentic portion of the text[25] - each with a self-contained segment of text and exposition; but this division, as Jeanotte has shown, is mediaeval. A guide to the beginning of each new chapter can be seen in the sections of the gospel which end with et reliqua[26] but this guide is not infallible.[27]

24. cf. 7.8 (PL 9.957A) ergo rerum tantarum, et tam diversarum ratio promenda est; atque ita, ut secundum continentem verum ordinem, et gravissimas veritatis ipsius causas, interioris significantiae intelligentia explicetur.

25. The final section of ch.33 (PL 9.1066f) has long been recognised to be from Jerome, and to have been added much later.

26. cf H. Jeanotte in Bibl. Zeitschr. 10 (1912) 36-48. The capitula, which begin to correspond to Hilary's own divisions after ch.24, were probably edited in the 5th or 6th century (Jeanotte, op cit).

27. A division by episodes might be made as follows: 1.1-2; 2.2-2.4; 2.5; 3.1-3.6; 4.1-4.8; 4.9-12; 4.13-22; 4.23-27; 4.28-5.4; 5.5; 6; 7; 8.1-2; 8.3-end; 9; 10.1-5; 10.6-21; 10.22-end; 11; 12.1-17; 12.18-20; 12.21-end; etc.

Since the material makes up not a series of scholia but a continuous commentary, each piece of text, though not each single verse, is taken up after the other and explained, often in terms of adjacent sections.[28] Not all of the gospel text is covered in this way, however. Apart from the missing prologue and ending, there is a system of choice of texts for exposition, which leaves out some and includes others.[29] Those left out are all classified (where mentioned at all) as intelligible absolute, and so requiring no further explanation. Those included have a hidden spiritual meaning, the unfolding of which is the purpose of the work. What this meaning is will concern us in a later section.

Each section always begins with a portion of the gospel text usually the beginning of an episode in the narrative. One or two verses are cited, and followed by an exposition into which following verses of the gospel text are then drawn. The relation in size between text and commentary depends, as do the lengths of the text and commentary themselves, entirely on the content of the material.[30]

The connections between the sections are not simply those of the gospel narrative, but there are definite references backwards (though never forwards) showing how the continuity of the sections is to be understood.[31]

28. In chs. land 2 the only verses precisely quoted are 1.1; 1.18; 1.20; 1.25; 2.1f; 2.13; 2.18; 2.21. The whole has an inner ordo cf. 1.2 'sequens est, secundum rerum fidem generationis istium ordinem nec numero sibi nec successione constare: huius quoque rei ratio afferatur etc.
29. e.g. 24.9 (PL 9.1051) Judicii forma is absoluto est etc. cf. the list below.
30. Here there is no fixed proportion. The lengths of Hilary's chapters themselves vary considerably, becoming much shorter towards the end (cf. chs. 26-8), perhaps an indication of haste.
31. cf. the reference to continuity at 5.4 (PL 9.944) continens sensus est, 18.4 (PL 9.1020A) Superius autem in abscindendis manu vel pede propin-
(contd.)

The absence of forward reference may, but need not necessarily, suggest original delivery of the material to an audience, who could recall but not anticipate.

There is always a definite break between sections, which is often underlined by the use of formulaic phrases.[32] Within the sections themselves, too, much of the exposition has stereotyped characteristics, though complex patterns are not found repeated. We do not find large differences in the shape of these patterns, of the kind found by Adler in Philo. Instead there is a fairly consistent structure of text, exposition and citation of further verses within the text of the rest of the episode being dealt with, though there are differences, for example, in the formulae introducing the citations. Occasionally there are no extra citations, and here the exposition often consists of paraphrase of the text.[33]

Biblical citations in the exposition are taken on occasion from outside the episode being commented upon. Sometimes single words from cit-

31. (contd.)
   quitatum contineri nomina exposuimus, 4.21 atque ideo etc. 27.3 dictis superioribus tractatum est, 14.6 sermo igitur ad originem proposit- ionis referendus est 21 post superiorem competenter nunc, and a rather different but connected use at 10.8 quae ergo dictum proprietas monstranda est. cf 20.5; 32.4; 19.11.

32. Notably the connectives post quae 2.1 etc. post haec (1.7) and the instances in 30 above.

33. cf. 8.3. First a list of the events of the narrative is repeated. All hanc habet causam. The whole is then explained in detail, epit- omising phrase after epitomising phrase; not only does the passage as a whole have a thematic theological meaning, but there are key phrases which must be picked out as indicative pointers to the theme. These pointers may each in themselves sum up the theme of the whole episode. This is a consequence of the theological conception of the gospel text; cf. below. Occasionally we find verse by verse expos- ition e.g. cf. the beatitudes at 4.3ff.

ations are singled out and stressed, but the usual practice is simply
citation as a 'proof text'. The function of all these citations is not
to add something new to the sense, but to confirm, illustrate, prove,
underline the meaning of the text under consideration. This use of additional citations to stress main points helps to provide a unifying element
and to balance the atomising tendency of much of the technique of exposition.

Sometimes individual words from citations are singled out and
stressed. The texts of the citations are more often cited as proofs,
confirmations and illustrations than actually exegeted. Thus in 1.1 Lk 3.2
is cited as a piece of evidence for the purpose of historical explanation.
Jn. 19. 26-7 is used as a proof of the explanation of the position regarding the brothers of Jesus at 1.4 (cf. Tert. De virg. Vol.6, De Carne
Christi 6, for whom Jesus' brothers are the sons of Mary) and at 1.7 Jer.
31.15 and Mt 2.18 are used as 'proof texts' for the illustration of the
fulfilment of prophecy. In the commentary there are 67 explicit citations of texts apart from the gospel text under consideration in each
episode (not all entirely accurate), 26 from the OT (7 from Genesis,
6 from Is., 3 from Ex. and from Ezech., and one each from Lev., Kings,
Dan. and Jonah) and 41 from the NT (13 from Mt., 10 from Jn., 4 each from
Lk., Acts and Cor., 2 from Eph., and 1 Pet., 1 each from Rom. and Rev.)
Bonassieux counted 236 vv of Mt. cited out of 1060 i.e. 21.27%. Though
many of the citations are of traditional doctrinal proof texts e.g.
I Pet. 2.22 and I Pet. 4.8, sometimes the link may be simply that of
association of ideas e.g. calceamenta suggests Is. 52.7 at 2.3 and
Ex. 3.5 at 10.5.

Attempts to determine from citations the actual text of the bible used by Hilary have been a matter of considerable and largely fruitless speculation. Bonassieux's attempt to establish the text of the synoptic gospels used (1906) was demolished by Julicher almost at once (TLZ 1907) and this judgement is confirmed by Feder (WS 1919). It is not clear for example that Hilary used the same text in Gaul and in Asia Minor, and in any event, he may often cite from memory.[34]

The order of the episodes into which the material is divided is reinforced too by the use of technical distinctions from the rhetorical tradition - ordo, ratio, proprietas etc. the details of which we shall consider in a later section. An important feature of the In Matthaeum is that the text is divided according to the main themes as Hilary sees them, and not simply line by line as in many other commentaries e.g. those of Jerome and Origen.[35]

This brings us to the question of the kind of explanation given. The exposition is no scholiast's explanation of obscure words and grammatical oddities: Hilary's concern is with the gospel as a theological whole, and with each section as part of a wider context. For this reason he does not

---

34. cf Reinkens' 'Beilage' to his work on 'Die Lateinsichen Übersetzungen der Bibel in der Mitte der IV Jhdt'. cf Souter, Text and Canon 81 'Hilary used in the gospels a text having points of contact with the Irish Latin codex Usserianus of the VIth century.(r) No doubt Britain and Ireland first got the gospel from Gaul.' cf too Engelbrecht.

35. How is the choice between different interpretations to be made? For Hilary the text has its own ordo, which may be unfolded. cf. 1.3 generationis ordo simplex est. 2.2 In Johanne locus contuendus... atque ita ut meminerimus gestorum veritatem non idcirco corrumpi, si gerendis rebus interioris intelligentiae ratio subjecta sit. 2.11 typica ratio servata est 21.12 rationem quaerere coelestis intelligenitae admonemur, 25.5 momenta praeceptorum coelestium consequamur.

normally go through the passage phrase by phrase as e.g. Origen does, and so avoids much of the atomisation of the text endemic in much ancient commentary. But the penalty is a frequent alteration of the accent laid on the several facets of given episodes by the evangelist, in favour of harmonisation with Hilary's own total concept of the work.[36]

We have noted that a basic feature of the explanation given is its exclusively theological nature. This distinguishes sharply the shape of the work from that of Origen, with its many historical geographical and other details Hilary's is not in that sense erudite.[37] When an obscurity in the text is explained, this is at once related to a theological point[38] The whole work is explained in terms of basic principles for the theological interpretation which is applied to and extracted from the text according to given hermeneutical rules. These principles are never argued for

36. This is especially evident in e.g. his treatment of the miracles of Jesus; cf 14.9f the episode of the feeding of the 5000 where the elements of awe and wonder and the cosmic significance of Jesus disappear in the relation of all to the law/gospel axis (on this R.M. Grant, Miracle and Natural Law 211ff, also comments) cf. too on 32. the treatment of the betrayal. 'sed in osculo Judae haec fuit ratio: ut doceremur inimicos omnes eosque quis sciremus dessevituros in nos esse, diligere. Osculum enim Dominus non respuit: The passion takes the form of a celestial play, in which the depth of the issues of betrayal and suffering are lost. This is also strikingly evident in ch.33, the narrative of the crucifixion, in which the detailed typology obscured the scandalus crucis.

37. cf. Origen in Mt. 13.42f (GCS 10) where there is a long report on pearl fishing in India, Britain and in the Bosphorus (the Latin translation of Origen in Mt. dates from 600) cf. Hil. In Mt. 13.8 margarita a lege ad evangelium transiens.

38. as in the explanation of racha at 4.17, the linguistic gloss on hosanna at 26.3 and the historical gloss on Samaria at 26.1.

but referred to as given.[39] To this second stage of the interpretational
process we now turn.

We have alraedy noted the division of the text into material whose
significance was plain absolute and that which was not. The former may
be classified in three sections, referring to the fulfilment of prophecy,
historical details about the life of Jesus which are not of direct interest
for the exposition of the history of salvation, and some parables.[40] The
latter has a deep but hidden meaning, indicated by several synonymous
phrases, the most common of which is coelestis significantis, which as
mentioned is assumed to indicate the key to the interpretation. Such a
principle is, as we saw in section 2 above, common to most early biblical
exegesis: important for us is the nature of its interconnection with the
structure of the commentary form and the theological motifs which govern
Hilary's conception of the text, and which of course, vary from exegete to
exegete. For Hilary, these key motifs consist in the dialectic (for
these themes always occur in balancing pairs) between the law and faith,
the Jews and the Gentiles, the Synagogue and the Church, those who deny

---

39. cf.below.

40. Absolutus. cf. 22.1 quaestio omnis in absoluto est; 15.1 absolute
     ratio; cf.18.11; 19.9; 22.1; 24.8; 27.3; etc. Within the context
     of a purely spiritual sense, a passage with a 'simple' sense may
     also occur; cf 20.3 omnis itaque hic sermo est spiritalis. Sed
     Dominus brevi absolutaque ratione dicens, i.e. the absolute is not
     contrasted in every case with the spiritual sense. 'Absolutus' is
     applied to parables and to actions of Jesus which are self-explanatory.
     Usually mention of an 'absolute' sense implies only brief mention.
     Connected with the passages whose significance is clear 'absolute'
     is the complete omission of some passages: these refer either to
     (a) the fulfilment of prophecy or to (b) historical events in the
     narrative which are not of direct interest for the main line of
     interpretation or (c) to some parables, and occur at 1.22-7 (a);
     2.5-6 (a); 2.7-8 (b); 2.23 (a); 3.5 (b); etc. 6.7-15 (b - because
     of treatment by Tert. and Cypr.) 13.24-30 (c); 26.27f (b) etc.
     and 28.10ff (missing/lost).

the divinity of the eternal Son of God and those who do not. There is
then no attempt to argue in principle from the literal words of the text
towards a reconstruction of the hidden significance; rather this is known
and is the key to the illumination of the literal course of the text.
Whatever we may think of its usefulness, the reciprocal relation between
the text and the inner significance, which is brought about by the Spirit,
constitutes a legitimate hermeneutical circle, in which, for Hilary as
for Cyprian and for Augustine, a vital link in the chain of understanding
is membership of the Church.[41]

What then of the relation between the inner significance and the
external commentary structures examined at the beginning of this section?
We might illustrate the position by suggesting that in the first stage
the bricks constructed from the raw material of the text, and can then be
used to build the arches of the hermeneutical design. The processing of
the raw material is essential to the nature of the building as it is con-
ceived, but in the process the original colour and texture of that raw
material, the gospel text, has been altered drastically.

Finally, in this formal section, we may mention the manner in which
Hilary seeks to present the material to his readers. Clearly he is not

41. cf.ch.14, ergo Dei Verbum lege finita navem conscendens Ecclesiam
     adit, et in desertam concedit, de synagoga videlicet ad ecclesiam con-
     cedit and numerous others. For the spiritual significance in gen-
     eral cf,2.6 ordo enim in eo arcani coelestis exprimitur; 5.13 totius
     sub dictis coelestis significantia continetur; 20.15 rationem quaerere
     coelestis intelligentiae admonemur; 19.4 in scripturis coelestibus;
     14.9 responsio ad spiritalis intelligentiae ordinem tendit; 20.1 ut
     ratio spiritalis plana esset; i.e. Hilary makes changes for stylistic
     reasons rather than to suggest nuances of meaning. On the hermeneut-
     ical condition of membership of the Church cf,13.1 significat eos qui
     extra ecclesiam positi sunt nullam divini sermonis capere posse
     intelligentiam.

presenting this for learning in school, or for the information of experts on biblical background; he is simply concerned to explain the sequence of events in terms of the movement from the law to faith.

The peculiar character is Hilary's method of presentation may be further illustrated by comparison with related literary forms. Porphyrius's scholion-commentary for example, uses the categories of the literary tradition in the same ways as Hilary does, but here there is no literary unity whatever, and no continuity of theme.[42] Zeno of Verona's near contemporary homilies contain a fair amount of material on subjects outside the biblical narrative: Hilary's commentary, despite its homiletic elements has none, and though there is a certain amount of ethical exhortation[43] there is no direct appeal to the reader in the second person, and no long diatribe-like excurses of the kind frequent in homilies. The stress is more on the attainment of cognitio Dei through faith than of moral excellences. Again the series of questions and answers and the refutation of objections real or assumed which characterised the dialogue and some forms of commentary are absent from the In Matt; in Hilary the divisions of the narrative are for a better understanding of the theological themes, not for analysis for its own sake, as for example in that highly sophisticated Alexandrian product, the systematic scientific textbook.

42. Wessner, (Quaestiones Porphyrianae, p.159f) showed that the work being cited by C. Iulius Romanus, must have been written approximately at the beginning of the third century.
43. Mainly in the context of the Sermon on the Mount. cf. ch.4 passim. cf.too 5,3,13,9 etc. contemptum saeculi.

The above then are the basic formal characteristics of the commentary and the effects which these characteristics have on the biblical text itself. The next step must be to examine in detail the theoretical aspects of the main interpretational principles, and to attempt to clarify the processes of hermeneutical interconnection involved in the application of these principles to the structure of the text in its 'prepared' form in the commentary.

b) The nature of the hermeneutical principles

In this section we shall consider factors deriving mainly from the exegetical tradition of the church and the rhetorical tradition of the schools.

We have seen that both the exegetical tradition of the church and the rhetorical tradition of the schools developed sophisticated systems for the interpretation of texts, to both of which Hilary was indebted.[44]

The basic concept expressed by the phrase 'coelestis significantia' is of course, a corollary of the idea of a sacred book, and as such was taken for granted in the early church, referring from the beginning of the third century at least to the status of the material within the canon of Old and New Testaments.[45] For Hilary the scriptures were in a literal sense divinely inspired. What was not so obvious for some of his readers was that the coelestis significantia was not always to be identified with

---

44. cf, sect. 2 above and summaries of the exegetical tradition in PRE3 art. Hermeneutik, RGG3 Schriftauslegung, Hermeneutik, Geist und Buchstabe, EKL art. Hermeneutik. On the rhetorical tradition, Gräfenhan and Steinthal are still useful.

45. On the formation of the canon cf. H.v. Campenhausen, Die Entstehung des Neuen Testaments, Tübingen 1968.

the literal meaning of the text.[46] For Hilary the text has two levels of meaning. In principle any given text may have both, but usually he draws particular attention to one or the other. Both levels may be used by God in illuminating our understanding, but the inner meaning relates specifically, in this gospel, to the movement from the law to faith. There is not, as in Origen, a series of steps towards our deeper illumination and perfection, but the illumination as cognitio Dei consists in understanding the relation of prophecy to fulfilment in the church, in the history of the saving acts of God, the pivot of this movement from the law to faith is the recognition of the divine sonship of Christ.

Thus in 1.5 nihil a Judaea petere scientiae agnitionisque permittimur, sed in Christo salutem omnem et spem locantes, admonemur prioris vitae itinere abstinere. Fides brings cognitio Dei, but the infideles are lost in ignorantia. cf. 4.11 (935B) Igitur mundus extra cognitionem Dei positus obscurabatur ignorantiae tenebris; cui per apostolos scientiae lumen invehitur, et cognitio Dei claret; 7.11 (958A) filium autem hominis, se scilicet cui caput Deus sit, non reperire in quos collocata Dei cognit-

---

46. Despite the references to divinus sermo (13) sermo Dei etc., and the literalist tradition of the fusion of the virtus of the Spirit with the inspired text, scripture is not explicitly described as the Verbum Dei. Jesus is however so referred to, and his words are themselves the Verbum; so 6.1 ergo et concorporationem Verbi Dei, passionis mysterium et virtutem-resurrectionis non promiscue tractari nos convenit; 7.2 adest leprosus...Verbi virtute curatur; 5.8 In dictis Dei veritas est, et rerum creandarum efficientia omnis in verbo ist. Scripture itself has a special coelestis significantia which is given by God and confers divine truth upon its meaning in both literal and spiritual senses cf. 7.1 nihil enim veritati detrahit, imitationem veritas consecuta; as at 7.1 again, ne quis forte existimaret aliquid rerum gestarum fidei detrahendum etc. Sometimes both senses are employed in the interpretation as at 19.10 et haec quidem ad simplicis sensus intelligentiam pertinent. Verum eodem cursu interioris causae ordo retinendus est. But at 20.2 only one sense is relevant, omnis itaque haec sermo est spiritalis.

ione requiescat; 9.9 Dei quippe cognitione superstitionum omnium vesania effugata, et visus et auditus et sermo salutis invehitur...cum, cui per legem nihil afferri opis poterat, verbi virtute salvari; 23.6 Proprium enim Domini nostri Jesus Christi officium est, cognitionem Dei afferre, et intelligentiam nominis eius potestatisque praestare; (24.1 in omnibus enim Christi meditabatur adventum. Quidquid enim in es continebatur, in profectum manifestandae eius cognitionis assumptum est); 25.6 sed perinde hic etiam infirmitatem animarum, quae ad cognitionem Dei tamquam lacte adhuc alantur ostendit; quae perfecti cibi virtute indigentes, tenui divinae cognitionis infirmoque gustatu imbuantur; 33.4 locus tamquam in vertice huius universitatis insistens, ad capessendem Dei cognitionem universis gentibus esset sequalis. cf.too 20.13 Atque ut typus crediturarum gentium expleretur, coelestis gratiae cognitione percepta, qui caeci fuerant, videntes Dominum suum sunt secuti. Traces however of the Western moralising tradition remain, at 4.1 exemplo docuit ut boni sumus, or at 2.3 sed subest gestis rebus exemplum...ut ad omne ministerium Christi voluntate simus accincti.[47]

The centre of the lex/fides axis, which is the essence of the history of salvation, is the history of the dicta and facta of Jesus.[48] These themselves create faith, with the aid of the agency of the Spirit, and meditation upon the whole coelestis significantis unveiled within the scripture will deepen the faith of the reader, under the action of the Spirit as the

47. Here Luther who has borrowed much from the In Matthaeum explicitly contradicts Hilary, without mentioning him; Johannes non gestat haec vestimenta ut exemplum nobis donet. Es war um sein predigampt zu thun WA 27.458.2-4 (apud Ebeling EE 443).

48. cf.too below the references in the lex/fides citations and in the work of Jesus in dicta and facta.

virtus inspiring the words themselves. The text has its own spiritual significance and mediates the knowledge of God in Jesus, who is the object of its witness, to the reader.

It is because of this stress upon the coelestis significantia of the texts themselves in mediating the knowledge of God, rather than a stress being upon God revealing himself in the context of scriptures, (cf the De Trin) that the special hermeneutical principles of the rhetorical and exegetical tradition play such an important role, as much as in the final process of the understanding of scripture as the medium of revelation as in the intermediate stage of the correlation with the lex/fides central motif and in the preliminary stage of the preparation of the narrative into a suitably pointed series of narratives bearing on the history of salvation.

A variety of means are used in this intermediate stage to relate the conception of the Heilsgeschichte to the narratives and to the texts, the most striking of these being the lex/fides model, which is applied throughout the work. The Jews stand under the condemnation of the law, Jesus came under the judgment of the law and himself pronounced judgment upon it. Faith brings freedom from condemnation and saving knowledge of God, and is the inheritance which has passed from the old Israel to the new. Further illustration may be found in almost every section of the work.[49]

49. cf. 4.22-25 where lex is contrasted throughout with fides evangelica.
     cf. too 5.1 justificatio ex fide; 8.6 fide enim sola justificat; 9.3
     usque enim in eum (Johannes) lex et prophetae sunt; et, nisi lege
     finita, in fidem evangelicam eorum (Johannis discipuli) nemo conced-
     eret. Ac sic consummatum justitia ex fide; 12.3 evangelica fides
     operatur in Christo; 18.11 sed lex, ut scimus, futurorum umbra est;
     19.10 iactura legis with fides evangelica; 20.9 apostoli quidem iam
     ex lege crediderant, quae eos in fidem evangelicam nutriverat; cf. too
                                                         (contd.)

The sources of this strong Pauline tradition have been much debated.
A recent carefully argued suggestion would trace it, and the apparent
'Pauline renaissance' in the Latin West in general, to a continuing
Marcionite stream in the western tradition: this we shall examine in
detail below. But the problem remains. One factor was probably simply
reaction from the moralising quasi-legalist strain in western Christianity
deriving from Tertullian particularly and the influence of popular Stoicism.
But as we have seen above there were also traditional sources of the law/
gospel, people of faith/people of the law motif in the West. The concept
of the populus Dei was central in western ecclesiology e.g. in Hippolytus,
and the classic theologian of the oikonomia of the Heilsgeschichte was
Irenaeus, whose continuing influence especially in Gaul can hardly be
doubted, despite the relatively late date of the first extant Latin translation. The tradition too of the movement of the people of God in the
letter to the Hebrews played a much greater role in the West than in the
East in the first four centuries and there was another side even to

49. (contd.)
    20.15; 21.15; 26.5; 27.9; 32.2; 32.7; and characteristically 9.2
    nam si iustitia fuisset ex lege, venia per gratiam necessaria non
    fuisset. cf.too for complementary motifs 2.1 admoniti per visum,
    sancti scilicet Spiritus donum in gentibus contemplantes, ad eas
    transferrunt Christum, Judaeae missum sed vitam et salutem gentium
    nuncupatum; 11.11 fides gentium cf.18.4 iudaicum populum; 8.5
    gentilium universitas; 15.5 fides in gentibus; 13.5 mulier-synagoga;
    14.7 passim on the Jews and the Gentiles; 7.3 tribunus...principem
    esse gentium crediturarum; 12.23 grace for the gentes; 5.12 sub foeni
    nomine gentes etc., 2.1 magi-gentes crediturae. 12.18-25 ecclesia/
    synagoga, fides gentium/infidelitas Iudaeorum. cf.too 5.6 justitia
    ex fides nulla est...etc. 3.11 legis opus inefficax, 11.11; 12.13;
    14.8 finitis igitur legis temporibus).

Tertullian, in his stress on the fides motif.[50]

Our present concern is however with the use rather than the source of the motif. For Hilary in this work the Christian gospel is par excellence the gospel of faith and the Matthean text is a mirror/microcosm of this gospel.

The means by which Hilary's special interpretation of the concept of spiritual meaning are connected with the structure of the narrative are various. We consider first those categories of the rhetorical tradition, especially ordo, ratio, proprietas and exemplus.

The use of these categories is not of course confined to the rhetorical tradition. In most classical allegorical interpretation, e.g. of Homer, or of the Old Testament by Justin, a lack of proprietas or ordo in the literal sense of the text is a sign of a hidden inner meaning.[51] The use of ordo in Hilary has important theological connotations, in underlining that the inner interpretation is itself part of God's saving history; so too with ratio, when illuminated by faith (without which, according to Hilary, we can understand nothing of God).[52]

50. cf.the discussion of Wille below, and the references in the notes to sect.2 above from Iren., Hippol., and Tert. For populus Dei cf. too A.Oepke, Das neue Gottesvolk p.255f on Hippolytus. The thesis is also found, as indicated above, in Tertullian, Clement, Origen and Lactantius. But it is never used in a manner so concentrated as that of the In Mt. The refutation of the Jews and of the teaching of the synagogue was of course a standard part of early Christian apologetic: (Oepke p.287) cites Constantine's letter to the churches after Nicaea (PL8.501-6).

51. cf.sect. 2 above (details for Homer cf.Buffière, for Justin cf. Shotwell op.cit.29ff - largely from Philo cf p.35 above).

52. cf.15.8 ordo igitur idem in sermoni Domini est, qui in consequenda gratia manet; 2.6 ordo coelestis; 3.6 rei gestae ordo; 8.6 veritatis ordo; 9.8 sed manet nunc ordo mysterii; 11.27 ordo gratiarum. For ratio cf 15.1 absoluta ratio est; 17.12 subest praesentibus rebus
(contd.)

In the rhetorical tradition these concepts have not only descriptive but also hermeneutical functions, which are reflected in the commentary in the ease with which the transition from matters of literacy form to matters of theological interpretation is made.[53]

That Hilary was familiar with the methods of classical rhetoric is clear both from the nature of his own background and from the works themselves. Where precisely he was educated is not clear, but there is no reasonable doubt that he was brought up in that classical tradition which enjoyed its brilliant Indian summer in Gaul in the middle of the fourth century.[54] Evidence for the courses pursued in the schools is from the second half of the century, but undoubtedly in Hilary's day Quintilian, and textbooks based on him, formed a major part of the standard literature in literary criticism. My own reading of the results of the long controversy on the influence of Quintilian on Hilary is that though there are no deliberate reminiscences of Quintilian, yet the influence of his categories of literary criticism is to be affirmed. That there may have been

52. (contd.)
ratio interior; 17.2 where ratio is connected with exemplum - et in hoc quidem facti genere, servatur et ratio, et numerus, et exemplum. 14.1 interioris intelligentiae ratio; 9.9 ratio praefigurationis; 19.1 typica ratio etc. It will be clear from the above examples that ratio and ordo are often used in a practically synonymous way. (This we shall see, may also be the case, but is not always so, with typus and exemplus). Sensus, cf. 6.6 sensus est superioribus coniunctus, and causa cf. 8.3 dum hominum occursus etc. hanc habent causam may also be closely connected with the above. The importance of these terms lies more in the continuity which they suggest than in the precise use of the individual terms.

53. cf. the discussion of the individual cases below.

54. On the background to the Church in Gaul and Hilary's relation to this cf. Scott Holmes esp. 143f and Jullian op.cit. 6.104-15, 123-8 and VII 246-64.

intermediate sources is not excluded: that there were other influences in the use of the rhetorical terms as well, notably Cicero (cf. De Orat 3.18 etc.) Seneca perhaps and Tertullian, is highly probable.[55]

The possible influence of this tradition in mediating theories of knowledge (reflected in Quintilian's use of res in the interplay of philosophical and literary terminology in Cicero etc.) will concern us in a later section. The first main effect to be noted here of the transference of these categories to the interpretation of the structure of an originally Semitic narrative is the distinct Latinising influence. In Gaul this was the age of the declamationes and the panegyrici; the use of the colores rhetorici was expected, and it was no accident that Hilary was in Norden's judgment one of the two best stylists of later Latin. In

---

55. Hilary and Quintilian, H. Kling (De Hil. Pict. artis rhetoricae ipsiusque ut fertur institutionis oratoriae Quintilianae studioso., Freiburg 1909/diss. HD 1910) suggested (op.cit.12) that if Hilary had studied at the nearest high school to Poitiers at Burdigald, then he might have known Quintilian's Institutio through Ausonius, who valued Quint. and taught there from 334-8; but for this there is no evidence. Kling finds parallels with the institutes in the De Trin. (Trin 2.81 = Inst 12.3) and (Trin 1.20 = Inst 12.10) (K 78 and 83). But the case for direct usage has not been proved (so Buttel and Schanz Hosius). It seems unlikely that Hilary had Quintilian before him, took him into exile or modelled his work on Quintilian. On the other hand, literary training based on the work is almost certain, and comes out in the use of hermeneutical categories which share, with the whole tradition of Latin rhetoric many of Quintilian's assumptions cf below. Colson op.cit.44 finds few references to Q before the IVth century but this is not very significant. On rhetoric in Gaul cf. too Haarhof and Courcelle, Les Lettres Grecques, 210f, and Pichon, 958-9, where the scene in Gaul is set out in tabular form. Quillacq (worthless) Roger (150-1 on Hilary) and Feder (Kulturgeschichtliches) add nothing to the information available; cf too Arbusow Colores Rhetorici. On Poitiers cf. Griffe 127f Jerome's comment on Hilary (ep. in Gal praef. Gallus ipse et pictavis natus') has no external support. Nothing is known of the church at Poitiers before Hilary - even whether he had predecessors. The reference in Ps 67.20 'Quotidie autem per populi credentis accessionem' may refer to baptisms in quantity and so to a fairly young church community (Griffe).

the declamation schools men learned to divide narratives into the events and categories, to isolate the element of the surprising, the apparently absurd, for the purpose of effect, to conceive the guiding lines for a speech. The influence of rhetoric has long been acknowledged in e.g. Tertullian and in Gregory of Nyssa: it is also used as a technical tool by Hilary.[56]

The presence of the rhetorical element has many side-effects. For example, the rhetoricians were accustomed to give citations not exactly, but only according to the general sense, and this procedure is followed by Hilary in his method of citation.[57] Favourite topic of the schools, e.g. the humilitas motif, recur. The concepts of allegory and similitude, of typus, imago, figura and cognates have a history in rhetoric, partly through Stoic influence, as well as in the tradition of biblical exegesis, to which we shall return.

Another accompaniment of grammar and rhetoric was the production of lexicographical material, and it is possible that concordances of the Bible were available to Hilary. Stimulated by the flourishing of rhetoric, there sprang up too a new school of historiography in the west, which Hilary's interpretation may partly reflect. There is some evidence of his

56. The formal and interpretational aspects of a speech were in rhetoric dealt with in relation to each other. Thus the student learned to divide speeches for analysis into genos, meros, typos, schema and tropos (cf. the excellent discussions in Fuhrmann and in Krauss) and within these categories to distinguish times and persons in the narrative cf. In Mt 22.3 et haec quidem parabola distinguenda temporibus est et dignoscenda personis. Interpretatio is discussed in a classic passage at length in Ad Herr. 4.28f.

57. On the loose manner of citation in the rhetorical tradition cf. Peter and Hagendahl. This is an added reason for the problematic nature of the attempts to establish which texts of the Bible Hilary used.

knowledge of Sallust. This too was above all the time of 'historical outlines' and periscopes, of condensed presentations of large works in narrative form: the In Matthaeum is an example of a highly condensed narrative, and it is probably not without significance that Hilary's work was given to the public in this form.[58]

The rhetorical tradition has then a considerable influence on the commentary. Apart from the detailed incidental effects it serves to prepare the text for interpretation, as we saw in examining the formal structure above: it serves too to Latinise and render intelligible in contemporary terms the thought of the narrative both as a literary whole and in terms of the individual concepts: and in addition as we shall see in detail in the next section of our study, it plays a role in moulding the framework of the theological and philosophical orientation of the work. Here we concentrate on the intermediate stage of the articulation of the hermeneutical principles in relation to the text. A good illustration of the inter-connections here is provided by the term exemplum, which has a long history in the Greek (paradeigma) and Latin literary traditions (cf Tertullian etc.), and is much used by Hilary. As we look upon the example of the narratives, these are transfusa by the Spirit to reveal the inner sense. The exempla explain the dicta and vice versa. The exempla of Jesus have an inherent virtue which creates faith; in faith, we are then brought to follow Jesus' exempla in our actions and so faith and works are not in

58. cf. Humilitas at 18.10; 20.12 and 24.2 and Auerbach, Publikum. (cf. too on Basil above). On rhetoric in Gregory of Nyssa cf. Meridier, and for Tertullian Welter, passim. For the panegyrici cf Monnard, 41f, and on epitomae and periochae Peter, Geschichtsschreibung p.341f. Nothing can be said definitely for the use of concordances by Hilary. For Origen cf. Cadiou and for the beginnings in the middle ages art, Bibelkoncordanz in PRE3.

tension. We are justified only by faith, and at the same time, we
remain in faith by producing bona exempla caritatis (an anticipation of
the classic mediaeval resolution of the relation of faith and works,
which reflects the fusion of a Pauline doctrine of faith with popular
originally Stoic moral teaching).[59] We see too that in speaking of res
of events, Hilary is speaking not only in terms of the Irenean tradition
of the Oikonomia of God (though that too is important to recall) but also
in the classical tradition of the res in the rhetorical division of the
elements of speeches and in the eclectic Stoic influenced philosophy of
the later empire which it partially reflects: likewise with ordo and ratio,
and possibly even finis (notably in the In Ps.) may owe something of its
interpretation as much to Cicero as to the theological tradition of Pauline
eschatology. On the detail of these interconnections, a great deal of
study remains to be done.[61]

59. On the use of exemplum in rhetoric and in Christian exegesis see the
studies of Petre, Kornhardt and Welter (Tert.). For Hilary cf. In Mt
2.5 exempli sui auctoritate; 10 ut exempli se passionis subsequatur;
2.3 operum exempla; 18.6 comparationis exemplum; 18.10 and similit-
inem nos humilitatis instruit, et confirmat exemplo. cf too 5.9;
9.16; 13.7. For discussion of exempla in the rhetorical tradition
cf. Cicero De Inv. 20.49, where exemplum is connected with ordo, res
and virtus; and Quint. Inst. Orat. 10.5.2.

60. cf. too in the In Mt the uses of ordo and ratio cited above; and in
the De Trin, 2.27 tenet autem ordinem prophetiae evangelica doctrina
and In Mt 2.2 veritatem non idcirco corrumpi si gerendis rebus
interioris significantia ratio subjecta sit.

61. We have already noted the close connection of exemplum with similitudo
in Hilary. This connection is to be found already in Ar. Rhet. 2.20
(in which parabole is de Orat. 2.41; De Inv. 1.3046; Quint. Inst. Orat.
5,2,23 and also 8.8; 8.14; 8.46; 8.49 and 8.54 (discussed by Petre
passim and Pirot 3.6f). On similitudo cf. Quint. Inst. Orat. 2.2.22
and on analogia 5, 2, 34 ibid. On the other hand there is a different
use in Quint. cf. for a parable, as metaphor: inst. Orat. 8.6.5f;
8.6.14 and 8.6.4-9 in general (cf. Hermaniuk 177). These different
interpretations were to lead to different lines of biblical inter-
(contd.)

A second important set of images employed in articulating the coelestis significantia in the texts consists in those related to typology,
allegory and metaphor in general. These too are to be found in the rhetorical tradition, and are clearly related to the categories taken from that
tradition by Hilary,[62] Hilary's usage is also however here derived from
the exegetical tradition of the Church and particularly (cf. too the notes
to section 2 above) from Tertullian, and possibly Irenaeus. Though we
shall seek to consider these motifs here in themselves, as we shall see
later their use is intimitely related to basic theological categories of
Hilary's thought. (Neglect of these areas accounts for much of the tedium
of a great deal of discussion of the history of patristic biblical interpretation!)

Allegory, typology and parable may be dealt with together. After
much discussion, it has become clear that types and allegories may belong,

61. (contd.)
pretation which come together again in Augustine, in Hilary and to
a lesser extent in e.g. Tert. (cf. sect.2 above, and below). To Quint.
too we may trace Hilary's concern with proprietas (cf. Inst. Orat.
8.2.1f 'quare proprietas non ad nomen, sed ad vim significandi refert,
nec auditu, sed intellectu perpenda est. In Quintilian too we find
the res/verba contrast e.g. Inst. Orat. 8. proem 6. cf. too the exx.
from TLL below.

62. Discussion for and against allegorising was a major topic of the late
Hellenistic philosophical and rhetorical schools. The most ancient
word for allegory was probably hyponoia (PL, Rep 2.378D etc - cf. LSJ
and Buffière 45f) Cicero who uses the Latin word allegoria (Orator
27.94) opposes the allegories of the Stoics. Quint Inst Orat 1.61
54-60 translates allegoria by inversio; for discussions of the
Alexandrian/Antiochene controversy on allegory cf. Hanson, Greer, and
esp. Barr 103ff: for the use of historia in rhetoric cf. Arbusow 109f.
v. Dobschutz (Harnack Ehrung op.cit.) pinpoints the significance of
the Philonic stream of allegory in Christian exegesis 'würde alles
früher auf das Gesetz oder den logos bezogen, so jetzt auf Christus'.
For almost all writers, the problems lay not in the fact but in the
nature of the christological application.

and usually do belong, to the same category of material, and that there is no 'necessary' distinction based on the fact that typologies are more 'historical' and so more legitimate than allegories. At the same time, these concepts have often been used to express, and have in fact, often corresponded to, a distinction between more and less 'historical' lines of interpretation.

Hilary in the In Matthaeum neither discusses, defines nor distinguishes his use of allegory and typology. He never mentions allegory, and hardly ever uses the form without reference to types. His use of typus and cognates is far from precise, and these may be exchanged synonymously with different models from the rhetorical tradition. Yet in accordance with a long western tradition he uses the concept of typology to elicit in 'cash value' the details of his interpretation of the Heilsgeschichte, in the sense of the Irenaean oikonomia rather than in the common modern sense of the term. In this sense, Hilary's understanding, like that of Tertullian noted above, may be said to be typological rather than allegorical in the terms of the popular distinction, in that he supposed a historical (historisch and at the same time heilsgeschichtlich) relation between the events involved in the types.

Hilary himself again uses a number of different terms synonymously. For this reason it is misleading to read too much into any one of them (cf. below on interpretations of species.) cf. 7.1 sensus allegoricus nihil detrahit litterae veritati; 12.11 imago futurae veritatis; 21.2 species futuri cf 19.3 futuri species; 11.2 legi forma; 19.3 infantes. gentium forma; 19.6 Christ shows the umbra veritatis; 32.3 vestis-velamentum legis; 9.2 velamenta verba legis. The most frequent figure however is that of typus (or typicus, as at 2.1; 7.9; 8.4; 12.24; 14.6; 17.8; 19.7; e.g. 8.4

typica ratio) cf 20.13 duo caeci are typus crediturarum gentium; 2.7 in genesi ecclesiae typus; 15.4 typum ecclesiae Chananaeam filium cf.too typus at 7.8; 7.9; 12.1; 14.3. Often used instead of typus is praefiguratio, as at 12.4 praefiguratio futurorum dictis praesentibus continetur. This says nothing different from 21.2 omnis autem haec species futuri ordinem tenet. cf.too 8.8 sed manet etiam nunc ordo mysterii; ut veritas praesentium, futurorum species adiecta sit dictorum et factorum Domini virtutem turbae timent. Mysterium is here used in the same sense as sacramentum, as in e.g.prophetiae sacramentum. Further exx may be seen at 9.9 praefiguratio; 15.4 interius mysterium; 17.2 praefigurare; also at 18.12 and 18.13; 1.1 forma; 1.8 species; 7.9 ordo typicae significationis; 8.4 typica ratio; as at 14.10 typicus ordo. 17.8, 19.1 and 7 typica ratio. 20.11 typicus ordo; 33.3 typica ratio. Connected too is imitatio e.g. 7.1 nihil omnim veritati detrahit, imitationem veritas consecuts.

In his special study of sacramentum in Hilary, Malunowicz noted 537 instances of the word, of which 68 translate the Greek mysterion, 36 refer to an oath, 305 to doctrine (284 to specific doctrines) 44 to a figural sense, 27 to worship and 57 to other miscellaneous objects. He offers the following comparative list:

	Hil.	Tert.	Cypr.	Ambr.	Lact.
sacramentum	537	136	64	4	26
mysterium	84	6	1	-	27

For the In Matthaeum cf.20.8 iam sine scandalo auditurus apostolis sacramentum crucis Dominus exponit; 28.2 ut sacramentum crucis admixtum esse gloriae aeternitatis agnoscerent; 20.9 de calice sacramenti passionis; 23.4 sacramentum scripturarum; 32.6 in hoc prophetiae sacramentum; 33.6 occultum mysterium totibus creationis; 10.9 sacramentum pacis coelestis. V. Soden,

Mysterium 225, notes that the oldest Latin Bible translations seem to have translated mysterion by sacramentum. The Vulgate version is usually mysterium.

Interior is used in the same way as spiritalis to refer to the figural meaning cf 19.10 rerum eodem cursu interioris causae ordo retinendus est; 9.2 Matthaeus interioris eius habitatione illuminatus cf interioris conscientiae nitor. We are inclined to see definite Neo-platonic influence here; on the other hand Cicero uses interior of mental feelings e.g. de Or, 3.49.190 ne insistat interius oratic etc. and so this does not in itself amount to a direct indication of such influence in a degree significant for the moulding of a given interpretation.

In the process of relating the figural interpretation by means of the literary categories of the rhetorical tradition to the gospel text, there are certain characteristic features of the narrative to which this interpretation may be connected. Thus people nearly always represent more than simply their persons (Joseph is a type of the Gentiles etc). Places may have no particular significance (there is little interpretation of Nazareth, Bethlehem or Golgotha) but movements between places have a typica ratio e.g. from Judaea to Egypt - from the Jews to the Gentiles etc. The ordo temporum always has a coelestis ratio, relating either to Jesus himself (to the time of his passion, ascension or resurrection) or to the time of the end of the world (the theme of judgement recurs). Dress is significant. Numbers indicate a coelestis ratio. The presence of a ship on the water is the Church sailing over the hazardous waters of the world. In these cases, often the categories of figural languages are omitted, and the equivalents are simply stated. Simonetti, who has also noticed these 'signposts' adds the figurative significance which is always attached to the presence of

animals. This last is common elsewhere, e.g. in Philo and in Prudentius'
Peristephanon (I am indebted to a seminar of Professor Courcelle on the
latter). Simonetti also notes that Hilary's interpretation often begins
with exaggerated literalness, which he then resolves by invoking the
coelestis significantia.[63]

Typus and cognates are used strictly of the main line of interior
significantia and are not applied to other metaphorical interpretations
in the gospel text. The literary categories of the rhetorical tradition
give shape to the typological illustrations, which are then related to the
lex/fides motif. Many of the types are traditional, Hilary's contribution
lying in the continuity and in the exclusive nature of the interpretation.

Often connected with the treatment of allegorical interpretation is
the treatment of parable. But for Hilary all parables are designated
'absolutus', and receive no further interpretation. This concept of
'absolute' significance is used by Cicero and Quintilian to designate passages where no figural meaning is present.[64] The meaning of the parable
in Hilary is made clear either by the text itself or by the words of Jesus
or by the actions of the characters in the narrative. There is no hidden
sense, possibly because the direct words of Jesus are thought themselves
to speak to faith, and to require no interpretation pointing to the source
of faith.

There are in the text of the gospel, of course, many other non-alleg-
orical metaphorical expressions, some of which are taken up into the inner

63. cf. Simonetti, Note, op cit.
64. On 'absolutus' in Quintilian and Cicero cf. Cic. Inv. 2.57.
    170 necessitudines quasdam simplices et absolutas, and Quint,
    9.3.19.

significance by Hilary and some of which are not. Hilary's concern is not
so much with the surface texture of the text, in terms of metaphorical
and non-metaphorical language as such, as with the points for which the
content of the episodes themselves suggests a special interpretation.[65]

The relation between the interpretational principles from the
rhetorical and exegetical tradition and the events in the history of salvation past and present for Hilary is complex and its full significance
will be best seen in the light of the analyses of the next section. Some
aspects may however be clasified from the above analyses.

How do we come to understand the inner meaning of the text? Understanding comes through perception of the correlation of the dicta and
facta of Jesus which is present in the text itself. But this understanding comes only through faith, which is given by the Spirit. The manner
in which this is done is described in concepts taken from the rhetorical
tradition itself, and from biblical exegesis which has already drawn on
that tradition. There is interestingly no trace of the res/signa dialectic
of Augustine. Instead Hilary, like Tertullian, in many respects uses the

---

65. On the relation of allegory to metaphor in general Lausberg (op cit
    p.421f) expresses the basic relationship neatly 'Die Allegorie ist
    für den Gedanken, was die Metaphor für das Einzelwort ist: die
    Allegorie ist eine durch einen ganzen Satz (darüber hinaus) durch-
    geführte Metaphor. In distinguishing allegory from typology -
    'Die Typologie ist wie eine Semantik der Realitaten, die Allegorie
    wie eine Semantik der Worte'. Lausberg describes in semantic terms
    the concern of those who have sought to distinguish allegory from
    typology, by stressing that typology is and should be grounded in
    historical events, and not open to the whims of metaphysical specul-
    ation. In the In Mt Hilary stresses that the whole of the gospel
    narrative is rooted in the events of the Heilsgeschichte, but he is
    not, as in the De Trin consciously opposing certain types of alleg-
    orical interpretation. For good discussions of typology and allegory
    in exegesis cf apart from Goppelt, Hanson etc., J. Barr in 'Old and
    New in Interpretation' 103-48 and A Bjorndalen in T.Th.K. 1966,129ff.

concept of 'virtus' in a manner which probably comes from originally Stoic influenced sources through the rhetorical schools to Christian exegesis,[66] (as too in Cyprian and Lactantius in the Latin tradition). A particular theological anthropology is created (and also partly presupposed) in the conception of the transfusion of the exempla of the text into our understanding by the Spirit to reveal the inner significance, the advantages and disadvantages of which we shall consider in our next section. For in dealing with these issues, Hilary is involved in questions not only of hermeneutics but of general metaphysics, of knowledge and existence and their relations to each other. The man who is transformed by the virtue of the dicta and facta through the Spirit and comes to cognitio Dei is ontologically affected by this, and this view of the story of salvation has more than only epistemological implications, both in Hilary's theology and in the background of fourth century philosophy, with its strong, neoplatonic overtones against which the work is done. These wider implications, and their effects on the details of his interpretation, we must now examine.

66. An examination of the background of the main concepts examined above in TLL produces the following results: the dicta/facta contrast is stressed by Cic. Att. 2.1.3; Quint. Inst. Orat. 1.4.2a; 1.4.29; 6.1.14; 10.5.10; Seneca Oed. 520; Ennius Ann. 31.4; Ter. Andr. 328; Tert Spec. 17; ib. idol. 23; Sall. Cat. 32; Cic. Inv. 2.117; i.e. this was a rhetorical figure in widespread use at all periods. Gentes: many refs in Tert. Lact; Arnob; Vict. Pet.; Cypr; Aug; Imago is used by Quint; Tert; Rufin; Cypr.; Aug; etc. Coelestis: Tert; Prisc; Panegyrici etc. Competenter: Chalcid; Rufin etc. Absolutus: Rufin; Donat; Cassiod, etc. Intelligentia: Rufin; Tert; Cypr; Mar Vict. Interior: apart from Cicero, Tert, adv. Marc. Porphyrius. Panegyrici: Orig in MT (Lat, P. Suet: Sulp. Sev. etc.) i.e. the technical terms used in his interpretation by Hilary are part of the common language of 4th century Latin literature and in no way unusual in occurrence or in usage.

c)   The theological conception of the gospel

in its intellectual milieu

To see the In Matthaeum in terms of the application of hermeneutical principles of exegesis to texts is indispensable for an understanding of the work, but it is not to see the text as Hilary saw it in the
first instance. For him the primary issues are theological issues, - of
God's dealings with his people in bringing them from the bondage of the
law to faith through his eternal son, Jesus Christ, in creating faith and
bringing men salvation through Cognitio Dei. Until we have explored the
approach to the commentary in terms of these theological concerns, our
picture of the whole will be incomplete.

Needless to say, the theological reflection takes place within the
general intellectual background of the fourth century, its prevailing
tendencies and its controversies, in agreement and disagreement, conscious
and unconscious, implicit and explicit, with these. Here we shall attempt
to limit ourselves as far as possible to matters which are explicit in the
commentary itself or implied in its construction, in the belief that too
much hypothesis has been built on too little evidence in this area in the
past.

Though the In Matthaeum displays a clear theological unity of conception, it is an exercise in biblical interpretation and not in systematic theology in the modern sense of the term. Having no other evidence
than the In Matthaeum for the development of Hilary's thought before exile,
we shall seek to be cautious in reading too much into or out of the work,
for establishing of general conclusions about Hilary's theology. Since the
time of Irenaeus, there had been no first rate theologian in the West, with

the possible exception of Tertullian, and the immense developments of the
fourth century itself are not widely reflected in the commentary with the
partial exception of the stress on the eternal Sonship of Christ. It has
been customary to see the work as a continuation of the theology of
Tertullian and Novatian, and we have seen that influence from that quarter
is to be affirmed - yet this stream does not account entirely for the particular stress on the centrality of God's actions in the events of the
history of salvation. It has been noted that there is no developed
doctrine of the Holy Spirit in the work, nor indeed as we shall see, in
the De Trinitate and this has been seen here as an example of a Gnostic
dualism and for the De Trinitate as deriving from a Stoic metaphysic which
led to binitarian characteristics. Yet not all theologians writing in the
West or in the East before the full development of trinitarian theology
were binitarian - cf. Irenaeus, and we shall seek to remain within the
evidence of the texts.

The focal point of the movement from the law to faith which is the
main theme of the work, is, as we have seen above, Jesus Christ himself.
Faith in God is faith in Christ the Son of God. In this process, the dicta
and the facta together are equally important: cf. 10. 1f - paria in dictis
atque in factis significationum momenta consistunt; cf. at 24.5 the stress
on perspicuitas verborum et locorum. The words as we have said above,
possess their own virtus cf. 10.1 verborum virtutes non minus oportet
introspicere quam rerum. (cf. 6.7 in verborum virtutibus, 8.3 verborum
virtus etc). The combination of dicta and facta constitutes the res evangelica: cf. 19.3 res evangelica, ut dicimus, inter praesentis et futuri
effectum, mediam utrique rei et congruem rationem temperavit ut his, quae
efficiebantur, futuri species adhaereret. To this res we are not to bring

our own theories, but we are to observe; cf. 7.8. neque enim res intelligentiae, sed rei intelligentia subsecundat. The centre of the res evangelica is Jesus himself. cf.12.7 quaestio omnis in verbo est. 12.4 evangelica fides operatur in Christo: 13.7 thesaurus enim in agro, ut diximus, Christus intelligitur in carne.; cf.23.6 proprium enim Domini nostri Jesu Christi officium est cognitionem Dei afferre, et intelligentiam nominis eius potestatisque praestare. cf.16.3 ne doctrina pharisaeorum Christum nesciens, effectus veritatis evangelicae corrumperet.

Christ is Deum ex Deo, Filium extra patris substantia atque intra patris substantiam consistentem (5.14) de infinitate paterna 31.3, has eadem substantia as the father (substantia here does not mean a 'material' state as in naive Stoic realism, as may be seen in 10.20 substantiam spiritalis animae) His is the mediatoris officium (Simonetti op. cit. 57 derives this from Tert. De Res. Mort 63.1 and adv. Prax, 27.15 cf. on Wille below). The height of blasphemy is in Christo negare quod Deus sit (12.17).

Stress is laid upon the fact that Christ is eadem substantia with Father, and is the aeternus filius of the Father, points which may reflect the Nicene and Serdikan formulae and indirectly too the Arian controversy, Christ is vere Deus, vere homo.[67]

The Spirit is spoken of as the Holy Spirit, the Spirit of God and the Spirit of Christ. It has been suggested that Hilary echoes here a 'Geisteschristologie' in which the Spirit represents the divine nature in the human Jesus, but it is not clear that this leads Hilary into all the consequences imagined. The Spirit acting on man created faith: this has been thought to be heavily indebted to the Stoic tradition. Stoic influence

67. The question of sources and antecedents will be dealt with in detail in discussing Wille's thesis below.

and 'Spirit Christology' have often been used in a pejorative sense. But
what counts in theology is not concepts and origins but the critical use
made of these.

There are indeed only scattered references to the work of the Holy
Spirit in the In. Mt. cf. 1.3. in the credal phrase: Nam conceptum ex
spiritu sancto and 9.6 of the woman with the issue of blood 'Fimbriam
vestis per fidem festinat attingere, donum scilicet spiritus sancti'; this episode
is recalled at 14.19, in which thevirtus of the Spirit is linked with
Jesus Christ. Sed ut ex veste tota fimbriae, ita ex domino nostro Jesu
Christo sancti virtus exiit. Connection of the spirit with Christ and
with God occurs at 12.15; ergo si discipuli operantur in Christo, et ex
spiritu Dei Christus operatur; adest Dei regnum, iam in apostolis
mediatoris officium transfusum: and 12.17 quid enim tam extra veniam est,
quam in Christo negare quod Deus est, et consistentem paterni spiritus
substantiam adimere, i.e. there is no systematic development of a Geisteschristologie. (cf. too the discussion of the De. Trin. below).[68] The

68. cf. too the further connections of spiritus at 3.3 quia ipse non solum
     homo, sed et Deus, licet usque in tentatonis diem cibo hominis
     abstineret, Dei tamen spiritu alebatur; ostendens non in pane hoc
     solitario, sed in verbo Dei alimoniam aeternitatis esse sperandum.
     4.17 racha vacuitatis opprobrium est; et qui sancto spiritu plenum
     con vicio insimulat, fit reus convicio sanctorum; contumeliam spiritus
     sancti sanctorum iudicim animadversione luiturus. 10.12 plebum
     Dominus miseratur, quia nullus adhuc eius pastor esset, custodiam
     sancti spiritus redditurus donum Spiritus sancti, messorum copiam Deus
     praestet; 10.14 spiritus Dei; 11.2 spiriti sancti gloria in carne
     cf. too 13.5, which tells against the 'Geisteschristologie' quamquam
     ad fidei sacramentum. id est ad Patris et Filii et spiritus sancti
     unitatem etc; in patri autem et filio et spiritu sancti, sine admixti
     extrinsecus fermenti necessitate in Christo, omnia unum sint. 17.3
     sed loquente adhuc eo, nubes eos candida inumbravit et divinae
     virtutis spiritu ambiuntur; 19.3 mu nus enim et donum spiritus sancti,
     per impositionem manus et precationem, cessant legis opere erat
     gentibus largiendum. 32.7 vestis autem nuptialis est gloria spiritus
     sancti, et candor habitus coclestis.

suggestion of on the one hand the reduction of the trinitarian concept to a Gnostic/Stoic dualism in which the world and God are irrevocably separated, and on the other hand a monist epistemology also from Stoic sources (the combination is indeed difficult) in which faith and knowledge are no longer distinguishable, since faith in God is without remainder direct, immediate knowledge of God, is consistent with the charges of docetism with regard to the person of Jesus as the Christ, on the one hand, and Christomonism on the other, which have been brought against his theology. To this has been added the corollary, (since scripture is understood in terms of the pivot of the story of salvation in Jesus,) of a docetic separation in exegesis of the spiritual and the corporeal and an inability to interpret in practice such matters as the pain of Jesus, on the one hand and on the other a naive understanding of the effect of the inspired scripture on the reader.[69]

Some further light is shed on the problem by considering the question of Hilary's doctrine of scripture as such, though he himself never raises the question in this form. There is no formal statement of the authority of scripture in the In Matthaeum.[70]

---

69. cf.below on Wille, and in sect. 4 below.

70. Apart from the reference already shown above, cf.5.8. in dictis Dei veritas est, et rerum creandarum efficientia omnis in verbo est. Ita nec quod spopondit ambiguum est nec inefficax quod locutum est. 5.14 Nihil in verbis Dei leve aut inane tractatur: omnisque hic ultra sensum gentilium aurium sermo est. cf. 6.7 of Jesus' teaching 'in verborum enim virtutibus effectus potestatum metiebantur.' These are set down in scripture, but linked too indissolubly with his person cf, 12.7 curatio omnis in Verbo est. cf. too 23.4 Atque ut ita publica opinio accepit..... sed Dominus ait 'erratis nescientes scripturas, neque virtutem Dei'. Ergo scriptum est; et cessare debet ambiguitas, quam auctoritas tanta condemnat ....

As in all fourth century theologians, the place of the canon of inspired scripture is taken for granted. Scripture may only be understood
in the Church, i.e. in the context of faith. The influence of Gnosticism
has been seen in this faith condition: but the need for faith in illuminating the basic significance of the gospel was a universal postulate in the
early Church, and too much may be made of alleged gnostic parallels in the
language of illumination and cognition Dei as a means of salvation. It
would also of course have been possible for Hilary to adapt models from
Gnostic terminology without himself maintaining gnostic positions.

We noticed above (cf. too section 4 below) that there is in the In
Matthaeum no developed doctrine of the Word, with which scripture is identified, as in Origen and in a different way in Augustine. The verbum Dei
consists in the words of Jesus and the events of the history of salvation
as these point to him and his significance for us, the dicta and facta
explaining each other and through the Spirit provoking faith.

It is never actually said that the whole of scripture is to be interpreted in terms of the lex/fides concept, as was to happen later in some
Lutheran interpretations of scripture (if not always in Luther). Rather,
the purpose of this particular gospel is to shed light on the relation of
lex and fides.

Again, though the impropriety of disparaging one sense or the other
is mentioned, there is no statement of the relation of inner and outer
sense (or interna and externa claritas) to each other. The inner sense
where detected is simply stated to be there. There is neither a progression in steps to a higher state of knowledge nor a relation of inner and
outer in analogy with the incarnation. Such traces of the distinction
between the spiritual and the corporeal as are present may be attributed

82

as much to the commonplace expression of the age as to the influence of
any one given source, Origenist, Marcionite, etc.

As we have already mentioned, and will reconsider at length in analysis the De Trinitate, understanding of the cognitio Dei in the In
Matthaeum is pictured in terms which borrow from the originally Stoic
epistemological model of the efficacy (virtue) of the events themselves,
qualified by the words of Jesus[71] rather than in terms of the Neoplatonic
schema of events and signs pointing to them. The modified realism of this
model, later to appeal to mediaeval and Reformation exegetes, is to be
distinguished (as has not always been the case) from the naive realism
of the Stoic schema as it is sometimes found in, for example, Tertullian
and Methodius, in which everything that is real is material. Since the
Middle Platonism of the apologists at least, it had been perfectly possible to conceive of non-corporeal reality within such a schema.[72] But if
Hilary had only succeeded by replacing realist monism by an idealist
monism, then the results are equally unfortunate, and the incarnation is
merely a particular case of the general Stoic schema of transcendence
and immanence. He is however concerned to stress that it is because the
events are the events surrounding the life of Jesus and the words are the
words of Jesus, that they create faith and bring cognitio Dei.

71. Apart from the references given above and discussed in connection
     with Wille below. cf. 8.6 veritatis deinde ordo succedit in gestis,
     quamvis futuri species expleatur in dictis. cf. 8.8. Atque non nos
     intelligentiam fingimus, sed gesta ipsa intelligentiam nobis impert-
     iuntur. cf. 10.17 constanter enim Dei ingerenda cognitio est, et
     profundum doctrinae evangelicae sacretum lumine praedicationi
     apostolicae revelandum.
72. cf. Holte 'Spermatikos Logos' in St. Theologica 14 for 1960, and
     Andersen, Nomos and Logos, passim.

The question of the Stoic-derived influence on Hilary is hard to answer precisely. We believe that Paul Löffler overstated his case in seeing Hilary's whole doctrine of God in terms of Stoic influence (and so as basically, binitarian) yet that this factor (with strong neoplatonic additions) is indeed important for the understanding of some of Hilary's characteristic thought. One may look in vain for direct borrowings from Stoic sources. But the cumulative evidence is strong: the main points are 1) the frequent use in the In Matthaeum of categories from rhetoric, and especially the preoccupation with the res concept, echoing Tertullian, Quintilian, Cicero and Seneca, all of whom much influenced by Stoic ideas. 2) The consequent extension of this strongly realist strain to the theological concentration on the event of the incarnation itself. 3) The theory of knowledge in the In Mt. in which the concept of 'virtus' plays a prominent role. 4) The assumption that the words and events produce without interpretation through a special sign theory their own instant effect on the mind, bringing cognitio Dei through the Holy Spirit. 5) Hilary's use of the image concept. 6) The use of the rhetorical categories in close conjunction with typology. In the In Matthaeum the Stoic influence leads Hilary to concentrate on the dicta and facta of Jesus; in the De Trinitate the concept of the incarnation becomes a controlling category in its own right, and influencing more directly the role of the rhetorical categories, the typology etc.

In adopting this model rather than that of a Neoplatonic sign theory Hilary avoids some of the theological difficulties of the latter, as seen in Augustine.[73] In the mediaeval tradition of exegesis and in much modern

73. On Augustine cf. Strauss, Duchrow and Schindler, and the discussion on the De Trin below. In other respects Hilary was influenced by Neoplatonism cf. below , esp. 130ff.

hermeneutics, namely that of positing a special language of the incarnation which has to be learned by the theologian and then retranslated for the people, and in which the relation between sign and thing signified was to raise many theological problems. It seems reasonable to suggest on the basis of his work as a whole that it was theological reflection upon the centrality of Christology rather than fortuitous accident which led him to stress these elements from the fourth century synthesis which avoided these particular dangers, (though of course, he could not foresee all the implications involved in the choice and the serious problems raised by his own sort of approach).

The methods of the In Matthaeum were still however only a first stage. Here the action of the Spirit in illuminating the events of the incarnation is still tied to the inspired text of scripture in a literal sense. The words and events are those of the narrative itself, which has its own virtus; still a special hermeneutic of the scriptures is required to articulate the operation of the virtus within the scriptures. Thus, though he does not share the Platonic and Neoplatonic sign theories of Origen and Augustine, Hilary in the In Matthaeum still uses, as Augustine was to use, the whole hermeneutic of the rhetorical tradition, along with its metaphysical implications with regard to the inspired text of the Stoic theory to which in Quintilian and in rhetoric in general it is indebted.

The problems are not yet solved, and as we shall see in examining the 'De Trinitate', Hilary was himself to produce hints (along with a large number of mutually contradictory other usages alongside these hints) of a further step. The concept of incarnation might, though did not necessarily make possible a new theory of knowledge in the Greek world. This could be taken up and combined with existing theories in different ways.

The concept of a special hermeneutic of the incarnation is however, theologically problematic, since it is often held that the incarnation qua incarnation is to be understood in the same way as any other event, and the truth of its happening is of the same kind as any other truth. The continuing apparent difference between the truth of the world as God's world and the reality of the world as man's world, which accounts for the 'odd' nature of religious language, (if not for the obscurity of much theological writing), reflects the tension of the life of faith between being 'in the truth' and being 'in the world'. For Augustine this problem was in any case resolved in the dialectic between civitas terrens and civitas aeterna, and for Origen in the realisation of eschatology in mystical illumination, and so never arose in an acute form. In the mediaeval world Platonic dualism was to provoke an Aristotelian dualism in understandable reaction: the alternative in mysticism, ever present in the world or later mediaeval Platonism, being theologically suspect as leading to monism and so hazarding the uniqueness of the incarnation.

In the De Trinitate, there are elements which go some way, as we shall see, towards a further step in the solution of the problems, and it was not for nothing that the Reformers, not indeed seeking for a new hermeneutic but under the impulse of their unsystematic rediscovery of neglected aspects of the personal dimensions of faith, were to look with interest to Hilary again.

However that may be, the insistence in the In Matthaeum that in the words and deeds of Jesus, man is brought coram Deo, that God acts directly in word and event, and not simply in signs of his presence, in creating faith and knowledge of himself in faith, was an important step in the history of interpretation. That the material for its articulation may have been fortuitously to hand in part in Stoic-derived theories of

knowledge does not detract from the achievement. (This does not mean of

course that we can simply repeat his method today, as we shall see below.)

In the nature of the case, we do not find in this short commentary

an explicit exposition of the relationship between the doctrine of God

and the doctrine of scripture. The issue is however worth pursuing for

the light which it throws from a different angle upon Hilary's method.

Though there is no explicit analogy, e.g. christological analogy between

the two, yet christological considerations play the same dominant role in

the development of the interpretation that they play in the theological

basis of that interpretation; the pivot on which the understanding and

the events themselves turn, is faith in Jesus Christ, God and man. It has

been remarked that a great deal of early exegesis is christocentric, even

'staurocentric'; important is how the christology operates. For Hilary it

is through the illumination of the events of the Heilsgeschichte which cul-

minates in the incarnation that the Holy Spirit brings faith and cognitio

Dei, to which we then respond in producing bona opera caritatis (the lack

of emphasis on the relation of the incarnation to the atonement leaving

room for that characteristically western tradition which was later developed

by Pelagius). In this picture, several strands of thought are involved,

the connection between them not yet being made precise. On the one hand

it is the peculiar nature of the deeds and acts of Jesus himself, which

have their own special capacity to evoke faith. On the other hand, the

Spirit, which is related as closely to the inspired text itself as it is to Christ and to God, creates faith and so understanding.[74] The presence

of different conceptions side by side and unresolved ambiguities doubt-

less accounts for the wide variety of more or less plausible theories on

the nature of Hilary's theology which have been constructed. Some steps

towards a resolution of the tension will be found in the De Trinitate.

74. In addition to those discussed above, the following comments in the
     In Matthaeum aptly illustrate the main themes of Hilary's theology:
     cf. on Wille and in sect. 4 below.
     1.1 (Jesus Christus) qui est aeternus et rex et sacerdos, etiam in
     carnali ortu utriusque generis gloriam probavit. 4.3 quia per man-
     suetudinem mentis nostrae habitaverit Christus in nobis, nos quoque
     gloria clarificati eius corporis vestiemur. (Note the tense - which
     is future rather than present). 4.14 Lex enim sub velamento verborum
     spiritalium nativitatem Domini nostri Jesu Christi, et corporalitatem,
     et pasionem, et resurrectionem locuta est. Jesus enim Domino nostro
     nomen ex corpore est, itaque et corporalitas eius et passio, voluntas
     Dei et salus saeculi est; et ultra humani sermonis eloquium est, Deum
     ex Deo, Filium ex patris substantia atque intra Patris substantiam
     consistentem, primum in hominem corporatum dehinc morti hominis con-
     dicione subjectum, postremo post triduum in vitam ex morte redeuntem,
     consociatum Spiritus et substantiae suae aeternitati materiem ad
     coelum assumpti corporis retulisse. 5.15 peccatum autem in Spiritum
     est, Deo virtutis potestatem negare, et Christo substantiam adimere
     aeternitatis: per quem, quia in hominem Deus venit, homo rursus fiet
     in Deum.
     6.1 porcorum vero haereticis est nomen; quia quamvis ungulae bifidae
     sint, acceptam tamen Dei cognitionem non ruminando disponunt. Ergo
     et concorporationem Verbi Dei, et passionis mysterium, et virtutem
     resurrectionis non promiscus tractare nos convenit. 8.8 sed hoc soli
     Christi erat debitum, soli de communione paternae substantiae haec
     agere erat familiare.
     10.5 in sancta terra, et peccatorum spinis atque aculeis non obsessa,
     ut Moysi dictum est, nudis pedibus staturi; admonemur non alium
     ingressus nostri habere, quam quem Christo acceptimus, apparatum.
     11.4 num quid existis videre hominem cognitione Dei vacuum et ad
     immundorum spirituum flatum vagantem? 11.9 plures enim eludere dictum
     apostolicum, quo sit Christum Dei sapientiam et Dei virtutem (1 Cor.
     1.24) his modis solent.
     11.12 atque ita in hoc mutuae cognitionis secreto (of Father and Son).
     12.18 abnegata paternae substantiae communionem decerpas etc.
     16.4 est ergo filius Dei ex Deo Deus. 23.7 quia lex et prophetis
     Christi deputabatur adventum, et adventus eius per supplementum eorum
     cognoscendi Dei intelligentiam praestabat.
     23.8 significabat et de consortio nominis substantiae unitatem.
     25.2 evangelii veritas
     33.5 in his autem omnibus Christus dum illuditur adoratur.

Throughout the foregoing analysis we have seen how the gospel text itself, has taken on many colourings foreign to the original, which then affect the interpretation over where Hilary remains true to his own theological intention. The unconscious translation of the gospel into the terms of the fourth century, the closing of the gap of strangeness due to the absence of historical perspective, is the price paid for the continuity and consistency of interpretation achieved by the technical apparatus of the commentary form. Some kind of translation is of course inevitable. It is also the price of relevance in any age.

It is clear that Hilary like any human being makes use of the thought forms of his age in developing his thought. Our particular concern must be with the manner of this reflection. To what extent are his theological intentions themselves the reflection of contemporary philosophical problems? How far is he conscious of the problems involved in the interrelation of philosophy and theology? Full answers to these questions must await the De Trinitate, but some preliminary comments may be made on the basis of the In Matthaeum.

In the nature of the work, that of concise exposition of the story of salvation in the context of the gospel text, no explicit reference to philosophical issues is made. Nevertheless, we have seen that Hilary develops a Stoic stream in contemporary theory of knowledge in his explanation of the process of understanding scripture. This explanation is in accord with his purpose of showing how understanding comes through faith, and it would clearly be inaccurate to suggest that the latter is really a product of the former. Hilary's theological anthropology is clearly much indebted to Stoic anthropology, both in terms of epistemology and in its stress on moral values and the need for good works. Proposals of large scale dependence on Marcionite and Gnostic systems, which we shall examine in detail below (cf. Chapter 4) raise rather more problems than they solve, much of the 'Marcionite' evidence being better explained in terms of Neoplatonic influence, which I believe to be clear.[75]   But this is more a general colouring than a use of the technical theories of a system, as may be seen from a comparison with, for example, Origen, and there are divergences too at vital points.[76]

By accident perhaps more than design, Hilary is eclectic in his philosophical choices. Yet in using various philosophical concepts for the articulation of and under the controlling category of the witness of scripture itself to God in the words and deeds of Jesus, he also demonstrated considerable theological acuteness. What matters in theology is not the presence or non-presence of philosophical concept but the nature of the decisions taken concerning the sphere of their application.

In the preceding analysis we have examined the means by which the text is used in making dogmatic points and dogma is used in explaining the meaning of the text: this interplay we shall again examine in the context of the De Trinitate. At this point it will be pertinent to consider further the relation of the text to the doctrine. We have already seen in examining the formal structure and principles of interpretation how in the harmonisation of the text into a consistent whole, Hilary loses many of the individual emphases of the gospel, but themes apart from the lex/fides context are rarely mentioned. In expounding the text in terms

---

75. Especially in the juxtaposition of the realm of the spiritual and the realm of the corporeal, and in the understanding of substantia (cf. on De Trin. below and Huber etc. ad loc).

76. e.g. in the power of the dicta and facta of Jesus in carne. cf. above.

of the Pauline Heilsgeschichte, he gives the narrative a consistency different to that of the evangelist's narrative, even though the latter too was concerned to insist on the transfer of the inheritance from the Jews who remain under the law to the Church.

Despite this Hilary has produced a profound meditation on the text which is no less concerned than was the evangelist to bring out the central significance of the words and deeds of Jesus, the Son of God, however that relationship may be at different times expressed - Messiah Son of Man, vere Deus, vere homo. Though he completely missed many of the particular insights of the gospel,[77] and though we must look elsewhere to understand the message of the evangelist in its historical context, yet quite apart from his interpretation as a whole, he was able to make significant improvements on the theological understanding of the gospel in the history of the exegesis on individual episodes, a full enumeration of which we cannot attempt here.[78] That is why his interpretation was valued by later theologians. At the same time, its value today will lie more in its function as an example to compare with other methodological examples in analysing the ongoing task of interpretation rather than as a guide to St. Matthew's gospel.

77. A good example, showing the Neoplatonic and possibly an anti Arian influence, is the comment in 33.5 quoted at 75 above.

78. For the parables cf. Fonck. le Parabole, who provides a large number of comparisons: for Romans cf the references in Schelkle, 'Paulus'. Schelkle notes (193) how in the In Ps. (in contrast with the In Mt) Hilary attempts to soften the accent cf. R.5.20, in order to stress now the value of the law. Hilary often in the In Pss interprets Romans with Origen. Köppen, Versuchungsgeschichte, stresses the importance for Hilary of continuity in the treatment of the temptation narratives, and his work bring out the independence of much of Hilary's characteristic exegesis.

In the commentary we have been dealing with a situation in which doctrinal considerations are used in the service of exegesis. In the De Trinitate though the relationship changes, it remains as fluid and reciprocal as before, the one concern illuminating the other. Without duplication of detail, we must now attempt to see what fresh light may be thrown on the relation of exegesis and theology in Hilary's exegetical methods from an analysis of the De Trinitate.

Before turning to the De Trinitate, it will be convenient to take up again, on the basis of the previous two sections, the question of the sources, direct and indirect, of the In Matthaeum, and the influence if any, of these sources upon it. Some of the matters in question, as far as they relate to Hilary's theology as a whole, will be further discussed in our next section, and others relating specifically to the Psalms in Section 5. A certain amount may however be said here. It will be useful to discuss these matters in the context of an examination of the recent studies of W. Wille and of J. Doignon on the In Matthaeum and its sources, parts of which Dr. Wille generously made available to me in advance of the completion of the whole.[79]

Wille begins his careful analysis of the In Matthaeum, in which he deals with all aspects except that of the literary structure of the commentary form itself and its hermeneutical implications, by noting the striking absence of the concept of 'nova lex' in the work (16). For Hilary exegesis is 'heilsgeschichtliche Selbstvergewisserung an Hand des Evangeliumtext': this need for assurance comes 'primar aus der Weiterexistens des judischen Volkes'. The text has two levels of meaning (42). The movement

79. Diss. Hamburg, Spring 1969.

of the text is not from the aistheta to the noeta, but is 'ein erkennendes Fortschreiten von der Gegenwart zur Zukunft.' Hilary's use of 'species' in his interpretation suggests contact with the Platonic tradition, being also found in Chalcidius (Tim. Komm 5.304.9f).

The discussion of the relations of Father and Son suggest the influence of Novatian (De Trin 31). The stress on the eternity and consubstantiality of the Son suggest indirect traces of the Arian controversy (59162). The presence of a Geisteschristologie (Hilary nowhere speaks of the Spirit as a person) suggests the use of Victorinus of Pettau and Ps Cyprian de montibus Sina. In discussing the eternity of the Son (1066D) 'Hilarius hat hier offensichtlich auf hermetische Aion-Spekulation zurückgegriffen'. In such speculation the incarnation is understood as a 'Spezialfall des weltdurchdringenden, welterhaltenden Handelns Gottes' (75) i.e. Hilary takes up archaic, philosophical positions (77). This is confirmed by his anthropology (81) 'wir halten fest, Hilary hat offensichtlich eine stark dualistisch geprägte Tradition aufgenommen', which he then tried to break away from. Typical of the influence in the work of this tradition is that salvation is understood as 'Erkenntnismitteilung' which is realised in mystical illumination (cognitic Dei) and salvation is fulfilled as 'Vergottung der menschlichen Natur'. The body of the believer is transformed into the substance of the soul (91). This may indicate the influence of Lactantius, and certainly reflects the Hermetic tradition.

In a further section, the sources of the understanding of history in terms of the Pauline contrast between law and gospel are considered. Wille notes a tendency to 'Entjuridisierung der Frömmigkeit'. This depends basically on a Marcionite tradition (not actually upon Marcion himself) which has been seen too in Arnobius the Elder. Agreement with such a tradition

is found in the use of language, in the understanding of Paul, and in the
antithetic use of the lex/fides motif. The Marcionite tradition too
speaks of veritas evangelii. Exegesis of details also corresponds with
this tradition (though there are also traces of an antimarcionite tradition). The interpretation of 'homoousios' is a further indication of the
influence of the aion concept (p. 104). Some further sources may be seen:
on Mt. 8.5 he is 'offensichlich' influenced by Victorinus of Pettau, and
'gratia als terminus technicus fur den inneren Sinn der Text ..... wird
durch die Abhängigkeit von de Montibus verständlich.' Some indirect influence of the Heilsgeschichte theology of Irenaeus, and of the populus
Dei concept of Hippolytus, is also likely.

Despite the careful and frequently illuminating argument, Willes'
conclusions can scarcely be regarded as established.

In the first instance, it appears from our own analysis of the In
Matthaeum that the scope of the work is much more than simply 'heilsgeschichtliche Selbstvergewisserung': as set out above, the interpretation
is an exposition of the events and acts of salvation in history in the
context of the creation of faith, the emphasis being as much on the description of the historical and theological 'state of things as they are'
as upon personal reassurances. We have seen that Hilary uses many terms
of figurative expression interchangeably: it is then perhaps less than
prudent to build too much on the presence of a word such as 'species':
though the general Platonic atmosphere of this commentary as a fourth
century document is beyond dispute, it is not clear that this particular
tradition plays a definitive role in his exegetical method.[80] Some con-

80. On Neoplatonism cf Wille (3); species and imago in Hilary and
    Chalcidius (W. does not suggest that Hilary actually knew Chalc.)
                                                            (contd.)

nection with Novatian, or knowledge of his work, there may well have
been:[81] yet Hilary was soon to range far beyond Novatian in his own De
Trinitate, and so was presumably not entirely dependent upon him, a year
or two before. There is no evidence of determinative influence. Indirect
traces of the Arian controversy there may well be, as Wille suggests with
others,[82] and even influence of that rather nebulous phenomenon, a
'Geisteschristologie' (in the sense that the doctrine of the third person
of the Trinity remains comparatively undeveloped). The fragmentary state
of the works of Victorinus of Pettau and their undistinguished quality,
indicated above, suggest a need for some caution in attributing significant influence to that quarter. The evidence for Ps. Cyprian, though
amounting only to a few verbal similarities (which may readily be found

80. (contd.)
    The alleged echoes of Novatian (A24) in substance but not in expres-
    sion (exc. deus ex Deo Trin 22) show no more than common membership
    of the western theological tradition of Tert, and Iren. Wille's
    relation to the formula at 4.14 Deus ex Deo, etc to the Nicene creed
    (63) is probably correct. The odd mention of theotes may as Wille
    suggests (64) reflect the creed of Serdika.

81. On Novatian cf. Smulders 79f, Gastaldi 28-31, and Doignon 357-365.
    Though Hilary may well have read Novatian's De Trinitate, Novatian
    does not appear to have influenced Hilary's exegesis to any signif-
    cant extent.

82. Hilary could have learned of the Arian controversy e.g. at Arles in
    353. In the absence of conclusive evidence, the balance favours a
    knowledge of the controversy at this period, but no primary preoccup-
    ation with this as yet. This would be supported by the strong
    emphasis on the consubstantiality of the Son, and the stress upon the
    eternity of the Son. Simonetti op. cit, deduced from the latter
    references that 'Ilario polemizza apertamente con gli Ariani!' (55)
    cf. Wille 59f.

with other sources where no connection is likely) is rather better.[83]

On the other hand, the strong influence attributed to the Hermetic aion speculation appears to be definitely improbable. The De Trinitate, written soon after, shows no such influence, where it might naturally be expected if the theory were correct. Neither Lactantius nor Arnobius the Elder were figures of the theological stature of Hilary: one fears that these apparent parallel instances have misled Wille. Likewise, the hermetical/mystical explanation of illumination by God in faith, though demonstrated in masterly fashion by Dr. Wlosok for Lactantius, is implausible in Hilary. None of the evidence, is unequivocal. And as we have mentioned, the taking up of an outdated system in all its ramifications is in any event, historically improbable for Hilary.[84]

83. The evidence for a Geisteschristologie (67f) does not perhaps, take sufficiently into account the references to the father, son and spirit cited above, and Hilary's imprecision in expressing the relation of the two natures in Christ in 4.1 is not in itself decisive. The parallels with the De Montibus (69f)(CSEL 3.3 104ff) and with Vict. Pett. (A33m93) I find weak, e.g. De Mont. 4. Caro dominica a deo patre Jesu vocita est spiritus, qui de coelo descendit Christus. etc cf. Hil 4.14 Jesus enim domino nostro nomen ex corpore est. cf. too the context of 4.44 cited above.

84. On hermetic aion speculation cf. 72f Wille's parallels with Asclepius are drawn, with the exception of cf. 31.2 (1055D) from the adv. Val. et Urs. In both cases Hilary is correcting asertions made by opponents (the parallel of Kraft's analysis of Hermetic influence in Novatian and Constantine's use of homoousios is not really relevant for Hilary. Whether the dualist tradition reflected in the distinction between body and soul in the In Mt. (80-83) reflects more than current neoplatonic sensus communis is also doubtful. W. perhaps relies too much here on Seeberg. Again Lactantius (cf A39. 144A) is not Hilary. Wille's evidence for mysticism (84 cf an 159 (A42) again relies on the hermetic tradition and Lactantius). There is however, no unambiguous mysticism in this sense in the In Mt. The exx, quoted for 'Heil als Vergottung des menschlichen Natur! all refer to Jesus, describing his two natures, and not to the state in the present of the Christian (949B. 1056C). The formulation is more likely to have some (not as yet demonstrable) connection with Irenaeus rather than with Lactantius. Doignon (352-9) also cites the Itala, with reference to Wille's thesis on umbra.

Wille's characterisation of Hilary's work as 'Entjuridisierung der Frommigkeit' fits well the general religious situation of the age: wearying of Tertullianist moralism, longing for something less banal. On the other hand, the evidence for a strong Marcionite influence on Hilary is thin. Veritas, umbra eternitas, lex and fides may be found in combination in many non-Marcionite traditions as we have seen above, e.g. in Tertullian, Irenaeus and Origen. The suggestion of a dualism from which Hilary attempted to break away probably reflects at least some of the facts: on the other hand it is not clear that this dualism was as consistent as has been suggested. The temptation to reduce a complex situation with a large number of unknowns or partially unknowns to a precise pattern is great, but it does not reduce the complexity of the facts.

The possibility of a Marcionite strain in Vict. Pett. (223 cf. B57) is as we have seen of negligible value for the determination of this factor in Hilary. This applies to its presence in Arnobius the Elder too. Though Hilary uses lex and fides in contrast as well as the adjective evangelicam, he does not use precisely the same formulation as e.g. the Marc. prologue to Paul 'verbum veritatis' etc. Frequent use of veritas is found in connections (cf. sect.2 above) where no Marcionite influence is likely. The alleged exegetical parallels though they would serve as conformation given direct evidence, fail to do so in its absence, just as the single occurrence of lumen scientiae (p. 84. A42) fails to demonstrate the presence of an originally hermetic theory of mystical illumination (despite its possible presence in Lactantius). It cannot be proved that some influence from these Hermetic and Marcionite sources suggested by Wille has not occurred, but I think the uncertainty of the foundations of these has been shown. This however does not detract from the value of the

97

careful manner in which most of the theological issues of the gospel are discussed.

The precise answers to the question of Hilary's sources and the influence of various traditions on the In Matthaeum remain unknown. The tradition of Tertullian, Cyprian and Novatian in theology is clearly followed, though at a distance and with considerable independence on Hilary's part. Traces of anti-Arian exegesis are present, though this was not yet the burning issue of the period of the De Trinitate. From Tertullian and Novatian and probably other sources certainly including Neoplatonic influence came dualist traits, though these may not be exaggerated. Some indirect influence of Origen is likely.[85] Cyprian was of theological importance. The marks of the rhetorical tradition throughout are clear. Hilary <u>may</u> have known Hippolytus' work, though this cannot be proved. The most likely single source of much of the inspiration of his theology of the Heilsgeschichte of the incarnation is Irenaeus: direct evidence for this is however entirely lacking.

85. Wille concluded that a direct knowledge of the Alexandrian terminology was unlikely, and that the Platonism was that of the fourth century Latin variety. Loofs 58f thought that there was no Greek influence in the In Mt, but Watson 8f concluded that Hilary was here already a disciple of Origen. The In Mt shows no use of a Greek text and this is a better indication than Jerome's remarks (Ep. ad Marc.3)(PL23.49) cf Hilary's difficulty with the language of little knowledge of Greek on his part at the time (and so almost certainly no direct reading of Origen (cf. sect.2 on the Latin trans. of Origen). Hilary must have learned Greek quickly (or relearned what he had learned at school and then forgotten) for as Bardy remarks, all the translations of the De Synodis are by Hilary himself. (Langues p. 211f) i.e. direct influence of Origen is improbable but indirect influence is likely to have been everywhere felt in some degree – though that has not been significant for the determination of the main themes of the In Mt. The above criticisms of specific conclusions by no means detract from the considerable value of Wille's work, from which I have gained much.

Much of the characteristic force of the commentary may however be

understood from examination of the work itself, of the literary structure

and its effects on the text, of the principles of interpretation in con-

junction with that structure, in the context of the rhetorical tradition,

and in the exegetical tradition of the church, and of the interplay of

theological and philosophical considerations which it reveals.[86]

86. It is encouraging to observe that Doignon's recent magnificent study
     comes to substantially the same conclusions as those offered above.
     Extremely interesting, but to my mind unconvincing comments on Hilary's
     theological method are to be found in the work of T.F. Torrance,
     especially in Theology in Reconstruction, pp. 92f, Theological Science,
     20f, and articles published in Abba Salama, 1975, 37ff, which the
     author has kindly sent to me. Professor Torrance finds in Hilary a
     prototype for his own brilliant but problematic concept of a theolog-
     ical science. This leads him, inter alia, to some unusual historical
     judgements e.g. the influence of Origenistic exegesis is most apparent
     in Hilary's first work, the commentary on Matthew (art cit.p.37).
     (On matters of scientific method cf, esp. M. Hesse, The Structure of
     Scientific Inference, London, 1974).

Christology and Hermeneutics

4.   The Middle Period

The De Trinitate

The middle Period: De Trinitate.

The De Trinitate, or more probably De Fide,[1] differs in many respects from the In Matthaeum. It was written not in Gaul but in Hilary's place of exile in Asia Minor,[2] it is not a commentary on a book of the Bible but a theological treatise. Yet its purpose, of setting out a particular doctrine in the context of the biblical teaching on the subject, and in doing so, of defending the doctrine, that of the divinity of Jesus Christ against Arian attack,[3] is by no means remote from that of the previous work.

A high proportion of the text consists of the theological interpretation of biblical texts:[4] indeed it had been shown by Martinez Sierra that much of Hilary's argument includes a direct refutation of arguments based upon the same biblical texts.[5]

1. Hilary does not in fact mention the title in his work. Cassian (de inc Dom. contra Nest, VII 24) and Rufinus (HE 10.32) refer to it as the De Fide. Jerome speaks of it as the adversus Arianos, Venantius Fortunatianus and Cassiodorus as the De Trinitate (6th cent.) cf the discussion in Reinkens 137 and Borchardt 40. The word trinitas occurs within the work only twice, at 1.36. and 1.22.

2. The beginning and end may have been written in Gaul before and after the exile. The problem has been much debated; cf. the summary in Borchardt 40f. cf. 10.4 loquemur enim exsules per hos libros (PL10. 346C). The evidence does not permit of a firm conclusion, except that part of the work was written in exile, and there is no evidence to suggest that the remainder was not written there too. The exact place in Asia Minor is also unknown.

3. cf. De Trin 2.2(PL10.51A) (sufficiebat credentibus Dei sermo) sed compellimur haereticorum et blasphementium vitiis, illicita agere. ardua scandere, ineffabilia eloqui, inconcessa praesumere. etc. cf too 1.16 where two groups of opponents, Sabellians and Arians are characterised.

4. Löffler op.cit.p. 88f counted 1272 biblical quotations, 231 from the Ct and 1041 from the NT; including the following: Genesis 62, Exodus 26; Dt 22, Psalms 39, Isaiah 43, Synoptic Gospels 255, Johannine corpus 428, Pauline writings and pastorals 324.

5. Martinez Sierra op. cit. Bardy too (Paul de Samosate) stresses the Arians concern with clarity. On Arian exegesis cf. too Athan.v. the tropici in Ep. ad Serap.2 (PG 26.532) quoted by Pollard.

Apart, however, from its occasional character the work was clearly intended to be a theological treatise in its own right, and as such was constructed with careful attention to style and structure.[6] As with the In Matthaeum, it is notoriously difficult to say which sources, oral or written, Hilary may have drawn upon: at all events it seems clear that his theological horizons had broadened considerably since the days of the In Matthaeum.[7] The order of the composition of the books remains debateable.[8] That the autobiographical character of the prologue contains at least an element of historical truth need not be doubted.[9]

a)   The formal structure of the work.

Much less need be said of this aspect here than in the In Matthaeum, since the literary structure, being much less rigorous in form, has considerably less impact on the argument. The texts are exegeted in a rather different way than in the In Matthaeum, the differences lying in part at

6.   Norden. Antike Kunstprosa, notes the 'auf stärkste sallustisch gefarbten Einleitung' to the De Trin and Hilary's desire to speak for God in his work 'verborum significationem, intelligentiae lumen, dictorum honorem (De Trin 1.38 In Ps 13.1)

7.   On the sources of the De Trin cf. Loofs, Löffler passim, Borchardt 136f, Doignon 85f,

8.   cf. Borchardt's discussion, op cit p.40f. In 4.1 there is a reference to the books which 'iam pridem conscripsimus'. In 4.2 there is a reference to the first book, and 1.19 is intended; 5.3 the fifth book is called the second book. In 6.4 book 4 is described as the first and then as the 6th book is 10.4 Hilary says 'loquemur enim exsules per hos libros'. In 4.2 there is a reference to 1.19 and in 9.10 to 1.13. Evidence from the subject matter is inconclusive. There is no basis for Watson's conclusion (xxxiii) that the first book was written last.

9.   The prologue compares well with the biographical comments of Jerome and Fortunatianus who may of course have derived their information in turn from the prologue itself.

least in the absence of the pressures for continuity and consistency of
the commentary form which had affected the exegesis of individual texts
in the commentary.[10] There is a marked lessening in the use of figural
interpretation in the De Trinitate. The relationship may be illustrated
by a random sample: we shall choose book 7 of the De Trin.

The first thing that strikes us is the rarity of the occasions upon
which the text is actually exegeted in detail. Usually the text is used
as an 'epitome', in condensed reiteration and scriptural confirmation of
the theological point which is being made.[11] This means that even fewer
extra scriptural citations than were occasionally brought in in the In Mt.
to explain particular points in given passages, need to be invoked.[12]
Here further citations which follow the main text being cited as an epitome
are more frequently used in confirmation of the theological point at issue
rather than in explanation of the text. For this epitomising use of

10. We have seen that in the In Mt. though individual phrases were often
treated in an epitomising manner with little regard for the original
sense, nevertheless the whole is still exegeted in the context of the
gospel narrative as Hilary understands this. Now, the same epitomising method is used but without the context being an integral part
of the exegesis. By 'epitomising method' we mean a procedure in which
a text is used as a summation of or pointer to a sense which is already
given, being either assumed, or established by some other means. The
text itself is here hardly ever exegeted (as it often was in the In
Mt) Instead all is referred to the main theme of the work, to the
divinity of Jesus. The result is that though the exegetical method
is not far removed from that of In Mt. the total effect of the exegetical operation is very different.

11. Both the shaping of the text through the literary categories, from
the In Matt.; and the linguistic and textual work of the In Psalmos
are absent. Compare e.g. Trin 7.22 with In Matt. 3.1f and In ps 124.
4f.

12. Thus in book 7 all four of the scriptural citations (Ps 76.6 at 7.10,
Rom 1.2 at 7.24, Mal 3.6. at 7.27 and Ex 7.10) are from St. John's
gospel.

scripture it matters little whether whole passages, parts of verses or individual words are cited. Many of the texts involved are cited as showing the opposite of what the Arians wish them to prove; though Hilary demonstrates this more by doctrinal assertion than from an analysis of the contents of the texts themselves.

These texts are usually introduced by means of a phrase of introduction: the formulae of recapitulation and repetition in the In Matthaeum tend to disappear in the nature of the case.[13] Where single words are stressed atomisation of the text still occurs, yet since the role of epitome is essentially different from that of continuous exegesis, this matters less.[14] The main theme is introduced in an epitomising text, and thereafter the argument proceeds, on occasion over several paragraphs, as a meditation upon the adduced text.[15] Such an approach differs distinctly from that of an evaluation of the text in its biblical context and an exegesis based on the strict content of the text itself. It is not so much the biblical context as the nature of his own argument which determines the meaning of the text for Hilary; this leads to changes in the accentuation of the given text in whole and in part.[16] (This factor

13. e.g. at 7.5 hoc dictum Domini; 7.9 legimus enim; 7.10 dictum est, ubi dictur; 7.15 in quo scriptum est; 7.17 ait; 7.19 ait.

14. cf. the treatment of 'ego et Pater unum sumus' at 7.24. The fact that the texts involved are almost all doctrinal texts from St. John, and not narrative episodes or parables, helps to lessen the effect of the splitting up into single words in the De Trin.

15. Extended meditation on a single text is seen at e.g. 7.10f; 7.16f; 7.22-27; 7.39-41.

16. So in 7.5 the phrase 'I and the Father are one' is treated as if the gospel writer knew in advance of the heresies to come. In 7.22 Jn 10-27-30 is read as if it were part of a 4th century theological treatise, and 7.23 the roles of the Jews and the heretics are exactly identified.

clearly occurs to some extent in all theology and is not always undesirable, but awareness of the phenomenon is important for the understanding
of a writer's thought.)

Common to the exegesis of the De Trin and the In Mt is the central
strictly theological concern: apart from this the special features of
exegesis in commentary-continuity, cross-references and the like are no
longer necessary in the structure of the De. Trin. But the importance of
the biblical texts in the doing of theology, as Hilary understands this,
is in no way reduced.[17]

Elements of other literary forms may also be found in this work. In
an important sense the whole of the De Trin. is a theological and exegetical dialogue with the Arians,[18] except that the formal structure and the
introductory setting of the scene is not present, as in the classical
dialogue. Again, the work exhibits strands of homiletic paraenesis, with
elevated exhortations concerning what we ought to do[19] - we have mentioned
that theology without a homiletic strain was practically unknown in the early
church. This element was to be developed considerably in the final period
of Hilary's writing, in/tractate on the psalms.
                                        the

17. As at 7.33 Non enim fides ex arbitrio nostro, sed ex dictorum est
    ineunda virtutibus.
18. This was well brought out by Martinez Sierra cf.below.
19. Exhortation is addressed either directly to the heretic, in the manner
    of classical rhetoric as at 7.23 at 'tu vero, heretice, quid agas ac
    profitearis agnosce' etc or to the believer, as at 8.69-70 throughout.

b)   Principles of interpretation, especially interpretation of scripture.

A striking feature of the De Trinitate is the relative influence of coelestis significantia and cognates in comparison with the In Matthaeum.[20] This is a consequence of the epitomising use of scripture explained in the previous section, in which the first object is not to draw out a hidden sense by exegesis, but to support an argument which is held to be equally evident in open and hidden senses alike;[21] since the Arians made use of allegorical interpretation to defend their positions (like the Gnostics and most defenders of special interpretations), Hilary is concerned to show that his interpretation is clear from the simple sense of the text. Typology is, as we shall see below, limited to the interpretation of Old Testament prophecy.

This lack of detailed exegesis (except in special cases) reflects the fact that Hilary is here concerned not with the theology of the Old and New Testament as such, but with the use of biblical texts to illuminate specific theological issues.

In the De Trinitate the lex/fides motif has receded entirely from the foreground.[22] The leading motif is now the divinity of the Son, Jesus Christ; but since the use of texts is different, the apparatus used in the

20.   There are in fact no references in Bk 7 to coelestis significantia. Hilary prefers to speak instead of scripture as Dei sermo, as at 7.38.

21.   cf. Io.1 Non est ambiguum, omnem humani eloquii sermonem contradictioni obnoxium semper fuisse. This is contrasted with varitatis sermo (ibid) which is the veritas Dei patris (10.3) The importance of the context is stressed at 4.14 and 9.59. cf too 2.3 and 7.4 where the faith of the Church is contrasted with the misinterpretation of the heretics.

22.   cf. the relations of gospel and law at 5.17-18-23 and 9.28. These are now no longer contrasted but complementary.

In Matthaeum for making the inner sense refer exclusively to the main motif
is no longer required.[23] Whatever Marcionite influence there may have
been is now gone, another indication that its supposed earlier presence
may have been due more to the character of the interpretation which he
wanted to make specifically of St. Matthew's gospel than to his general
theological outlook at that time. At the same time, there is no trace in
the De Trinitate of the traditional Alexandrian doctrine of a series of
steps towards the deeper mystical illumination of scripture:

Though as we have seen scripture is normally used in the De Trinitate
in a manner different from that of the In Matthaeum, the question of how
scripture is to be understood correctly is still involved, and may be
looked at from a number of different angles. An important feature of the
work is that it presupposes faith, which brings us a corollary with itself
the illumination of scripture by the Holy Spirit.[24] The change in the role
of scripture brings in its train changes in the setting out of the manner
of its functioning. The category of exemplum is much less frequent,[25] and
there is less stress upon the virtus of the words. The dicta/facta
dialectic of the rhetorical tradition now being bridged by the one Verbum

23. References to ordo still appear as at 7.16 propositionis ordo, and
    8.40 doctrinae ordo, but the category itself no longer plays a signif-
    icant role.

24. It is from God that we can learn about God cf 8.38 esp. It is from
    faith that we learn to deepen faith (i.18-19)(Grabmann 1.121f sees
    this as an important anticipation of Anselm's famous 'fides quaerens
    intellectum). It is in the Holy Spirit that faith is nourished (cf.
    8.31, 8.34, 2.33) Faith depends on the spirit of Christ rather than
    the spirit of heresy (8.25).

25. Again the change in character of the narrative, and the absence of a
    long series of historical narrative episodes, largely explains the
    lack of exempla. The Word is not however deliberately avoided, e.g.
    at 8.9. Christ gives an exemplum unitatis.

of the incarnation: 'at veri hic verbum Deus est: res exsistit in Verbo,

Verbi res enuntiatur in nomine'.[26] Thus the literal sense could refer as

much to the verbum as the spiritual sense, and there was no need for

constant invocation of the inner sense. One could see this as a decisive

breakthrough comparable to the change in the understanding of hermeneutics

at the Reformation (the Reformers themselves did) but, as we shall see,

there is need for caution: with Hilary all is still in flux, and different

modes of thought exist side by side and even intermingle.[27]

26. Virtus still appears too e.g. at 7.33 Non enim fides ex arbitrio
    nostro, sed ex dictorum est inuenda virtutibus. But the central
    preoccupations have changed apart from the explicit references to
    the Verbum, the whole emphasis throughout on the centrality of faith
    in the Son of God, not always directly related to scripture, plays
    a major role in revealing God and guiding men to faith may be seen
    at 1.18-19, 3.9; 9.52 and 12.45. The Incarnation is The res of
    scripture, and in Hilary's basic dictum, non sermoni res, sed rei est
    sermo subiectus (4.14). The Verba lead to the ratio and so to the
    veritas who is God (5.36). The whole word is a sermo veritatis
    (6.4.).

27. With the Reformers Hilary shared the insight that Christ was the
    interpreter of his own word, though the manner of interpretation
    naturally differed. The reasons for the differences are varied.
    1) Differences in other areas of theology related to this, e.g. the
    doctrine of man and of eschatology were also involved, so that Hilary
    was not as close to Luther on grace an justification as Luther him-
    self thought. Their realist emphasis brings points of convergence:
    Luther's realism is articulated within a nominalist (and so despite
    his stricture in some ways Aristotelian) framework, Hilary's and
    Calvin's within a Platonist framework. 2) Though Hilary stresses
    that God is only known through God in Christ, it is important to bear
    in mind that he does not always draw the explicit conclusions that
    Christ reveals himself through the scriptures. The influence of the
    general patristic understanding of scripture deriving from Philo
    remains, though here again the greatest problems raised by the philonic
    theory of verbal inspiration are partially resolved by the stress on
    the events themselves rather than the words. Modern theologians who
    elect to ignore the historico-critical method find impressive
    correspondence at the cost of anachronism.

Hilary is much concerned to stress that God can only be known through God: Non potest Deus nisi per Deum intelligi, sicuti nec honorem a nobis nisi per Deum accepit (5.21 neque enim nobis es natura est, ut se in coelestem cognitionem suis viribus efferat. More precisely, God is known in Christ: dum eo cognito Pater cognitus est, dum eo viso Pater visus est. (8.18 cf. 7.31, 5.27 and 5.20 above).

The scriptures point to God (cf 6.19) and he in turn illuminates the meaning of the scriptures. The important implications of this shift from the divinely inspired scripture as itself the creator of faith to Christ as the one who initiates the disclosure of the knowledge of God in scripture we shall explore below. Here we must attempt to understand why Hilary came to take such a step. The crucial factor which prompted his revised conception was probably the pressure of the Arians' argument.[28]

Contrary to the popular belief that makes all heretics first fools then impious fools, most Arians were probably neither. As theologians they were well aware that theology was not simply to be equated with philosophy and even bad philosophy, and they sought as much as did their opponents to work for the glory of God. Therefore an appeal to scripture as the basis of his position (cf. De Trin. 6.19 and 1.17) was not enough, for the Arians too based their case on scripture.

28. In the De Trin. as in all Hilary's work it is important to recall that his central concerns are practical rather than theoretical. He is here concerned to refute the argument of the Arians and to stress the divine sonship of Christ. He is NOT concerned to develop a systematic hermeneutic of scripture. Nevertheless his practical concern forced him to develop a theory of understanding in general and of scripture in particular alongside existing theories, and the scattered nature of his basic points need not detract from their often considerable theological acumen.

The problem for Hilary lay in a correct understanding of scripture, which would yield the true interpretation if not read with false pre-suppositions (cf.7.4; 2.3; 8.6; 10.1-2; 12.3; 3.23); attention must be paid to the proper context and to understanding the words in the light of the events which they indicate, and not vice versa (9.2; 4.14). In any case, the words have their own virtus, which may be understood provided that we avoid imposing our own preoccupations upon them (7.33). The intention of the speaker must be considered (6.41) and where the sense appears ambiguous comparisons must be made (11.22-31) and parallel texts must be used (9.58f). If this is done, then scripture will be sufficient for the disclosure of the knowledge of God (11.7) and is so when inter-preted within the Church (7.4).

Having said this however, it must be stressed that though we may detect here the beginnings of a new understanding of scripture, this understanding is not always carried through into the exegetical practice. Must of the exegesis of the De Trin. follows traditional lines, continuing the pattern of the In Matt. without the features peculiar to the commentary structure. It is mainly in specific anti-Arian expositions that the new accent is carried through. But at the same time, the factor of christolog-ical reference remains an important element in the work as a whole.

Hilary's understanding agreed with the Antiochene tradition (though apparently without any anti-Origenist intention), in referring the literal sense direct to Christ, but went beyond this in its understanding of the validating function of the Verbum (to be distinguished both from Augustine's detailed doctrine of the 'inner word' and from the Reformers' understanding of the hearing of the Word alike). It is distinguishable too from Origen's ontological understanding of the allegorical process and

110

from the popular "Origenist" simplification of this.

Augustine like Hilary (through the same Latin rhetorical tradition) sees the differences between the literal and the spiritual senses in scripture more in terms of res and signum than of the spiritalis/corporalis distinction of Origen. But the sign theory which he elaborates, and which was to be the basis of mediaeval exegesis, involving a dualism of signs and res, was in important respects closer to Origen than Hilary. It is therefore understandable that the Reformers, especially Luther, were to see Hilary's understanding of the self-authenticating function of the Verbum, as being essentially their own criterion 'was Christum treibet'.[29]

29. For Augustine's theory of the interpretation of scripture cf. De Doctr. Christ. esp. III De ambiguitatibus in scriptura enodandis and also De Trin. 15.10f; also the studies by Duchrow esp. 213f, Schindler 95ff and G. Strauss 84f (cf. too 96f and 147ff), also Gadamer 397ff. Ebeling, art, Hermeneutik in RGG3, offers an excellent short summary of Augustine's method. 'It becomes clear in the wider context of his epistemology, ontology and philosophy of languages why he made the relationship between sign and thing signified (signum and res) the basis of his hermeneutics. In doing this, he combined a theory of the purely significative character of language with the metaphysical idea of sign-giving property of the reality of time and space which must be transcended (and which to this extent has linguistic character and becomes as the object in the foreground the sign of the true thing signified). This schema, based on the double concept of signum and res, provides two possibilites: an exact concern for the literal sense coupled with an interpretation by extrapolation from the sensible to the intelligible world. The bridge is formed by the fact, known from rhetoric, that words may act as signa in a double way; in their own right (propria) and in a transferred sense (translata). Difficulties for both interpretations arise from the fact that words may be unknown (ignota) or have two meanings. In the first instance, the artes liberales may be adduced to provide explanation (including the rhetorical theory of tropes) and in the second case, there is need of a criterion for the understanding of what should be understood literally and what metaphorically; because so intended by the author.
Ebeling characterises thus the relation between Augustine and Origen (RGG art, Geist u. Buchstabe) 'The Schema of a double sense of scripture is retained by Augustine, but for A the sensus litteralis is the rule, and the sensus spiritualis (mysticus) is the exception. It is not the ontological difference between the corporeal and the spiritual, but the (not always sharply differentiated) language event
(contd.)

111

Augustine was also indebted to Aristotelian sources for his doctrine of the Word and the dualism which it involved. Quite apart from the important indirect influence through Cicero's Hortensius in his early years, he had read the Categories and in his work on the Trinity made extensive use of the psychology of the De Anima, possibly in a Latin translation but conceivably directly. His understanding of verbs as signs of a hidden res has its roots, if only indirectly, in the beginnings of Aristotle's De Interpretatione. On the relations of Augustine and Aristotle, in general cf. D. Ritschl, Memory and Hope 105ff and lit. cit. ad loc.

The wider consequences of Augustine's work are excellently summarised by Gadamer, op, cit, p.397. 'The external word, and with it the whole problem of the multiplicity of languages, is expressly depreciated in value by Augustine, who nevertheless still mentions it. The external word, like the internal word which is merely reproduced within (the recipient) is bound to a particular language (lingua). The fact that the verbum can be said in different ways in different languages means however only this, that it is unable to show itself in its true being to the human tongue. Augustine says in entirely Platonic devaluation of the appearance in the sensible world 'non dicitur, sicuti est, sed sicut potest videri audirive per corpus'. The 'true' word, the verbum cordis, is

29. (contd.)
(signum res) which is the basis of Augustine's hermeneutic and allows more attention to be paid to the literal sense and the narrative itself. Corresponding to this the scopus is not the spiritual alone, but faith and love. Nevertheless, Augustine's hermeneutic like his understanding of the letter and the spirit, remains in close affinity with Neoplatonic thought'. The works of Strauss, Duchrow and Schindler (like that of Krause on Luther referred to above) are essentially expanded paraphrases of the work of Ebeling.

entirely independent of such an appearance. It is neither prolativum nor
cognativum in similitudine soni. Thus this inner word is the mirror and
picture of the divine word. When Augustine and the scholastics deals with
the problem of the verbum, in order to find the (appropriate) conceptual
apparatus for the mystery of the Trinity, it is exclusively the inner word
of the heart and its relation to the intelligentia, which they make their
theme.' As for Hilary we have already seen how in the In Matthaeum Hilary
uses models derived from what was originally Stoic epistemological theory.
Stoicism itself had early absorbed much Platonic material (at least since
Poseidonius) and in the Neoplatonic tradition there was a general complete
blending of the old Platonist and Aristotelian schools (often but not
exclusively taking the form of a combination of Aristotelian epistemology
and Platonist ontology.) The importance of this blending of the traditions,
which in itself combined to produce all kinds of new possibilities, cannot
be sufficiently underlined. Reconstructions, too, which see the 'key' to
fourth century discussions philosophical or theological, and not simply
individual strains in these, in terms of the strict applications of conceptual categories and distinctions from Plato and Aristotle themselves,
are usually untenable, though of course they may stimulate further study
of the precise nature of the problems involved.

Epistemology was for the Stoics intimately connected with the theory
of language and with logic, which according to Mates, was a logic of
propositions and of inference schemas, in contrast to the Aristotelian
logic of classes and of logically true matrices. In understanding there
are three main factors for the Stoic-the significans, the significate and
that which exists: cf. Sext. Adv. Math. 8.11f οἱ ἀπὸ Στοᾶς τρία φάμενοι
συζυγεῖν ἀλλήλοις, τὸ τε σημαινόμενον καὶ τὸ σημαῖνον καὶ
τὸ τυγχανόν.

113

Where the impression of an object formed in the soul corresponds to the object itself, this is a true impression and the soul itself immediately grasps the reality and is in harmony with the world, inner logos corresponding to outer logos. Stoics appear to have distinguished several different meanings for the true and the truth (the true, according to Sextus, differing from the truth in essence; in constitution and in meaning). A distinction was made between the truth of being, equivalent with to hyparchon, and the truth of statement. Correspondence to the truth is established by the general logos itself, which infuses all matter and the soul, so that the object of perception itself becomes an active sign signifying itself and setting up a corresponding image (imago) in the soul of the observer. This relationship has corporeal substantial character - later through Middle Platonism modified to incorporeal substance - and sets the soul of the observer in harmony with the names of the universe, in a general monist framework (realist or idealist in character as the case may be). Knowledge of the truth then produces virtue.[30]

Whatever the dilemmas of monism, the Stoic model certainly avoided the equal disadvantages of Platonic dualism.

30. On Stoic epistemology and logic cf. Bochenski, Ancient Formal Logic 77-100. History of Logic 114f, also Mates, Stoic logic, Merlin in CHAMphil 126f, Prantl, Geschichte der logik 1.6.401f. *On Latin Neoplatonism esp. Huber op.cit, and the arts in RGG3 Platonismus, Aristotelismus. For the De Trin. cf esp. the notes on p. 143 and 160ff. In stressing the presence of Stoic vocabulary and epistemology in the In Matt, and the continuing realist emphasis throughout Hilary's work, it should not be forgotten that Neoplatonist logic sought to relate itself to Plato's logic as well as Aristotle's logic, and to questions of general metaphysics (cf. A.C. Lloyd in Phronesis 1.58ff and 146ff) and that Aristotle too tried always to obey the Platonic injunction to look to the thing rather than the word (cf. W. and M. Kneale, The Development of Logic, 21).

(*Long (ed) Problems in Stoicism and Doignon 116f, 494.)

There was however a further alternative to or radical modification
of the conceptual world of Platonic (and likewise of course Aristotelian)
dualism available, namely that provided by the incarnation itself.
Reflection upon this concept could introduce new possibilities for the
understanding of the relation between knowledge and being, and for the
understanding of the problems of perception, which might be taken up in
various ways. The significance of this concept has been well expressed
by Gadamer (W. & M. 396, cf 395ff and 405) "Wenn das Wort Fleisch wird
und erst in dieser Inkarnation die Wirklichkeit des Geistes sich vollendet,
so wird damit der Logos aus seiner Spiritualität, die zugleich seine
kosmische Potentialität bedeutet, befreit. Die Einmaligkeit des
Erlösungsgeschehens führt den Einzug des geschichtlichen Wesens in das
abendländischen Denken herauf und lässt auch das phänomen der Sprache aus
seiner Versenkung in die Idealitat des Sinnes heraustreten und sich dem
philosophischen Nachdenken darbieten. Denn, im Unterschied zum
griechischen Logos gilt: das Wort ist reines Geschehen (verbum proprie
dicitur personaliter tantum Thomas Iq34). As we have mentioned, Stoic
epistemology, Platonic dualism and incarnation could be thought together
in different ways along with additional ingredients, as required.

The obvious and attractive combination of the realism of Stoic
materialism with the concept of the incarnation into flesh could simply
lead to a disastrous 'christomonist' system in which the difference between
the divine and human in God and man, in Jesus Christ in particular and in
other men in general was confused to the detriment of all concerned: Hilary
has himself been accused of this, but as we shall see the Arian controversy
caused him in fact to lean in the opposite direction.[31]

31. cf, too below p.162f.

The tradition provided examples of numerous other options, which we cannot elaborate here, but the existence of which is important for the understanding of the fourth century situation.

In the apologists, the Logos doctrine of the Stoic had been used to show how God could become incarnate and still remain God. But if monism was avoided, the basic Platonic dualism between the material and the spiritual, between God and men, inherited from Philo (and which was not the biblical differentiation between creator and creature) made it difficult to emphasise the saving significance of the coming of Christ. Of course for the apologists the significance of the incarnation consisted in bringing knowledge of God to men, and since in the Platonist tradition it is knowledge which brings virtue and so transformation of being, they felt no serious difficulty. But though the importance of knowledge in transforming existence has been stressed by all theologians in the Platonist tradition including Hilary, that sphere alone has been felt to be inadequate to express all that Christ has brought about.

In the work of Origen, the basic dualism of the Platonic sign theory remains and the significance of Jesus Christ for the interpretation of scripture is articulated in terms of this background. Thus Philo's allegorical interpretation can be taken over and 'baptised' by christological imagery without reconstruction. But the metaphysical element involved (also present in Philo) makes use of the incarnation concept in effecting the unification of the human and the divine; thus attempting to avoid both the problems for theology of a Stoic monism and a Platonic schema of immanence and transcendence. The union is expressed epistemologically as mystical illumination and ontologically (and also doxologically) as deification.

116

Opinions differed even in his own time about Origen's relation to his Platonic heritage and its effect on his theology. It seems clear that Athanasius, taking up the Stoic legacy of the logos doctrine as it had come through Philo and the apologists to Origen, and using it to reinterpret the incarnation in such a way as to avoid the dualist dangers which led to Arianism intended not so much to contradict Origen as to remove the ambiguities.[32]

Hilary shares with early Latin theology in general the originally Stoic influenced legacy of the logos doctrine, along with the Platonic exegetical and metaphysical tradition, as this had come through the Apostolic fathers (esp. Barnabas) to Irenaeus and so to Tertullian. Part of the legacy may have come to Hilary through the direct though not proven influence of Irenaeus, who in fighting the Gnostics was conscious of the difficulties raised by the kind of Platonic dualism used by the apologists. For Hilary too the Stoicised epistemology of the In Matt, coming from Tertullian, with its tendency to monism and still without the strong Neoplatonism of the later Latin West, coupled too with the res/verba dialectic and the use of virtus etc (cf, sects 2 and 3 above) of the rhetorical tradition of Cicero and Quintilian, avoids the dualism of the Origenist/Augustinian pattern, while the traditional exegetical distinction between the literal and the spiritual (from Philo through Irenaeus) help to preserve him from monism.

32. Coulange, Metamorphose 199, concluded that "Hilaire ne semble pas rien devoir a Athanase, il n'a probablement rien de lui" But for the suggestion that Hilary might have been encouraged in his fight by Athanasius' stand and on Athanasius and his relation to Middle Platonism cf, now E.P. Meijering 'Orthodoxy and Platonism in Athanasius' Leiden 1968. The doctrine of the Inc, as logos/verbum is discussed by Hilary at 2.1-21: 7.11 and 10.21, 50 and 54. Meijering, op.cit.p.183ff, makes the point that Platonism need not be undesirable in theology.

It may perhaps be added, on the use of different epistemological frameworks at different times, that though of no theological significance in themselves, these gain their significance when applied to the solution of specific problems. The history of doctrine would appear to show that none of the above frameworks is in itself 'to be preferred' in theology, nor indeed are formal ways of approaching problems inherently better than informal approaches or vice versa. Different frameworks may be used in different circumstances to articulate clearly the Christian conviction of the action of God in creation, in history and in the lives of men. Often a 'realist' framework of some kind, Platonist or Aristotelian, has served well to express in objective terms the significance of the incarnation – as with Athanasius in combating the theological legacy of Arianism, or with Luther in combating the abstractions of a late scholasticism in which the living God appeared to have been removed and obscured from men in a late mediaeval 'death of a thousand qualifications'. Yet realism may be corrupted into a positivism, in which the infinite difference between the divine and the human is obscured, as in Tertullian and Methodius of Olympus on the resurrection of the body, or in e.g. some 17th century understandings of sacramental grace, Catholic and Protestant. (Excellent work on realism and naive realism is now to be found in the unpublished Ph.D. thesis of A. Millar Cambridge 1974.) All such frameworks partake of the limitation of the human, so that their usefulness depends not on a supposed appropriateness to the divine per se but on the theological situation of the time, in which the faith of the biblical writers is to be articulated.

Having sketched the general background to the issues involved in the hermeneutical focus of the De Trinitate, we must now return to the details of the hermeneutical principles themselves. Origen had selected arguments

118

from one school of philosophy to refute the arguments of another opposing school with great versatility;[33] Hilary too, though with less intellectual virtuosity, selects out elements in the fourth century synthesis which originally came from varied traditions, to suit his purposes. As we have said, the De Trinitate shows Hilary's thought in development, in which contradictions and strictly incompatible elements may be found together: but the lack of finished consistency does not obscure the basic directions. Traces of the earlier explanation of the transformation of the words and exempla into our understanding by the spirit in the Stoic tradition are still present. But now the role of the Holy Spirit, which is not central in the De Trinitate despite the popular title, is given a distinctive place in illumination of the incarnation as the key to scripture rather than in the immediate illumination of the words as in Philonic theory.[34] It is often pointed out as part of general theories on Hilary's 'system'[35] that the idea that God can only be understood through God himself reflects the Aristotelian view of the aseity and impassibility of God. But this is not peculiar to Aristotle, (whose views on deity are in any case highly complex) and in Hilary's case more likely to be a product of general reflection on the tradition. After all the proposal that like can only be known through like is a locus communis of all ancient philosophy from the Eleatics onwards.

33. On Origen's relation to the Stoa cf. esp. H. Chadwick, Origen, Celsus and the Stoa, HTR, 1947.
34. A full list of references to Gloria in Hilary, many of which come from the In Matt. is given by Fierro op. cit. esp. p. 74n2. References in the De Trinitate include 2.26f; 3.18; 9.4f; 9.38ff; 10.7. cf, Trin 2.33 'fidem nostram de Dei incarnatione difficilem, Sancti Spiritus donum quodam intercessionis suae foedere luminavit' Further references to the Spirit of God are found at 1.36; 2.1; 2.4; 8.20f; 12.55f.
35. cf. p. 172ff below.

From the rhetorical tradition, the literary categories of ordo, ratio and proprietas play a much diminished role in the exegetical work.

Now their role is largely limited to the literary function of stressing the consistency and reasonableness of the interpretation in the classical manner, complementing the highly polished prose and careful stylistic construction, e.g. of the prologue.

Since in the De Trinitate texts are rarely exegeted as fully as in the In Matthaeum, and since, as we saw above, the Arians resorted to allegory, Hilary himself makes sparing use of allegory and typology in this work. Had it not been used by the Arians, he might have learned to use allegory more fully as in the Alexandrian tradition without embarrassment for his own purposes, as he was later to do in the treatise on the Psalms. Typology, not as important as it had been in the In Matthaeum, in articulating the movements from past to present, is here almost entirely limited to the traditional role of pointing to the fulfilment of the Old Testament promise in Christ and in his Church.[36] The problems involved in the understanding of the realisation in the Church now of the Pauline eschatology, despite the distinction between ontological and doxological categories often made, existed neither for Hilary nor for his opponents,

36. Figurae. Particularly important is the typological use of Abraham as the type of justification by faith, cf. esp 4.23ff and also 5.15-36 (also In Matt. 2.3, Ps. 127.7, 134, 51 etc.) But figurae are not to be used to distort the plain sense of the text, by heretics even if the Lord did on occasion speak parabolicis et allegoricis dictis (9.70) Analogy is discussed by Hil. at 1.19; 4.2; 6.9; and 7.29f. On analogy in the ancient world cf. Lyttkens op. cit. On the special significance of the words of Christ himself cf 1.32 (Trin) These are illuminated by the Holy Spirit to awake faith in us: cf 2.32-33.

as indeed they did not arise for the community around which the fourth gospel itself arose.[37]

Corresponding to the freedom gained, in contact with the eastern tradition and through the stress on the divinity of the Son as a focal point, from the rigid interpretation of the In Matthaeum, we find a greater use of all kinds of illustrative material, which is used in the same way as biblical parables and similitudes in illustrating aspects of the doctrine of the incarnation; though again Hilary stresses the limitations of all human analogies.

Figural illustrations, both in the rhetorical tradition of Stoic descent and in the Platonic tradition from Philo have an ontological significance, which as applied to the incarnation by Hilary explain the suggestion of the presence of the beginnings of the mediaeval doctrine of substantial grace: in addition however Hilary's use of figurae in analogies has a strong doxological as well as an ontological element. (There is nothing necessarily bad about ontology: all depends on the particular application.)

Also, though in Origen and in the tractate on the Psalms we sometimes find a point by point correspondence between the analogans and the analogate, the incarnation: in the De Trinitate, in the analogies for scripture, this is not the case.

In the De Trinitate as in the In Matthaeum there are passages where the word 'absolutus' shows that the meaning of the biblical passage cited is in itself clear. Due to the epitomising use of scripture, and the lack

---

37. Stuhlmacher op. cit, 13, concludes that "Die paulinische Rechtfertigungslehre verschwindet darum, weil die Situation verschwand, fur die sie geschaffen war".

of detailed exegesis of a continuous theme in the biblical narrative,
these passages are here more frequent, and in contrast to the In Matt.
are not limited to the parables of Jesus and the fulfilment of prophecy,
but can be applied to any type of passage. Indeed one of the pivotal
passages of the De Trin. Ex. 3.14 (De Trin. 1.5) is described as 'absolutus' in meaning. It is significant that whereas in the period of the
In Matt. and of the rules from the rhetorical tradition for the understanding of scripture, only some parables and some of the words of Jesus
were alone clear 'absolute' in the midst of the darkness of the rest,
now in the De Trinitate, the meaning of any part of scripture may be seen
in the light of the incarnation: the purpose of scripture is to induce
true faith by pointing to God in Christ. In the In Psalmos this scope
of scripture is extended to include the life of man in the light of Christ,
specific detailed information being extracted with the aid of the
Alexandrian rules, as we shall see below. Where further information, on
ethics and on all aspects of human activity and questions about the world
in general has been brought from the Bible, as was to be done later in
some mediaeval interpretation further resort to detailed allegorical rules
has been required.

c)   The theological structure

Before going into the examination of the theological structure it
will be convenient to recall the argument in the De Trinitate. Fairly
straightforward in outline, it has often been summarised. The first three
books, opened in a quasi-autobiographical manner, are concerned with a
general and mainly non-polemical introduction to the nature of the Christian faith, and the way in which Hilary came to faith, not through phil-

osophy but through the guidance of God who reveals himself through the scriptures. The roles of faith and reason, of scripture and philosophy and their relations to one another are explained.

Hilary then turns to the arguments of the Arians from scripture in detail, and proceeds to refute them individually.[38] Despite Deuteronomy 6.4 there is a distinction within the Godhead. The other person is the Son who is God; Christ is the true Son of God. The Son is God by nature, the Son is eternal. The Father and the Son are perfectly one, Christ is true God and true man, Christ's passibility is discussed. The equality of the Father and the Son is stated, and in conclusion that argument is summarised and Hilary prays to God, asking that he may remain in the faith of three persons in one God.[39]

Hilary is concerned in this work to stress the full manhood and the true Godhead of Christ. It must be emphasised that he is not specifically concerned with the doctrine of the Trinity or of the Holy Spirit.

He sees Christ in terms of the three times of pre-existence, kenosis and exaltation. Against the Arian stresses on the weakness of the man Jesus, he insisted on the impassibility of the logos, and of Christ's soul

38. Martinez Sierra lists the following as texts used by the Arians and defended for orthodoxy by Hilary (op. cit. 152) Dt.6.4; Mk 12.29; 1 Tim 2.5; Rom 16.25f; Is 65.16; Jn 17.3; Mk 10.18; 1 Tim 6.15; Mal 3.6; James 1.17; Ps 7.12; Mt 6.26; Mt 10.29; Dan 13.42; Is 6.61; Ac 17.28; Ps 17.28; Ps 138.7f; Jn 4.24; 1 Tim 6.16; Jnl 18; Ex 3.14 and Jerem 1.6.

39. For the refutation of the concept of a distinction in the Godhead cf. Trin 5.23-24. The Son Jesus Christ is the true Son of God (5.25-26) and is thus divine 6.36ff. The Son is God by nature (7.9f) and is eternal (12.17f). The Father and the Son are in all senses a unity (9.43ff). Any indication of suffering or sadness on Christ's part was no indication of weakness (9.70f and 10, passim), Father and Son are in all things equal (11.2ff). Apart from the monographs of Smulders and Galtier good discussions of Hilary's Christology are provided by Grillmeier, Kelly, and A.B. Bruce.

and body (a feature we have already encountered in the In Matthaeum) and made much use of the Johnannine concept of gloria in explaining the advent of Christ (he never uses the word incarnation). At the resurrection Christ enters into the glory of God himself and in him man has entered. We may say, doxologically, as it were, that men have already become the sons of God, but only through adoption in Christ, who was God before he became man; the nature of the union of Godhead and manhood in Christ, and the nature of our relationship to the risen Christ were to be the subject of much debate over the next hundred years.

The structure of the treatise, as usual in the patristic age, is not that of a formal system of dogmatics. Rather, the case against the Arians is built up point by point in answer to their own case, by theological reflection on the texts cited by them. At the same time the material scattered throughout the first three books provide a kind of prolegomena to his theology. It would be anachronistic to regard this as a theory of hermeneutics, though hermeneutical questions are involved. Still less it is simply a hermeneutic of scripture, for the theological process is not for him simply the interpretation of texts.

Hilary begins with an area often overlooked but always vital to theology, that of theological anthropology. Man cannot arrive at knowledge of God by himself. This has important consequences for the language we use in speaking of God. Knowledge of God must come from God himself: God has revealed himself, in Israel and especially in the incarnation of his Son Jesus Christ.[40] The record of this revelation is the scriptures,

---

40. cf.esp. I 18-19 (also sect. 6 below) also 4.14 Nemini autem dubium esse oportet, ad divinarum rerum cognitionem divinis utendum esse doctrinis etc.

and the occasion of the awakening of faith is the reading of them.[41]   The

Names in scripture are not mere names, but through them the things which

they signify are themselves revealed.[42]   Through them Christ reveals him-

self, and brings understanding of all else in the Bible and in creation.

It will be seen that the role of the Bible here is of basic onto-

logical significance.   It is not simply a source of information.   The life

of faith is awakened in the context of scripture by Christ.   But the theo-

logical task is the reflection upon Christ himself in the context of his

church, though the indispensable guide to the articulation of this activity

remains meditation upon the events portrayed in scripture, and is devel-

oped accordingly in the De Trinitate by the epitomising use of the Bible,

to suggest directions in which talk about God can proceed.   Such talk

becomes not biblical language about God but language in which the specific

concerns of the biblical witness are regarded: (cf. the discussion of

'pointiertes Reden von Gott' sect 7. below).

Many problems have been felt to exist in the De Trinitate and con-

sideration of some of these will take us further into the heart of Hilary's

thought.   God, it has been suggested, is regarded by Hilary as being in

himself impassible and unknowable.   This is so both in the Neoplatonic

tradition of fourth century Greek theology and in the Stoic/Aristotelian/

41.   Hilary was never tired of insisting of the primacy of scripture in
      fighting the Arians cf 9.8. sequimur ergo, adversus irreligiosas et
      impias de Deo institutiones, ipsas illas divinorum dictorum auctor-
      itates, cf too in addition to the references already given 2.1; 11.7;
      5.7; 1.6; 2.2; 11.7; is by implication a warning against Arian
      allegories.   Quae enim simpliciter et ad eruditionem fidei divinitus
      dicta sint, ut ad id quod dicta sunt, non alienorum atque extrinsecus
      dictorum confirmemur exemplis.

42.   For the stress on the name of God (a feature found already in Philo)
      cf. 1.5 on Ex 3.14 cf. too in I. 18-19 passim).

Latin tradition. God inspires the word of scripture, so that the words and the things to which they point are ontologically related. The spirit sends knowledge of Christ as God and man in the incarnation, and infuses us so that we may rise on the knowledge of the risen Christ to God.

In this process it has been argued that the humanity of Christ plays no role in the communication of knowledge of God - because this was the starting point of knowledge of Jesus for the Arians. This change is scarely rebutted by simply pointing to e.g. Hilary's reference to Christ as witness (cf De Trin 3.9). The result of what has been thought of as an immanentism of the Spirit, a counterpart as it were of the Aristotelian view of the aseity of God would be to reduce the role of the incarnation to that of providing merely descriptive knowledge of God. There being no real gulf between God and man which knowledge cannot remove, the significance of the cross is gone and is characteristically replaced by the motif of glorification.[43]

The roots of this problem have been traced to Hilary's use of the imago concept.[44] Here is found the Stoic/Platonic doctrine of the one

---

43. Apart from Fierro op. cit p.94n2, the many references to gloria cited in the Migne index 11.960f. It is above all in Christ that our glory is to be found. cf.Trin 1.36 subdimur autem gloriae corporis sui, ut in ea simus claritate, qua regnat in corpore; quia corporieius conformes erimus. The word 'substantia' and cognates is frequently used in the De Trin (cf.PL. 11.1025) But the case for 'massive use of Aristotelianism' requires more careful study. Against the stress on full knowledge, glorification and sanctification must be set grace cf Trin 4.2; 4.14. Loffler's summary of Hilary's effort against the Arians is worth citing: 'Auf jeden Fall hat er sich bemuht, das offenbarte Geheimnis dessen, was Gott selber ist, nicht an die halbe Wahrheit einer menschlichen Denkform zu verraten'.

44. For imago Dei cf.10.16; and for the general background apart from Loffler and Wille, Jervell, Imago Dei.

perfect archetype which can only have one perfect copy. In such a basically binitarian system there is then no room left for the Holy Spirit,
which is relegated to a role of immanentism in the world, with the result
that the doctrines of creation and redemption are confused. Further,
because of the ontological nature of Christ's relation to us through the
Spirit, our knowledge of him partakes of a character corresponding to his
own substantia, which means that faith once acquired is a concrete perm-
anent possession whose contingent Character has been lost, while the asym-
metry of God's knowledge of men and man's knowledge of God disappears in
what has been seen as a massive use of the Aristotelian category of substance.[45] Here is analogia entis disguised as analogia fidei, docetism
unbounded. In his zeal to overcome the Arians, Hilary has himself gone
to opposite extremes which reproduce the very errors which he sought to
combat.

We have already seen that it would be odd in the fourth century synthesis if the entire thinking of a man like Hilary, for whom there is no
evidence of his previously having been a professional philosopher, were
governed by the detailed philosophical system which had long since been
out of general use. There is however a general agreement on the presence
of elements in the fourth century cultural background which indeed lead
to particular difficulties in presenting doctrines of the incarnation.
On the one hand because of his aseity God cannot become a real man, and
the transmission in incarnation can only be of knowledge, the humanity of
Christ is of negligible importance, and on the other hand the ontological

45. On Aristotle and substance in patristic theology see now the fine
    analysis by G.C. Stead in 'the Concept of Divine Substance', V.C.
    29.1 (1975) 1-14, and Divine Substance, Oxford, 1977.

relation set up between God, the risen Christ and the believer is such that the eschatological orientation of the Church is lost. Much of the depth of the Pauline understanding of man, of grace and of eschatology is lost in the transformation into a different historical situation and a different context of Greek philosophical terms. Yet within this framework, Hilary does attempt, by differentiating between the ontological and the doxological, to retain a difference between the life of faith now in the church and the union with God in Christ which comes only at the end of time.

Monism, docetism, binitarianism - other charges reflect the above - Hilary's refusal to admit that the Son of God could suffer, his alleged doctrines of analogia entis, of the divinisation of man, the suggestion that for Hilary the maxim holds 'anima Christi habet per gratiam, quae Deus per naturam'. Neoplatonist mysticism is deprecated by one critic (Wille) while the lack of the mystical is deprecated by another (Grillmeier). Evidence of binitarian tendencies is found by Loffler at 2.26; 10.15; 12.56; 4.41; of monism at 1.16, of Stoic doctrine of the imago at 10.16 and 11.16, of the assertion that the Son of God in Jesus did not suffer at 10.27 cf.11.2 and 10.22 and of man being able to know God as new being at 2.35.

It will be desirable to consider the text cited in support of these assessments in some detail (as far as this is possible in a work dealing with exegesis).

Examination of 2.26, 10.15 and 12.56 and 4.41 shows that when the theory of an all comprehending Stoic metaphysic (which as we have seen is inherently less likely than e.g. a Stoic influenced epistemology in the fourth century) is removed, the evidence is weakened considerably. Where
128

the stress is upon the sonship of Christ this is clearly to be seen as a
rebuttal of Arian claims. Where it is said that the Holy Spirit is incom-
prehensible, this need only mean that like many of his predecessors, e.g.
Irenaeus and Cyprian, Hilary is not yet working on a theological basis
into which the implications of the doctrine of the third person of the
Trinity are fully integrated: it does not mean that a third person is a
priori unthinkable. Though at 1.6 there is language reminiscent of monist
theory e.g. ut circumfusus et infusus in omnia nosceretur, this is not
developed in an explicitly monist direction. As Waszink has shown, similarity of Latin Language does not always indicate identity of subject
matter in this period (Waszink in Fondatien Hardt, Entretiens, p.158,
'schon bald wird es klar, dass Sätze, die auf den ersten Blick völlig
neuplatonisch scheinen, in Wirklichkeit ein spezifisch christlich
Bedeutung haben, weil dieselben Worte allmählig ganz andere Begriffe zu
bezeichen haben'). On the other hand, one does find in the use of virtue
in connection with the Spirit (e.g. at 10.26) traces of the Stoic epistemology which was so marked in the In Matthaeum.

Occasional echoes may also be found in other works of Hilary: Hadot
(p.88) cited De Syn 35 'ut latitudo deducta quodam naturae suae tractu
assumensque hominem filius nuncuparetur'.

The suffering of Christ is dealt with at 10.27f; 11.22; and 11.2.
Hilary says at 10.35 'collatis igitur dictorum atque gestorum virtutibus,
demonstari non ambiguum est, in natura eius coporis infirmitatem naturae
corporeae non fuisse, cui in virtute naturae fuerit omnem corporum
deppellere infirmitatem: et passionem illam, licet illata corpori sit,
non tamen naturam dolendi corpori intulisse: quia quamquam forma corporis
nostri esset in Domino, non tamen in vitiosae infirmitatis nostrae esset

corpore, qui non esset in origine, quod ex conceptu Spiritus Sancti Virgo progenuit. This argument is clearly docetic and Hilary' position need not be defended. But in discussing Christ's suffering Hilary always has in mind the Arian argument from that suffering cf. 10.27; 10.28; 11.2, and he occasionally takes care to add a specifically anti docetic qualific- ation e.g. at 10.24 (neque enim tum, cum sitivit aut esurivit aut flevit, bibisse aut manducisse aut doluisse monstratus est; sed ad demonstrandam corporis veritatem, corporis consuetudo suscepta est, ita ut naturae nostrae consuetudine consuetudini sit corporis satisfactum (cf.too 10.27).

How far does Hilary teach that man may come to the full knowledge of the glory of God here and now? There are many passages in which the emphasis on gloria and on the gift of the Spirit which led to the sug- gestion of such an anticipation of the eschaton, involving a Gnostic understanding of faith (Beumer) and a mystical doctrine of illumination by knowledge. A characteristic reference is to 2.35, in which it is said of the gift of Spirit 'hoc usque in consummationem saeculi nobiscum, hoc exspectationis nostrae solatium, hoc in donorum operationibus futurae speci pignus est, hoc mentium lumen, hic splendor animorum est'. Yet even here a distinction is drawn between what we possess in via and what we shall know at the end of time. Again, Hilary is prepared to describe faith as fides crucis[46] - 'placuit Deo praedicatione stultitias salvos facere credentas, id est crucis fide aeternitatem mortalibus provenire'. The situation may be summed up by saying that the desire to refute his opponents decisively leads him into extreme positions[47] Again the presence

46. Fides crucis cf.De Trin. 3.25.
47. Hilary can be flexible when not standing in statu confessionis cf De Syn, 71. 'potest una substantia pie dici et pie taceri.' On the docetic element cf.A.B. Bruce, The Humiliation of Christ, 1898, and A. Grillmeier, SJ, Christ in Christian Tradition pp. 395ff.

of Gnostic and other vocabulary is not necessarily indicative of Gnostic
or monist orientation (cf in a different context, G. Bornkamm Zur Interpretation des Johannesevangeliums in Ev. Theol. 1968.1.8ff). At the same
time, it is clear that the role of the human nature of Christ in the
atonement and the role of the Holy Spirit were left largely unexplored
by Hilary: in this he reflects the state of fourth century Latin theology
in general. Particularly in the case of the role of the humanity of
Christ, the Arian charge had led Hilary to an opposite extreme.

It might be thought from the foregoing that Hilary's use of the
Bible was only occasional to the development of his theological thought,
present in order to refute the Arians' use of the Bible, and that it was
only the weight of quotation, the colouring given by the presence of so
many instances of biblical imagery which lend the biblical tone to the
work. This would be confirmed by the numerous instances of interpretation contrary to the intended meaning of the text in its exegetical
context.

Yet for Hilary, theology without the direction of the biblical text
is impossible. Allegory even is unnecessary because the truth of his
position may be seen from the open meaning of the texts. It is through
the scriptures that God intended to convey the doctrine of the divinity
of Christ, pre-existent, incarnate, risen. The relation of the Old
Testment to the New is seen in terms of the relation of witness to the
pre-existent Christ and that to the incarnate Christ: thus the whole of
the Old Testament and not simply the passages referring specifically to
prophecy, becomes a witness to the incarnation. Though the Johannine
tradition is predominant through the use of the concept of gloria, the
Pauline doctrine of the pre-existence of Christ serves too to illuminate

the divinity of Christ as the Pauline doctrine of justification served
to illuminate the doctrine of the story of salvation in the In Matthaeum:
a reminder of the continuities with the earlier period which remain despite the important differences.

As a theologian Hilary was careful to avoid slavish adherence to
particular philosophical systems for their own sake. His vision of the
God of Christian faith remained the focus of all his work. He was also
completely a child of his age, and his thought was steeped in the philosophical climate of his day. Later theologians admired his work, and
especially his christological concentration. But this should not of
course be seen as an invitation to take over his sorts of techniques
today. To do so would be to learn nothing from the vast development of
human thought in the interval, and especially in the last hundred years.
To such a prospect Christian faith is certainly not invited.

The New Humanity

5.   The Late Period

The Tractatus in Psalmos

The Late Period: Tractatus in Psalmos.

The Tractatus in Psalmos has been, at least in modern times, the
most neglected of Hilary's works.[1] The In Matthaeum has interested
scholars as a prelude to the De Trinitate and because of its unique position as a commentary: the De Trinitate has long been a source of reference for the historian or dogma: but the In Psalmos has usually been seen
as a pale imitation in devotional form of Origen's exegesis, of no particular interest in itself.[2] In the following analysis, the attempt is made
to show that the work is of considerable significance for the assessment
of the role of exegesis in Hilary's methodology as a whole.

The Tractatus was written in the years of comparative calm after
Hilary's return from the east, some time after 361.[3] The contents are best
described perhaps as a series of devotional meditations. This is not a
commentary like the In Matthaeum, in which an inner sense involving a
single consistent motif of interpretation is brought out. It is probable,
despite the gaps in the work as preserved, that Hilary commented on all

1.   As usual the chapter in Reinkens is excellent. There is study in
      detail of the use of the different senses of scripture in the In
      Psalmos by Nestor Gastaldi (Paris/Argentina). Père Gastaldi most gen-
      erously made available several sections of his work in advance of com-
      pletion, and these have illuminated many aspects of the work for me.

2.   Following Jerome (cf.Apol. in Ruf 1.2; Vall. 2.1). The view of un-
      critical following of Origen has already been questioned by Watson in
      his excellent short notice on the In Psalmos (xliii-v and 235).
      Gastaldi confined himself strictly to the analysis of the different
      levels of significance of scripture.

3.   Dates. Hilary died in 367/8. Ps 67.15 (PL9.453) refers to the De
      Trin 1.15. From this it is clear that the work on the Psalmos was
      written after the exile.

of the psalms.[4] The work contains many homiletic elements, and is clearly

written for use within the Christian community. Its tone is devotional

throughout, rather than explanatory, philological in the strict sense. It

probably came into existence as the expansion of a series of homilies in

Church. As in the In Matthaeum there are practically no references to con-

temporary events, and it is never said for whom the work is intended.[5]

The formal scope and method of the In Psalmos is set out in the pro-

logue, which is in this instance preserved. Much is derived from Origen:

the rules set out are not strictly adhered to throughout the work.[6] The

main points may be summarised as follows: the book of the psalms is a

unity, secundum apostolicam auctoritatem,[7] but is composed by many authors.[8]

The whole book secundum evangelican praedicationem intelligi oportet[9]....

totum illud ad cognitienem adventus Domini nostri Jesu Christi referatur.

This understanding is not at once apparent to the reader: sunt enim

universa allegoricis et typicis contexta virtutibus.[10] There is however a

4. The authentic commentaries by Hilary preserved are those on Ps 1; 2;
    9; 13; 14; 51-69; 118-150. Inauthentic are 15; 31; 41.

5. Though there are no direct references to recipients, there are fre-
    quent references to activities which go on in church, e.g. 'psalmus
    qui lectus est', the ref. in Ps 67 to baptisms etc., which suggest
    the context of a congregation in church. cf n. 42 p.70 above.

6. cf below, where it appears from the evidence that Hilary was more
    independent than Jerome suggests.

7. Prol, 1.1, 1 CSEL22 pi. (13)

8. Prol, 1.2, (ibid p.4, 14t)

9. Prol, 1.5, (ibid p.6, 1 2t)

10. Prol, 1.5 (ibid p.6,18)

clavis scientiae, per fidem adventus eius.[11]   It is then always correct to

look for the key in Christ (cf the In Matthaeum, where the key - never

mentioned as such - lay rather in the whole history of the movement of

the people of God to faith). The whole is carefully supported by quot-

ations from scripture.

The Hebrew text is sine ordinis adnotatione:[12]   all was put in order

by the LXX seniores, who, spiritali et coelestis scientia virtutes

psalmorum intelligentes....in numerum eos atque ordinem redegerunt.[13]

Yet in theory the importance of the literal sense of the text is also

affirmed: tamen absolutissime in gestorum et temporum historia edocemur.[14]

The psalter has a threefold purpose: cum enim primus gradus sit ad

salutem, in novum hominem post peccatorum remissionem renasci, sitque post

poenitentiae confessionem regnum illud Domini in sanctae illius civitatis

et coelestis Jerusalem tempora reservatum. et postea consummata in nos

coelesti gloria in Dei patris regnum per regnum filii proficiamus[15] (in

psalms with the number 8 there is a special rule, as also in the case of

Ps 118; these are secundum ogdoadem evangelicam destinatus.[16]   et hoc

---

11. Prol, 1.5 (ibid p.9,5,12)

12. Prol, 1.8 (ibid p.9,15)

13. Prol, 1.8 (ibid p.9,15f)

14. Prol, 1.9 (ibid p.10,16)

15. Prol, 1.11 (ibid p.10,5ff)

16. Prol, 1.13 (ibid p.12,9) cf.Ps. 118 which 'perfectum virum secundum
     doctrinam evangelicam consummat'. The three languages of the Old
     Testament have a special significance (1.15) and the last 15 Pss have
     also a special significance 'qui ogdoadis et praesenti religione et
     sperata exspectatione perficitur, isto cantico graduum in coelestia
     et aeterna conscenditur'.

istius textus et sermo testatur).   These are directed ad percipiendos
fructos evangelicos.

The titles also have a special meaning: non enim sine causa tanta
rerum diversitate hic titulorum ordo convertitur.[17]   For example 'at vero
cum Canticum tantum in titulo praeponitur, scientia in eo spiritalis, et
intelligentia coelestis',[18] or 'per corporalem superscriptionem significationem spiritalis psalmi intelligatur editio'.[19]   Where there is a diapsalma, cognoscendum est, demutationem aut personae aut sensus sub con-
versione modi musici inchoari.[20]

Some preliminary indication of the effect of these rules on the treatment of the text, the exceptions made to them and the change in the shape
of the work in comparison with that of the previous periods, may be gained
from a brief analysis of selected psalms.

Psalm 1 begins with an introduction.   Ex cuius persona does the work
come?[21]   Here we note the technical structure of the literary criticism of
the schools common to Rome and Alexandria alike.   Nunc ex persona Filii non
posse intelligi, res ipsa absoluta docet.[22]   Despite the emphasis on the
prologue on the significance of the title, the explanation of the correct
interpretation is grounded at once too in the text itself.[23]   Despite the

17.   1.17 (ibid p.15,6)
18.   1.20 (ibid p.16,15)
19.   1.22 (ibid p.18,2)
20.   1.23 (ibid p.18,9)
21.   In Ps 1.1 (CSE122 p.19,6)
22.   1.1 (ibid p.19,22)
23.   1.1 (ibid)

stress of the prologue that all may have a coelestis significantia, and
though Christ is the key to the understanding of the book as a whole,
this does not mean that every detail, or even the interpretation of each
psalm, is to be related directly to him.[24] This is an important distinction.[25] The whole is a reflection not simply of Christ but of the
life of man in relation to Christ. What the criteria for direct reference to Christ himself are, we shall consider in detail below. The next
question runs: de quo viro?[26] This cannot be Christ, for the contents
do not correspond to the dignity of his person.[27] This characteristic
argument, which we have already encountered in the In Matthaeum, is
supported by a citation from the gospel (though without reference to the
commentary).

Here the tractate proper begins. The central theme is the forgiveness of sins, interpreted in accordance with the three tier structure of
the whole book as set out in the general prologue. An exemplum is given,
and then treated as a moral illustration[28] and not (as in the In Matthaeum)
as a key to the structure of the whole text. The mention of cathedra
pestilentiae evokes a question from St Matthew,[29] and is then interpreted
in relation to the words of Jesus. The concept of perpetua meditatio,
connected by association of ideas with similar thought in Paul and in

24. 1.1 ex persona filii non posse intelligi, res ipsa absoluta docet
(ibid)
25. 1.2 sed ubi et quando ad eum prophetiae ipsius se referat, ration-
abilis scientiae discernendum est veritate.
26. 1.2 (ibid,p.20,27f)
27. 1.3 (ibid, p.21,3ff)
28. 1.6 this is an exemplum not as always in the Mt. from scripture, but
ex usu conscientiae communis (ibid,p.23,20)
29. 1.10 Mt. 23.3 (ibid,p.25, 1.16f)

John, provides a Christologically orientated meditation on the life of
man before God which corresponds to the Old Testament prophecy and is
interpreted along the lines of that prophecy.[30]

The reference to 'lignum'[31] apparently irreconcilable with the
liberal sense, is illuminated by reference to Genesis 2 and Proverbs
(both of immense significance for the theology of the early Church).
The reference to Proverbs now provides a link with St Luke's gospel[32]
(a reminder that the tractatus can only be understood in the light of
the enormous exegetical activity of the De Trinitate) and to a meditation
on Christ, commented upon further by Isaiah and by Paul. The plants of
the psalm are analysed allegorically (like the fig tree in the In
Matthaeum) so that its leaves are the verba Dei.[33] The tree is related
to the redemptio ligni vitae of the cross,[34] and through a reference to
iudicium to the last judgment (a reminder that even in the late period
the themes of the cross and judgment are not entirely lost in the gloria
of the resurrection, as is often suggested).[35]

A short reference to hearers[36] and readers reminds us that the first
audience was very probably 'live', and the use of the formula 'virtus
ipsa verborum proprietatem dicti et intelligentiam continet'[37] indicates

30. 1.11-12 (ibid,p.26-7)
31. 1.13 (ibid.p.28, 4f)
32. 1.14 Lk. 23.43 cf De Trin, 32; 10.34 and 10.60 (ibid,p.29, 6f)
33. 1.11 (ibid.p.31, 12)
34. 1.18 (ibid,p.32, 11)
35. 1.20 (ibid,p.33, 25f)
36. 1.21 (ibid,p.34, 1.7) 'neglegentem audientium et incuriosum legentium facilitatem dicti dominici sermo perturbat.
37. 1.21 (ibid.p.34, 1.19)

that the concern for the literal sense has by no means entirely disappeared. The ductus of the whole is completed in the Church, in the name "Christians" and in Christ.[38] The knowledge of man by God and of God by man is articulated in terms of the Pauline Adam/Christ typology[39] (as in the contemporary Tractatus Mysteriorum) and the whole is brought to a close with a christological text from the fourth gospel, familiar to us from the De Trinitate:[40] both Paul and John lend their witness to that of the psalms and the prophets in testimony to Christ.

The above sample from the prologue and the first psalm is typical of the nature of the whole. The general prologue suggests a close connection with Origen, and since the first mention of this by Jerome, it has often been said that Hilary's work here is a translation or rough translation of Origin's commentaries on the psalms. Relations with Origen are complicated by the uncertainty as to which of his works on the psalms Hilary used, and by the lack of extant material from Origen dealing with the particular psalms extant from Hilary. Rather more helpful is the often forgotten suggestion that Hilary and Eusebius of Vercelli translated the commentary on the psalms of Eusebius of Caesarea, which was itself a revised version of the work of Origen. Hilary's version is often nearer to Eusebius of Caesarea than to Origen, but it cannot be said to be a translation of either, for there are as many decisive differences, both in method and in content, as there are similarities.[41]

38. 1.22 (ibid.p.35, 1.7ff)
39. 1.24 (ibid.p.36, 1.26f)
40. 1.24 (ibid.p.37, 1.14) Jn. 5.22 cf. De Trin, 4.29; 7.20; 11.12 cf. for the other two sections in Hilary's division of the psalter Pss 53 and 130 (ET in Watson op. cit).
41. Origen, Hilary and Eusebius (cf. Jerome Vir. ill.61; ep. 61.2; 112.20 cf.PL12..948) cf. Origen in PG 12 1053-1685, Eusebius of Caesarea, PG
(contd.)

In the psalms chosen above for illustration, Hilary follows the main
lines of the rules in the prologue (from Origen) as a general framework.
But within these general guiding lines there is ample scope for Hilary's
individual interpretation. Before going on to consider these relation-
ships in the context of the tractatus as a whole, it may be mentioned that
many of the differences from previous works in the In Psalmos derive
essentially from the nature of the material itself. Here there is no
history of salvation to be explained in terms of the lex/fides motif of
the In Matthaeum: as in the De Trinitate, the wider theme, with the
additional freedom derived from acquaintance with the eastern tradition
enables Hilary to use a much wider range of imagery and techniques.

Comparison with Origen is complicated, as already mentioned, by the
fact that we do not have the corresponding homilies/commentaries of Origen
for the surviving work on the psalms by Hilary, and it is not entirely
certain which of Origen's works Hilary is supposed by Jerome to have used.
Many features of Origen recall Hilary; cf the three homilies on Ps 36 in
which the christological emphasis is clear, 'Jesus Christus veritas est,
Dominus noster Jesus Christus justitia est etc, the heretici are those
who non spiritaliter intelligunt (671D) etc. A comparison of Origen's
commentary and homilies with those of Hilary show some similarities and
many differences. In the general prologue Hilary follows Origen in having
one book of psalms and not five, but there is nothing in Origen's prologue
on the diapsalms. The relation with Eusebius of Caesarea appears closer.
In Ps 1 there are no real parallels, and the explanations are often very

41 (contd.)
     2.3, 21-1457. The few fragments of Eusebius of Vercelli surviving
     (PL12) tells us nothing in this matter. On all this cf. now Doignon
     p.531ff.

141

different e.g. in 1.4. On Ps 13.7 there is a close parallel, and in
Ps 14 the quotations are the same but the explanations given differ.
Ps 66 is very different in both but Pss 59, 65 2nd 68 show many similarities. E. had very little on Ps 118. In Ps 121 Hilary is close to E,
but in Ps 124 very different. Ps 132.1 offers an exact verbal parallel
and 136 has parallels. In Ps 138 the general sense is parallel but the
words are not. Taking the cross-section used before, in Ps 1 and 53
there are close parallels neither with 0 nor with E. In Ps 130 Hilary's
stress is found in E but not in 0, i.e. in none of these cases can we
speak of translation, and of adaptation only in the widest sense. Comparison of the biblical citations provides a similar picture: in Pss 1-2
Hilary gives nearly all Origen's and nearly all Eusebius' citations. In
Ps 64 Hilary's quotations are nearly all in Eusebius but not in Origen.
The balance would indicate that Hilary's use of Origen probably comes
through Eusebius on the Psalms. The details for the individual psalms
compared follow the above sample: occasional striking similarities,
often no resemblance whatever, and the resemblances more often with
Eusebius than with Origen.

a) The Formal Structure of the work

Because of its very loose nature, the literary structure of the work
no longer plays the important role of the In Matthaeum but an examination
of it may still shed light on the development of Hilary's exegesis as a
whole.

It is clear that the In Psalmos arose from a series of homilies
delivered in Church - cf.the reference as already mentioned to readings
e.g. 14.1 psalms qui lectus est, 135.1 cum in lectionis tempore, etc. and

142

the frequent formulae of exhortation. These homilies were themselves
composed by reference to the homilies (probably not the commentaries) of
Origen, probably in the version of the homilies of Eusebius of Caesarea.
At a later date these were all put together by Hilary. It is likely that
he preached only on one section of each psalm on a given occasion. It is
very unlikely that the long textual discussions, referring to the
different Mss versions in different languages, listed above, e.g. 138.37,
in quibusdam codibus legimus etc, were mentioned in Church. But in the
revision no attempt was made to delete the references to the live situation
and to produce a polished unit in the manner of the De Trinitate.
Possibly Hilary would have done so if he had lived longer. It seems
probable that the homilies in Church, complete with ascriptions at the
end, were left more or less unaltered, and connections and extra notes
were simply inserted at the appropriate place, much of this coming from
Hilary's sources.

At the same time, it would appear that Hilary himself used 'tractare'
and cognates in the technical, classical sense of 'to treat, investigate',
as it was frequently used by Quintilian, rather than in the later sense
indicated by the well known line from Augustine 'tractatus populares quos
Graeci homilias vocant' (Aug. haer. 4. pref). This idea of investigation,
careful treatment of the theme, is used of the psalmist himself at 67.23:
sed suscipiendae ab unigenito Deo carnis, adeundaeque mortis, et per
Apostolum, et nunc per Prophetam grandior profundiorque ratio tractatur.
For Hilary it may also imply something close to exegesis of a text, as at
Ps 130.1 brevis psalmus est, et distinctione magis quam tractatu
explicandus. The relation of written and spoken tractatus in Augustine
is dealt with in A.J.H. Van Weegen's Preek en Dictaat bij Sint Augustinus

(cf.esp. p.8, n.4), Hilary's use would be close to Augustine's second use
of the word, as at DDC 4.46 tractator divinarum scripturarum, and in Sermo
170.3 scripturarum tractatores dicimur, non nostrarum opinionum affirm-
atores. (v.Weegen ibid, Bardy in RSR 33, 1946, 211-235 and Mohrmann in
La Maison-Dieu 39, 1954, 97-107).

Further details of the literary structure (which for our purpose
are more important for comparison with the In Matt. than for the direct
understanding of the In Psalmos itself) may be illustrated as follows:

Usually as in Ps 1 the exposition begins with a prologue in which
the main themes are stated. These may be set out in a series of questions
regarding speaker and addressee as in the above example. The length of
the text varies; in Ps 1, two verses are taken together at the beginning
then each verse is dealt with separately. The end of each section is
marked by a rhetorical finish. Each psalm may originally have been
divided up and covered in several homilies. Despite the presence,
examined below, of much philological material, Hilary clearly has in mind
a devotional context in this work.

The division of the text into verses to be dealt with 'absolute'
and verses to be explained in terms of a hidden meaning, as in the In
Matthaeum, has gone, and is not replaced by the epitomising method of the
De Trinitate. Open and inner senses are no longer dealt with distinctly,
nor is all referred to Christ directly, as was often the case in the
De Trinitate: all this is replaced by the heavily modified framework of
Origen's rules, the details of which are discussed below.

Each psalm being naturally a single unit, and the range of interpretation being much less strict in the In Matthaeum, the use of the
rhetorical structure by building up references and cross references and

144

in shaping the episodes for interpretation, though present no longer plays a significant role. Typical too of the looser framework is the presence in quantity of quotations from the OT and NT throughout. The division of the material in units of single words or verses depending on the course of the meditation and not upon the strict sense of the text, as usual in the early Church, again leads to the phenomenon of atomisation and change in the accentuation of specific episodes which we noted in the In Matthaeum. A certain amount of new material (for Hilary) in the form of grammatical, historical and philological explanation is present (doubtless a fruit of the exile) but this is always subordinated to and does not indicate a change in the essentially pastoral character of the work.

As in the In Matthaeum and the De Trinitate, due regard is paid to continuity of context, as at 64.1 opportune superiorem psalmum hic qui subiacet consecutus est, 67.30 quid illus sit, mox continuat ordo dictorum.

The old categories of the rhetorical schools are again evident, but their presence is no longer to vitally important for the interpretation of the whole. This may be illustrated from Ps.1 in exemplum:

1.1 et sumamus ex usu conscientiae communis exemplum

1.2 igitur secundum hoc propositum exemplum, impium...est

1.6 et quem im magnis aeternae beatitudinis constituat exemplis

1.8 Ridiculum hoc forte et ineptum comparatae beatitudinis
     credebatur exemplum

But the taut structure of the In Matthaeum in which the rhetorical categories plays a central role is no longer to be observed.

Much work has been done on the biblical quotations of the In Psalmos. According to H. Jeanotte, Hilary cites 1002 of the 2515 vv. of the psalter in the work, i.e. nearly 40%. Scellauf's analysis showed that Hilary often quoted from memory. He distinguished the biblical citations apart from the text actually being commented upon as used to clarify, to stress and to abbreviate. The imprecision in the form of the citation makes identification of the text which he used difficult. Zingerle in WS 1889 noted that Hilary's text was often close to that of the LXX, and elsewhere (Comm Wolfflin) suggested that Hilary probably had a Graeco-Latin glossary before him. On the other hand Hilary on occasions used texts other than that of the LXX (Buttell cites 118 Daleth, 118 He 13; 138.37; 43.2; 146.10)

A list of the comments made by Hilary on the latin translation of the Pss is given by Feder (Studien II 110f) including non satis proprie, non ita absolute, ambigua significatione, minus propria etc. The whole question of Hilary's text, comments on the text and philological work in the In Psalmos has been examined by Goffinet, who simply concludes (31f) that Hilary probably used the version of the biblical text current in Gaul in the 4th century. Critical comments are to be found at In Ps 2.35; 51.38; 54.11; 54.1; 56.1; 65.3; 65.15 etc; 118 (8 refs) 130;136; 137; 138; 143;. Goffinet draws the conclusion that "Origenes dat hij kritisch-filologisch element in zijn Psalmencommentaar" but he has not considered the possible role of Eusebius. Jeanotte, Le Psaultier, noted Hilary's habit of referring occasionally to minute details in the text e.g. at Ps 137.2 the use of ad templum rather than in templo, and of discussing carefully the details of translations e.g. at Ps 54.10; 118 Lamed 2.14 etc. and variant readings e.g. at 78.13; 138.6 etc.

(b)   The principles of interpretation.

The analysis of the first psalm has alraedy revealed several of the distinctive features of the principles of interpretation in the In psalmos. Notable among these and particularly important for the In Psalmos is the suggestion (present along with other suggestions) that scripture takes the forma dominici corporis;[42] its importance is increased by the fact that here Hilary returns to the more explicit exegesis of continuous texts after the epitomising use of the Bible in the De Trinitate. The concept of the Bible having the form of Christ's body is from Origen, but the manner in which it is developed diverges in important respects from Origen's treatment; we never find in Hilary a trichotomist treatment of scripture (which is present theoretically at least in Origen) but a dualism of spiritalis and corporalis. This distinction, which resembles in some respects (but is not identical with) the inner and outer senses of the In Matthaeum, leads to a renewed emphasis on the 'spiritual inter-pretation' which was noticeably much reduced in the De Trinitate.[43]

The details may be illustrated as follows:

Coelestis is very frequent cf. 13.1 exemplum nobis coelestis doctrinae etc. For spiritalis cf. 62.3 sed nos spiritalibus doctrinis eruditi, 67.11 animalia cum essent, facta sunt spiritalia 118. 1.5 in reference to Romans 7.14 quia lex et spiritalis est, et umbra futurorum; 118 Lade. 10 dona praecipue spiritalium gratiarum: 123.9 spiritales enim sumus. This is contrasted on occasion with corporalis e.g. at 134.13/ et in his quae

42.   cf. Prol. 7 and cf. below.

43.   Though Hilary does divide the psalms into three parts this is a rather different matter. On Origen's division of scripture cf. sect 2. above.

corporaliter gesta esse memorantur, spiritalia significari memininus, 134.16 Moyses non iam spiritaliter per doctrinam, sed corporaliter per gloriam fulgens ita meminit etc. cf.too 139.17 Recti autem habitantes cum facie Dei nihil in se corporale retinere intelliguntur. It is clear from the above that in the In Psalmos, the spiritual is much more important than the corporeal, a further indication of the influence of Origen.

In addition to the contrast between the corporalis and the spiritalis which, as we have seen, tends to depreciate the corporalis per se and clearly comes from Origen, many passages indicate a simultaneous continuation of the relation from the In Matt., now less sharply stated, between the literal and the spiritual. On the one hand Hilary can write, as in 1.9 absolutissime in gestorum et temporum historia; 123.5 fides historiae non periclitatur, si rebus effectis, inesse connexam sibi extrinsecus significantiam existimemus; 13.3 sed in singulis verbis singulae virtutes sunt explicandae. But on the other hand, as at Ps. 55.1: multa psalmi superscriptio comprehendit, quae praeter rerum gestarum notionem alterius intelligentiae intiment sensum, and as in In Matt., vellem percontari cos, qui etiosas spiritales psalmorum intelligentias existimant. cf.too 124.1 and 131.11 volunt ergo Iudaei, 138.39 sed aliqui etc. In 125.1 there appears to be no literal sense at all. Occasionally the spiritual sense is justified by reference to the New Testament with the comment, 'quia per Dominum dictum est' as at 1.11.

A major reason for this new accent is undoubtedly the problem posed by the material itself. In the In Matthaeum, Hilary stressed the abolition of the law. Now he returns to the law, in order to stress the role of the spiritual law in ordering the life of man as seen in the light of

148

Christt.[44] (There are similarities here to the tertius usus legis of 17th century theology.) As mentioned in the prologue, not all of the psalms can be brought simply under the motif of promise and fulfilment, though this theme is certainly present. Apart from the prophecy of Christ which they contain, they form a mirror, prototype and guide to the progress of man towards the finis of the kingdom of God. Some parts of a single psalm may refer to Christ directly, others to the life of man in the light of Christ. Technically, this change of reference is made by the Spirit in the individual psalm, and the change is indicated by the diapsalma.[45] Again, though much of Origen's language of mystical illumination and transformation is used, the completion of that transformation of man takes place, not now, but in the future finis of the Kingdom of God.[46]

At the same time remnants of the trichotomist division of nature and of the Alexandrian concept of deification in the threefold division of the psalms in terms of the progression of the soul, which Hilary retains.[47] It is characteristic of Hilary that alongside this model traces remain not only of the facta/dicta contrast and the virtus model of the In Matthaeum but also and more importantly, of the epitomising use of scripture in reflection of the De Trinitate. Hilary's strength as an

---

44. this theme is well illustrated by Ps. 118 A.5, passim.

45. cf.the references above to the diapsalma Typical is 54.8.

46. The final consummation is discussed, in accordance with the plan of the prologue, in the context of Pss 148-150.

47. as at Ps. 14.7 Sometimes he uses the Pauline twofold division of man as soul and body as at Ps 158 7-8 cf.M.J. Rondeau in St. Patr. VI 197-210 "Remarques sur l'anthropologie de St. Hilaire.'

exegete, like that of Luther, lay paradoxically in the fact that he was
not interested in a theory of hermeneutics for its own sake. The basic
concern was the communication of the Gospel itself. With this basic
intention in mind, it is possible to see the In Psalmos not simply as a
step back to the vagaries of Alexandrian allegorism but as the mark of a
stage of theological development in which, (given the premise the
scripture is what Hilary thought it was) all kinds of techniques may be
employed without any kind of self conscious inhibition.

This is also the case with the lex/fides dialectic of the In
Matthaeum, which here influences several passages but no longer plays a
central role: cf the references at 51.2 to evangelica fides, 59.3
justificans ex fide, 67.9 evangelia legis supplementa, 68.1 evangelicae
spei fideles, 123.5 quia lex spiritalis etc. Evangelica doctrina can
refer to almost anything in the New Testament, e.g. at 53. 1.5 in a
reference to Matt. 26.53. Even the ecclesia/synagogae contrast may be
found, e.g. at 67 28 non ad synagogae confessionem, sed ad ecclesiae
benedictionem nos cohortatur propheta.

An important result of this ecclecticism is that though the presence
of all of them may be traced, neither the stoicised doctrine of inspiration
nor indeed the categories of the rhetorical tradition can be said to play
the significant role of the early period. They may influence the interpretation on occasion but they do not reflect Hilary's main concern.

Such matters as the ordo are important, and as before the rhetorical
categories are interwoven in the spiritual interpretation: cf,118, A.1
dictorum ordo non neglegendus est. But since the whole structure is much
less rigidly organised than that of the In Matthaeum, the impact on the
whole interpretation is less. Further examples may be seen at 54.15 talis

autem temporum ordo non nisi ex prophetica scientia distributus est; 69.3
et idem est dictorum ordo, qui et rerum; 63.3 spiritalis ordo; 66 secundum
doctrinae ordinem, 65.2 rationem atque ordinem, 118B 10 sed retentus hic
ordo rationis est. cf. too 59.5, 67.3, 118A1, 118B7 etc. For ratio cf. 65.1
res ipsa et ratio demonstrat cf. 126.18. For exemplum, cf. 67.7 idque
exemplum omne ad ecclesiam etc cf. 122.8 comparationis exemplum etc. For
proprietas cf. 136.10. nos secundum graecitatis proprietatem, 53.4.
proprietates autem virtutesque verborum. cf 138.22, 138.38 etc. For dicta
cf. 1.12, 2.2, 2.15, 2.23, 51.5 etc. Gesta 51.2, 68.1, 141.3, Demutatio
2.9, 2.13, 53.6, 65.16 etc. Diapsalma 53.9, 59.3, 60.4, 66.2 etc. Sensus
53.4, 65.25, 69.9.

As the commentary in the In Pss. is usually verse by verse, the need
for the strict, condensed organisation of narrative is less, and this too
tends to lessen the role of the rhetorical categories. For the res/verba
pair, cf. the exx. above and e.g. 1.5. nunc et res ipsas et eorum verba
tractemus.

It is in accordance with this new freedom of expression that we may
regard the use of allegory in the In Psalmos, now on a larger scale than
ever before. The formal characteristics of Hilary's use of allegory
cannot be distinguished in any essential point from those of Origen, and
can be used in any exegetical context. The actual instances are developed
by Hilary independently, usually in terms of his own christology, but
Hilary is in no sense consciously 'anti-Origen'. Allegory and typology
are used in the In Psalmos almost interchangeably.

Hilary makes uninhibited reference to allegoria in the In Psalmos in
addition to the use of types as before cf. 5.13 secundum propheticam et
allegoricam intelligentiam but 62.8 quia litterae et legis allegoricorum

praescriptione cessante, Deus vivae intelligentisque hostiae sit laudibus
honorandus; 67.1 allegoricorum dictorum interpretatio Gal. 4.21 is cited
at 118. Phe.3 as a justification for the use of allegory, cf. too 146.9
parabolicam tamen, sive, ut apostolus ait, allegorumenam nobis doctrinam
ita commemorata praeberent,. The reference twice to Gal. 4.21 may indicate
an awareness of general misgivings regarding allegory. We have seen that
it was not his custom to justify his use of figural interpretation in the
In Matt. or the De Trin. cf. too for allegory the references at 147.10
and 13 to allegorica doctrina and allegorice, and at 147.5. allegoroumeni
consuetudine. cf. to 118. Phe.3. and 134.1.

Typus is found at e.g. 133.5, typicus at 146.7 and 54.9 etc.
praefigurare at 59.6 and 63.1 David qui passionem Domini praefigrativit.[48]
cf. too 124.6 futuri species and De Tit. 91.1 lex meditatio veritatis. On
occasion too the figural significance may be indicated by significare e.g.
124.5 cum enim et montem significare Ecclesiam, id est Dominum in corpore
legimus. cf too 65.11, 65.12; 67.24 etc.

Parallel again with the In Matt. is the stress on veritas e.g. 67.21
de divina veritatis scientia, 118.5.5. veritatis verba, verbum veritatis
etc. and virtus, cf. 138.32 interius verbi huius virtutem. For parabola
cf. 68.2 - this is now equivalent to allegoria cf. 146.9 above. New is the
use of textus (Prol. to Ps 1.13), and revelatio at 25.7.

Apart from the general prologue, esp. 5 and 6 a further report on
Hilary's method is given at 150.1. On the role of prophecy cf. 63.3 and
62.4, which recalls the In Matthaeum prophetiae scientia est pro gerendis

48. On David as the types of faith cf. 56.4; 121.10; 142.10; 141.3; 141.1;
    139; 62.1114.1; 55.1; 55.2; 58.1; cf. list in Reinkens p. 298.

gesta memorare. We have seen that in the In Matthaeum only those figurae

which were interpreted non-metaphorically were taken up into the

Heilsgeschichte. In the In Psalmos as in the De Trinitate, this is no

longer the case. All figures may now be referred directly to Christ or to

the life of man in the light of the gospel. The meditational/mystical

effect created by this exegetical procedure adds to the impression of much

greater freedom in the use of texts than either in the De Trinitate or in

the In Matthaeum.

To some extent, as we have already seen, the use of certain of the

above principles rather than others, depends on the nature of the psalm

according to the divisions of the book in the prologue.

This is reflected e.g. in the use of the designation 'absolutus'.[49]

Because of the great freedom in the use of figurae, the examination

of hermeneutical principles themselves is of less immediate value in

assessing the work than the wider context of the role of scripture in the

theological conception of the work as a whole: to this we now must turn.

49. References to absolutus and cognates are found at e.g. 118 Heth (8)
8 et sane absolutior ita sensus videbatur; 118 Daleth 4 quod utrumque
absolute docetur, 136.1 absoluta quaedem verborum species, 134.1.
secundum simplicitatem audientium absolutus etc. 137.5 absolutisume,
cf 1 1.4, 131.11, 135.14, 140.12, etc. At 134.1 the usual contrast
between corporeal and spiritual is replaced by that between absolutus
and allegoroumena. References are made to the LXX at 2.2; 2.3; 42.1;
118.D6, 118.He 13, 131.24, 133.4 etc. A full list is given by
Lindemann. At Ps 69 Hilary refers to Aquila. For translatio cf. 65.26,
67.12. 118.He5, 7 etc. Interpretatio cf. 67.14; translatores 145.1 etc.
The differences between latin and Hebrew thought are discussed at e.g.
138.22. Hilary holds the view that the Lxx is the best text of the
Psalms. A preference for the LXX is expressed at 118 1.4; 59.1; 131.2
and 4; 133.4; 2.3; Prol. 2.1; 142.1; 59.1; 138.32. Reference is often
made to the Hebrew e.g. at 65.25, yet the Greek is to be preferred to
the Hebrew, as at 138.25, and to the latin: verbi virtutem latinus
sermo non tenet etc. Such comparisons of text may be seen at 133.4;
38.32; 138.43; 142.1; 143.1. cf. Reinkens' discussion op.cit.283.

c)   The theological structure.

The theological background of the In Psalmos is basically that of the De Trinitate: differences in detail arise from differences in the nature of the main themes, which in the De Trinitate might be summed up as the defence of anti-Arian Christology, in the In Psalmos as devotional meditation upon the life of man coram Deo. In the De Trinitate the ground was dictated by his opponents, forcing a concentration on the theme of the divinity of Christ: here Hilary is free to develop a wide variety of themes in the course of meditation on the different motifs of the psalms. At the same time he is able to combine much of the exegetical legacy of Origen with his own exegetical method, developed through the In Matthaeum and the De Trinitate.

Continuity with the De Trinitate is suggested by many of the expressions. Hilary assumes that the celestial significance of the psalms is to convey the message of the gospel: cf the references to figural expressions above and e.g. 2.23 tenendus autem idem evangelicorum dictorum ordo, qui psalmi est.; 53.1. evangelica doctrina etc. This is also the case where as in 58.1 omnis a historia dissentit. This is the divinus sermo (56.5) and Verba Dei sunt, quaecumque prophetae locuti sunt (118.Phe). In the prologue (7) it was said that scripture has the forma dominici corporis. Further, sit totum illud ad cognitionem adventus domini nostri Jesu Christi, et corporationis, et passionis et regni et ad resurrectionis nostrae gloriam virtutemque referatur (11). Christ is the key to scripture. Of the scribes it is said - negant enim Christum. cuius adventus opus est prophetarum, clavem scientiae abstulerunt (5). Occasionally the exemplum of Christ is stressed: e.g. 118 Nun 8 hoc praecipuum a se doctrinae sumi exemplum mansuetudinis scilicet et humilitatis, per quae animabus requies

154

inveniretur. He is the ultimate reference of all the psalms: cf, 138.1
Non est ergo ambiguum, quin in psalmis de eo scriptum est. Nam tametsi
plerumque in his talis sint, ut ad personam patriarcharum, prophetarum,
apostolorum, martyrum, generationis quoque primae et generationis sequentis
referri oporteant: tamen quia omnia in Christo et per Christum sunt,
quidquid illud in psalmis est sub diversorum personis prophetarum, omne de
ipso est: quia doctrina omnis, diversis licet praeceptorum generibus
multiformis hoc per diversos praestet ut ipse noscatur. Knowledge of God
in Christ is given by God himself through the scriptures: Ps 134.3 per
cognitionem nominis Dei ad scientiam eius perficimus; 129.1 humana
infirmitatis confessio ... ex Deo hoc solum nosse, quod Deus est. cf
cognitio dei at 69.1 and 134.27. Here, and not from 'the philosophers',
of whom Hilary is rather scornful, is to be found knowledge of God: cf.
64.4 cernimus namque nudis philosophos corporibus algere ... tum hoc inane
atque ridiculum est, et cum ipsis superstitionis causis miserabile. There
is no developed doctrine of the hearing of the Word, as in Augustine, but
the knowledge of God is planted by him in the hearts of men: cf, 118 Phe. 5
corde enim per fidem patente, et per desiderium ad hauriendum hiante,
intelligentia doctrinae coelestis accipitur. Non animae hoc, sed cordis
officium est.

In the In Matthaeum the strict typological method of the West was
combined with the techniques of the rhetorical schools to produce a carefully controlled exegesis. In the De Trinitate detailed exegesis succeeded
by an epitomising use of scripture. In the In Psalmos detailed exegesis
returns, the whole being seen indirectly, but not always directly in the
light of the coming of Christ. Where this basis is secured, it is then
possible to make use of the whole range of Origen's exegesis in support of

it, to the extent of using his allegory of scripture as having the form of the body of Christ. That is to say, Origen's complex hermeneutical apparatus, can be adapted and used alongside techniques drawn from his previous exegetical works, in the context of Hilary's own theological meditation on each psalm.

The importance of the link both with Origen and with his own previous exegesis may be seen from a consideration of the inter-relation of theology and exegesis in some of the more controversial themes of the work.

It has been suggested that the In Psalmos shows the culmination of a transition from a western theology to an Origenist position in which deification and mystical illumination are the main themes. This is illustrated from e.g. the lack of emphasis on the sensus corporalis of the scriptures, which is thought to reflect Hilary's doctrinal difficulty with the human nature of Jesus, and from the passages in which it is maintained that God cannot suffer.

There are indeed grounds for this suggestion, but they are not the grounds usually given. It is clear that though scripture is said to have the form of the body of Christ, the whole exegesis is not in practice related by detailed analogy with the doctrine of the incarnation, either in Hilary or in Origen himself.

Though Origen's scheme of mystical illumination is followed and the language of deification is used, the theology is that of the De Trinitate: It would be misleading to suppose that Hilary had any qualms about the use of Origen's ontological categories of deification as such: it is simply that they are usually applied in accordance with the limitations upon human language about God detailed in the De Trinitate.

156

For Hilary as for Origen, scripture provides the ladder of meditation towards perfection. Hilary is careful to stress the concrete nature of the work of God in men now: cf. 51.3 verbum caro factum habitat in nobis; 123.9 spiritales enim sumus, et evolamus ut passeres. But at the same time it seems clear that he did not envisage the achievement of full mystical illumination in this life: cf. 118 Zain. 1 omnis Dei sermo qui scripturis divinis continetur, in SPEM nos bonorum coelestium vocat. What is desired here is praise of, but not union with, God: cf. 134.2. et contuendum in exordio psalmi est quod ad laudem nos Dei advocat, cum in superiorem psalmum ad solum benedictionem hortatus sit. cf. too Pss, 149-150 passim. When we find an expression like that employed at 132.1 per omnem doctrinae ordinem gradibus scanditur, nam per gradus ad superiora vehimur, we are at once aware of the background in Origen: but on the other hand the background of such a phrase as at 124.1 habitemus nunc ecclesiam, coelestem Jerusalem, ut non moveamur in aeternum, may reflect not so much a conscious Origenist ontology as a word of encouragement to a comparatively young Church in the midst of a still largely pagan population. If it was one of Hilary's main services to Latin theology to have introduced (or reintroduced) the Alexandrian exegetical tradition to the West, and so to prepare the way for the reception of the many translations of Alexandrian commentary which were soon to follow, it was at the same time his achievement to show how this work could be combined with important elements in the western theological tradition, coming from Irenaeus. His work of adaptation was to be overshadowed by Jerome, and then by Ambrose. Yet his pioneering work, as later theologians were on occasion to discover, was often done on a theological basis at least as perceptive as that of many of his successors.

In this achievement the role of the exegetical tradition, eastern
and western, lay largely in preparing text and context: the critical
factor was the theological method which then moulded the available
material into interpretations which, however we may view their contents
today, were often of much greater depth than those of his contemporaries.[50]

50. N. Gastaldi's thesis now casts further light on some of the issues
    discussed above in the following ways. It is possible to interpret
    Jerome's statement to mean that Hilary and Eusebius of Vercelli
    worked independently and not jointly in using E. of C's commentary
    on the Pss. So Gastaldi, following Kannengiesser. The stress on
    the realities in scripture, which we noted in the In Matthaeum as an
    echo of the western tradition, is found too by G. in the In Ps. cf
    Ps. 21.1-2 Tert, Adv. Jud. 10.13: non omnia imagines, sed et veritates.
    G. has found echoes of Cyprian and Novatian in the In Pss too.
    After going thoroughly into the relation of H. on the Psalms to
    Origen and Eusebius of Caeseraea, Gastaldi finds no trace in Hilary
    of Origen's rabbinic or his gnostic exegesis. G. too found parallels
    with and differences from E of C, i.e. agreement on the titles of
    the psalms, but differences on the value of the LXX.. G. concludes
    that O's influence is greater than that of E but that the continuity
    with the In Mt. is still very marked. 'la tecnica qua usa Hilario
    para commentar los salmos, se funda en criterios en gran parte ya
    adquirados por el antes de su estadia en oriente' (66) Origen brings
    the linguistic, geographical and historical details, but little else,
    for G. while the only significant role of Eusebius' work is in
    providing a source of scriptural quotations appropriate to the
    various psalms. (op. cit, 68). The full list of diapsalmeis is given
    by G. op. cit 135f. They indicate 1) the author, or 2) the historical
    circumstances in which the psalm was written or 3) the circumstances
    of the translation of the psalms. For Hilary all the material in the
    psalms can be understood as prophecy of Christ, as may be seen in
    terms of the life, death and resurrection of Christ cf. esp. Ps 118.13;
    quia omnia in Christo et per Christum sunt, etc. For the citation
    of St. Paul in Hilary on the Pss cf. A. Souter in JTS 18. 1917 73-4.
    A complete list of references to the birth, life, work, death and
    resurrection of Christ in the In Psalmos is given by Gastaldi, op.
    cit, p. 291ff. Gastaldi (295-8) has collected a large number of
    references in the In Psalmos to the christian hope. This
    eschatological reference tends to contradict the popular image of the
    In Psalmos as steeped in Platonist/Origenist theology, in which all
    is already fulfilled in the present.

A Note on the exegetical material of the minor works of Hilary.

1.1 Tractatus Mysteriorum;

This piece composed towards the end of the In Psalmos is usually viewed in the context of the Alexandrian tradition, because of the numerous allegories in the christological interpretation of Genesis 1 and 2. To this extent its structure is the same as that of the In Psalmos. At the same time however, as Brisson has shown, much of the typology of the In Matthaeum is also to be found, another indication of the state of affairs already noted, namely that Hilary in no sense rejected his earlier views in going on to expand them in new directions in the light of new information. The details as might be expected show features of the theological principles of the In Psalmos and those of the De Trinitate, which as we have seen were also carried forward in the In Psalmos.[51]

2. The remaining writings interest us only in as much as they provide further material with which to compare the results so far obtained. They show no significant differences or changes, but serve to exhibit the extent to which the principles of theology traced in the De Trinitate were thoroughly integrated into all his thought, so that they could be turned easily to application in polemical and political contexts. The primacy of the claims of God in Christ, if need be over against the claims of synods or emperor, remains the central point.

51. for the T.M. cf,above all the excellent edition by Brisson (SC 19).

6.   Retrospect!

Comparison and Development

Comparison and Development.

Constant throughout Hilary's work is a concern to relate exegesis to the process of doing theology as a whole.[1] The exegesis is always related to a basic theme: in the In Matthaeum to the history of the salvation of the populus Dei;[2] in the De Trinitate to a doctrine of the incarnation,[3] or more precisely of the knowledge of God through Christ his eternal Son, in the In Psalmos to the progress of man from sin to transfiguration in Christ.[4]

1. It is not from our conjectures and opinions but from the gift of understanding given by God himself that knowledge of the meaning of the scriptures proceeds. cf. esp. De Trin. 1.17-19 passim: novis enim regenerati ingenii sensibus opus est, ut unumquemque conscientia sua secundum coelestis originis munus illuminet.... optimus enim lector est, qui dictorum intelligentiam expectet ex dictis potius quam imponat, et retulerit magis quam attulerit, neque cogat id videri dictis contineri, quod ante lectionem praesumpserit intelligendum. omnis igitur comparatio homini potius utilis habeatur, quam Deo apta, ...

2. cf. the many refs above; typical is In Mt, 8.8. De tribuno posuisse me satis est, principem esse gentium crediturarum.

3. cf. De Trin. 7.11 Res exsistit in Verbo, Verbi res enuntiatur in nomine .... nam cum audio et Deus erat Verbum, non dictum solum audio Verbum Deum, sed demonstratum intelligo quod Deus est (it must be stressed that in the De Trin. the main concern is with the understanding of the incarnation rather than the scripture text, though the two go together with reality to which for Hilary, scripture points rather than the words themselves).

4. cf. Prol. 11. qui consummationem diligenter advertat, providentiam dispositorum in hunc ordinem psalmorum cum dispensatione salutis nostrae intelliget convenire. Cum enim primus gradus sit ad salutem, in novum hominem, post peccatorum remissionem renasci, sitque post penitentiae confessionem regnum illud Domini in sanctae illius civitatis et coelestis Jerusalem tempora reservatum, et postea consummata in nos coelestis gloria in Dei Patris regnum per regnum Filii proficiamus, in quo debitas Deo laudes universitas spirituum praedicabit; cf too exx cited above.

Behind this relation of theology and exegesis lies the conviction common to this and other periods but expressed differently at different times, that beyond the open sense of scripture, or hidden save to the eye of faith in the open sense, there lies a spiritual teaching which may be unfolded, concerning the gospels in the life of man.[5] But since this theme of the gospel is the subject of all theological reflection, exegesis and theological reflection act reciprocally together - the key being the nature of the reciprocation.[6]

This concern, on the one hand to recognise the limitations of human language, and on the other hand, not to neglect the means of doing theology which have in fact been revealed in the incarnation, Hilary shares in the fourth century with Athanasius in particular.[7]

5. cf.In Matt. 14.3. Frequenter monuimus, omnem diligentiam Evangeliorum lectioni adhiberi oportere: quia in his, quae gesta narrantur, subesse interioris intelligentiae ratio reperiatur.

6. cf.De Trin. 1. 17-19 above and e.g. In Matt. 8.8 Atque non nos intelligentiam fingimus, sed gesta intelligentiam nobis impertiuntur. Neque enim res intelligentiae, sed rei intelligentia subsecundat.

7. The lack of explicit verbal parallels has led commentators to conclude that Hilary had probably never read the works of Athanasius. Their common theological and ecclesiastical concerns suggest that a personal acquaintance, and some direct influence of Athanasius on Hilary, is likely. This argument was mentioned by e.g. Albinus and Plotinus, and it is not impossible that Hilary too, e.g. in writing of names in the De Trin. cf 1.21 and 3.17ff, was influenced if only indirectly through the rhetorical schools, by the Cratylus. If the nature of things changes the words, then a substance can change the meaning of a word, and so words like ktizon, when applied to God, can have a different meaning than when applied to man. Arguments of this type are of course only viable within such a Platonic framework. The central concern in Hilary (and also in Athanasius) to interpret scripture on the basis of the Father - Son relationship has been examined in a chapter entitled 'Hilary and the Pilioque' by J. Pelikan in his 'Development of Christian Doctrine' pp. 120ff. Pelikan, who reaches conclusions very similar to our own, offers a full analysis of the congruence between the immanent and the economic Trinity, and of the crucial role played for Hilary by images used by God as he

(contd.)

Though the exegesis often reflects the interpretational conventions of
the day,[8] yet at the same time Hilary is concerned to work out his interpretation on the basis of adequate theological relation to his basic
concerns, neither selfconsciously avoiding nor uncritically following
current philosophical fashion.[9]

In the In Matthaeum, the concern for an integrated theological
interpretation enabled Hilary to produce what was probably the first
considerable biblical commentary of the Latin West. In doing so, he was
able to use the full resources of the rhetorical schools in the service
of theology to prepare the texts themselves for interpretations in terms
of this conceptual unity of the story of salvation as the movement from
the law to the Gospel. In this process of exegetical harmonisation, in
particular in the early work, many of what would today be considered the
key accents and concepts of the biblical passages are either applied in a
completely different way from that intended by the biblical writer (not
in itself a necessarily fruitless procedure, but still full of problems)
or else passed over in silence and so 'lost'.

The process of harmonisation is seen at its strongest in the In
Matthaeum, because of its special structure.[10] In the De Trinitate much

7.   (contd.) testifies about himself (esp. De Trin. 7.38 and 4.14).
      His analysis of passages relating to the divinity of the Spirit (esp.
      De Trin. 12.55) and to the relation of the Spirit to the Son (esp. De
      Trin. bks 2 and 8) are a further useful alternative to the interpret-
      ations of the place of the Spirit along the lines of 'Geistes-
      christologie' and 'Stoic monism'.
8.   cf. too e.g. In Matt. 17.2. Et in hoc quidem facti genere, servatur
      et ratio et numerus, et exemplum.
9.   cf. De Trin. 4.14. Intelligentia enim dictorum ex causis est assumenda
      dicendi: quia non sermo subiectus.
10.   As mentioned above, the worst example is probably in In Matt. 31-33
                                                        (contd)

of the consistency of interpretation arises from the very high proportion of Johannine texts dealing with the same material in similar ways. In the In Psalmos the taking over of the techniques of Alexandrian interpretation enabled Hilary to construct his exegesis in a much less tight fashion. Here was a technique which with modification allowed much more attention to be paid to individual texts than was possible in the tradition of western exegesis, which had accompanied a theology operating within a fairly narrow range of basic themes. This is perhaps an additional reason why western theology in general on reaching the complex proportions of the fourth century welcomed so eagerly and often uncritically the eastern techniques now available.

In terms of the theory of exegesis Hilary like Augustine was to break away from the structures of the western rhetorical schools. Unlike Augustine he did not develop a new special theory of hermeneutics, but attempted, as we have seen, to relate scripture directly to his doctrine of Christ itself.[11] Yet he never set this method down in formal terms, and in practice used it along with other methods (this indeed was partly a consequence of his own position - the basic point was the focus and not the theory). This was what attracted the Reformers to his work, whatever

10. (contd.) passim, in which much of the depth, cosmic significance, anguish and horror of the passion narrative is lost.

11. cf. e.g. above in De Trin. and In Matt. 5.8. In dictis Dei veritas est;nec inefficax quod locutus est. cf De Trin. 7.11. At vero hic Verbum Deus est: res exsistit in Verbo, Verbo res enuntiatur in nomine. Verbi enim appellatio in Dei filio de sacramento nativitatis est, sicuti sapientiae et virtutis est nomen. De Trin. 5.33 and the passages cited in sect 4 above referring to Christ as the point of reference of the biblical text are also relevant here.

the actual differences: had succeeding generations followed Hilary rather than Augustine, the course of the history of exegesis might have been rather different. But this was impossible because of the fragmentary and incohate nature of Hilary's work[12] itself, quite apart from other considerations.

Perhaps one of the greatest gulfs which separates the exegesis of Hilary, along with that of Augustine and Luther alike, from modern exegesis and the theological use of exegesis today is however the initial 'preparation' of the text for theological interpretation on the basis of the rules of Roman/Hellenistic literary criticism, in which the 'strangeness' of the historical perspective of the world of the biblical narrative, Semitic and Hellenistic alike, is lost. The history of God in Israel, the messianic hope, the prophecy of judgement and promise, the eschatological tension of the earliest communities, the understanding of God's righteousness and his wrath, all these had undergone enormous diffusion and transformation through the application of the techniques of the schools, and could not be recaptured. In this sphere, the revival of Hebrew studies in the Renaissance was to be an important aid to Luther and the Reformers, though as the case of Jerome illustrated, Hebrew was not enough.

A final illustration of the characteristic strengths and weaknesses of Hilary's exegetical method may be seen in his understanding of the relationship of Old and New Testaments, especially of the problem of the Law. The relation of promise to fulfilment, of the law to the gospel, of

12. cf, note 16 on Hilary's influence at end of ch. Aug. did however borrow much from Hilary in his De Trin. cf now Pelikan op. cit.

the Jews to the Gentiles, was from the beginning one of Hilary's special interests. In the In Matthaeum, lex is strongly contrasted with fides: in the In Psalmos the whole of the Old Testament can be seen as a lex spiritalis which is itself part of the gospel.[13] It is tempting to see this as indicating a transition from a strongly eschatologically orientated western Irenaean tradition to an Alexandrian tradition in which eschatology has been swallowed up in the process of sanctification in the present. But this as we have seen is too simple an explanation to fit the facts (Luther's understanding of the law follows a similar course and would be hard to accommodate in a similar explanation). It is rather a consequence of the theology of the De Trinitate, after which the most unlikely of theological models, that of the lex spiritalis, can be taken up and used in a new way.

13. cf. In Matt. 9.3 Usque in eum (Johannem) enim lex et prophetae sunt; et, nisi lege finita, in fidem evangelicam corum nemo concederet. In Ps. 131.16 Sed haec omnia eius quod hominis assumpsit corporis species est, omne in se sacramentum continens legis. Nunc et deitatis spiritu et origine carnis unitum, intus scilicet ac foris aureum est; est enim Dominus noster Jesus Christus in gloria Dei patris ... Testamenti intra se tabulas et legis librum conservans; sunt enim in eo verba vitae. cf. In Ps. 118.13.10 Ea enim lex, quam Moyses scripserat, paedagoga nobis in Christo fuit; et idcirco super docentes se et seniores intellexit, quia legem evangelicam, quae Moysi lege continetur, intelligit.

A Note on the influence of Hilary's exegesis and theology.

(cf note 12 above)

Hilary's exegetical achievements were rapidly over shadowed, as
mentioned in section 2 above, by the flood of translations of Greek
exegetical works in the late fourth century, then by Ambrose and above
all by Augustine, whose works set the pattern for all later western
exegesis. Hilary's work appears to have remained almost unknown in the
East and was never translated into Greek.

Nevertheless it was not entirely forgotten, and continued to exert
an influence on the western Church.

Ambrose and Zeno of Verona borrowed large quantities of the In
Psalmos for their own works on the subject and valued Hilary highly.
Jerome also borrowed, but was anxious to play down the importance of
Hilary's achievement to the advantage of his own. Augustine had read and
valued the De Trinitate, but did not make great use of Hilary's exegesis.
Pelagius often appeals to Hilary (De Gest. Pel. 14.31f) (De Nat. et Grat,
61, 71, 81,) and John Cassian calls him 'magister ecclesiarum' (Contra
Nest, VII 24) Thomas refers to him often and, according to De Lubac
(Exeg. Med) derived much of his theology from Hilary. Abelard refers to
the De Trinitate 14 times and Peter Lombard has 88 references (according
to Grabmann, Schol. Meth. p. 120-1). Jakob Perez of Valentia refers
frequently to the In Psalmos (Werbeck p. 74).

Luther valued the realist emphasis of Hilary's exegesis and its
christological concentration, with its stress on faith in the gospel and
rejection of the law. Hence the dictum 'Nemo illorum sanctorum novit
quicquam de spiritu sancto praeter unum Hylarium (WA 15: 566. 4-5): Ebeling

(EE. op. cit. 475f, 493) prints parallel paragraphs showing how Luther in his preaching on occasion follows large sections of the In Matthaeum almost word for word (many other references in Ebeling op.cit). Calvin too valued Hilary's theology for the same reason as Luther, but used the theology more than the exegesis as such (cf.refs, in McNeill/Battles index 1615). Others have found material of value in Hilary in more recent times, notably Karl Barth (cf.KD 1/1, 373, 374, 456, 461 etc), but it must be said that for reasons which are entirely understandable, Hilary has remained an almost forgotten theologian and exegete, and has not perhaps been remembered according to his merits.

7.   Prospect

The Role of the Bible in Theology:

Exegesis and Methodology in

Contemporary Theology

Exegesis and method in Hilary and in contemporary theology.

(a)

In the development of his exegetical method Hilary was able, particularly in his use of Origen, to step outside his own exegetical tradition,
to find new methods and to use without difficulty methods which in his
own tradition of exegesis had for good reasons been rendered suspect,
through particular historical associations and misuses. He did not
however (and could not!) take over the entire thought structure of a
hundred and fifty years before - the theological scene had altered too
much for that, bringing its own problems, and these were not to be solved
through methods evolved for dealing with a very different situation.

Like Hilary theologians today want to use the most accurate tools
available, the first of which, the historico-critical method, at once
leads to a considerable revision of the manner in which the text is
'prepared' for further interpretation. Many modern scholars wish too to
stress the common concerns of exegesis of biblical material and of systematic theology, which then as now has to work with extra-biblical concepts
in reflection on the testimony of the gospel. Not sharing the theory of
inspiration of the early Church in general, most theologians today would
not wish to answer all theological questions directly from scriptures,
and they are more highly conscious of the earthen nature of the scriptural
vessel. Like Hilary they too are concerned to take account of the problem
involved in applying analogies expressed in human concepts to God, even
when these are drawn from scripture, and yet they often wish to integrate
the results of biblical exegesis fully into the doing of theology. But at
the same time they will recognise that here there are two intertwined but
distinguishable problems, that of the process of exegesis of the biblical

170

texts , and that of integrating the results of that process into systematic theological construction.

To impose solutions upon contemporary problems on the basis of patristic or indeed any other discussion in the past without regard for the development of these present concerns would clearly be arbitrary and irrational. Yet it may be that the very distance of a patristic discussion from contemporary concerns can serve to illuminate some of these because of the unfamiliar light in which the issues (which are not identical but usually in some respect similar) are placed.[1]

A survey of the key areas of discussion on the process of exegesis of biblical texts and the role of the results of that process in systematic theology, shows that, though many of the different approaches to this subject cut straight across the confessions, others have developed especially in particular confessions of the Church. In assessing and developing aspects of these, the theologian in an ecumenical age (whatever the potential temptations of that may be) is at least in theory freed from the role of sitting in judgement upon the confessional contributions in the service of a 'truly Reformed', or 'truly Catholic' solution, as the case may be, in order to seek clues from the whole tradition of the Church (and from the whole world of learning) towards the development of concerns common to theology today.

Few scholars would today take issue with the affirmation that since the Bible is in many or its parts the product of an historical process, coming into being through historical events and experiences, and through

1.   cf. the use of patristic examples to illustrate present problems
      provided by M.F. Wiles, The Making of Christian Doctrine.

reflection upon them, the historico-critical method is necessary for the understanding of this process. The Bible contains a collection of very diverse literary documents, the contents of which often stand in tension with one another: 'where they are, as far as we can see, really contradictory, this may go back to real theological disagreements within the biblical period itself or may have been occasioned by different social or historical situations. The difficulties raised by this for systematic theology have not been solved by us. Although the truth in Christ is one, the human witness to it is manifold.[2]

Though theology may strive to present an overall picture which points to the same truth to which the Bible points, clearly forced harmonisation in exegesis is to be avoided. For Hilary this problem did not yet exist: given its presence the presentation of an overall picture is exceedingly difficult.

How is the text itself to be interpreted after matters of text and transmission have been settled? Assuming that both 'historical' and 'unhistorical' layers of tradition may be of equal theological relevance and may be relevant in different ways, how is the relevance of the possibly several meanings of a passage to be determined and related to systematic theology? How far may this be articulated in terms of radically different sets of philosophical categories, perhaps from different cultures? What kind of questions may be expect to be answered by references to scripture? What is the role of our previous knowledge and understanding in the study of the Bible? What of the 'keys' to the interpretation of scripture provided by the various confessions? The finding of the survey cited above

2.   New Directions, op. cit, p.34.

is that 'it is doubtful whether any one interpretative principle can be so stated as to become a prescriptive instrument applicable in all circumstances'.[3] It can be said that particular aspects of scripture come to the fore and demand special attention not by reason of a confessional standpoint, nor as a result of the application of interpretational principles, but because a particular historical situation has developed.

In considering the possible role of patristic material in providing assistance in the discussion, we shall concentrate in the first instance on the question of the status of scripture in theology, since the details of the historico-critical process develop out of modern exegetical methods unknown to the early Church.

Though popular tradition (following Harnack) speaks of the threefold patristic criteria of scripture, the creed and the episcopal office, it is generally recognised that within these three scripture was foremost in importance as a norm for the church's life and teaching. Origen in taking over Philo's allegorical system clearly believed that all truth was to be found supremely in scripture (facets of this truth being found elsewhere too) and that the system of interpretational principles which he imposed upon the text was to be found already reflected in scripture itself. Provided the key to the enigma were known, scripture was self-interpreting.

3.   ibid. p.39.

This belief he shared with the whole patristic tradition including Hilary and Augustine, though the nature of that self-interpretation was differently understood, different stresses being laid on the literal and the non literal sense, etc. Most early church exegesis was 'christological' in orientation, but in different ways. For Hilary in the De Trinitate, Christ reveals himself through scripture, in direct creation of faith; the middle ages however, followed in general the allegorical scheme of Augustine, the authority or the allegory being an elaborate series of rules, sanctioned by the Church, under the general heading of fides, spes and caritas, again with differences in nuance between the Platonist and Aristotelian schools. The swift rise of Aristotelian views in the later middle ages brought a new emphasis on the authority of the Church, beside and eventually above scripture: where there were several sets of rules, who was to judge which was correct but the Church?

In the face of this dilemma Luther came to the conclusion, already anticipated in some respects by Hilary, and others, that Christ is his own interpreter in the context of scripture. Instead of an enigmatic mixture of the obscure and the less obscure, to be interpreted by the allegorical key, all is plain (it was held) when it is seen in faith that the texts of scripture refer ultimately to Christ himself. The preaching of scripture is the preaching of Christ: scripture interprets itself as Christ reveals himself.[4] Calvin added the modification that the Holy Spirit reveals Christ through the scriptures in the heart of the believer, so avoiding the limitation of Christ to the word of scripture itself, but

4.   cf esp. the work of Ebeling and Krause already cited.

not of course, excluding the place of the written word in the process.[5]
In the period of orthodoxy there arose a new legalism which amounted to
a return to the allegorical interpretation of scripture.[6] Theologians of
the Enlightenment, seeing the sterility of the method, attempted by the
use of historical research and philosophical method to purify the faith
and to return to the pure simplicity of the gospel. Thus was born the
historico-critical method.[7] The difficulty was that an increasingly
exclusive concentration on the historical problems was to lead to a loss
of the awareness that Christ witnessed to in scripture was the living and
acting Lord. For Roman Catholic theology the problem was not so acute,
for scripture since the Tridentinum had been understood as subordinate to
the Church which was in itself a kind of extension of the incarnation.
Though the effect of historical method was to make itself felt with the
modernists, this was essentially part of a larger and in some ways a
different problem.

One important response to the problems of historical method came
from the 'dialectical' theologian. It will be useful to recall the basic
features of this approach. For Bultmann as for Luther and for Origen,
scripture interprets itself (though both Luther and Bultmann reject Origen's

---

5.   cf. R.S. Wallace, Calvin's doctrine of the Word and Sacrament, and
        W. Krusche, Das Wirken des Heiligen Geistes bei Calvin.

6.   cf. R. Preuss: The inspiration of Holy Scripture.

7.   cf. K. Scholder: Die Anfänge der Historisch-kritischen Methode. For
        the development of biblical interpretation in the 18th and 19th
        centuries cf. H. Frei, 'The Eclipse of the Biblical Narrative.'
        Troeltsch, of course, is in a category of his own. cf. The Absolute-
        ness of Christianity, passim, and on the problem of text and context,
        below, p.187ff.

doctrine of mechanical inspiration). For Bultmann as for Luther, Christ reveals himself to man from within the text of scripture in the act of proclamation. Since man confronted with the text of scripture is not only a sinner who needs to be convicted of sin, but also a modern man for whom the gulf between the thought world of the Bible and his own world has to be bridged, this bridge, which removes the false scandal of unintelligibility in order to allow confrontation with the true scandal of the cross, is provided by the programme of demythologising. This programme provides a special theory of hermeneutics. The epistemological problem is not simply to be treated as part of the general estrangement of the sinner from the open truth of the gospel (as for Luther) but arises from the difference between the thought world of the Bible and that of our own time. Therefore, a Vorverständnis, both of the historical particularity of the text and of the nature of the existential decision to which he is summoned, must be reached by the exegete before he can grasp the impact of the gospel; and equally unless he is summoned by Jesus, he will never understand the New Testament in its true historical and theological context.[8] The relation between eschatological summons and historical understanding remained somewhat unclear.

For Barth, following Luther too but also Calvin, the function of the hermeneutical programme is taken in part at least by his doctrine of the Trinity. With Bultmann he rejected the doctrine of mechanical inspiration, and he accepted in principle the historico-critical method.

---

8. On Bultmann's hermeneutics cf. esp. the famous essay of 1941 on The New Testament and Mythology. cf. too W. Schmidthals, Die Theologie Rudolf Bultmanns' Otto Weber, Dogmatik 1.370ff, and the excellent work by G. Hasenhüttl. 'Rudolf Bultmann'.

Following Calvin, he held (and this difference of nuance is paralleled in many respects in the history of Reformed/Lutheran controversy on the Lord's Supper) that Christ does not actually make himself present from within the text (however understood) but that God reveals himself in the history of Jesus Christ as testified in the scriptures, through the seal in the heart of the believer of the testimony of the Holy Spirit. The manner of God's approach is of waiting and asking, rather than of demand for decision. Unintelligibility to modern man is part of the general problem of man's anthropocentric rather than theocentric way of thinking, and is dealt with by the Holy Spirit in reorientating man's whole life in the context of the proclamation of the Word, and indeed in the ongoing life of the community, for the movement no longer has to be that of sudden demand for decision.[9] In practice fears of 'anthropocentric' method neutralised the application of historico-critical method.

As far as the Barth-Bultmann controversy is concerned attempts have been made to move to a new understanding which learns from both sides, despite the headshakings of the original protagonists. Reaction against early existentialist dogmatism, as it was thought inter alia to be, in both Barth and Bultmann led to a new quest of the historical Jesus. Following Luther in seeing Christ as the 'centre' of scripture and all

9.   On Barth's doctrine of Scripture cf. J.K.S. Reid, The Authority of the Bible p. 194f. Also J. McIntyre, The Shape of Christology, J. Barr, Old and New in Interpretation & D. Ford, Ph.D. Camb. 1977, Biblical narrative in the theological method of Karl Barth in the Church Dogmatics (lit.).

theology as interpretation of scripture, Ebeling built up a systematic

theology around the historical Jesus in which the historical Jesus is the

centre of the kerugma of scripture.[10] Fuchs combined this with Barth's

concern for ontology and for the charismatic element to provide a new

ontology of language in which Jesus reveals himself as language event in

the context of the preaching of the gospel from the text of scripture.[11]

In his book, 'Paulus und Jesus' Jüngel combined more explicitly the

exegetical concerns of both Barth and Bultmann. For him, the Pauline

theology of justification corresponds exactly to the witness of the

gospels to Jesus. God has revealed himself as the trinitarian God in

the history of the incarnation in Jesus Christ. Man cannot himself speak

of God. But in the parables, which are a pointed, ostensive mode of

discourse about the kingship of God which also involves his own person,

Jesus reveals himself as a language event, which is repeated in the

preaching of the word, as Jesus is brought to expression through human

words, as God's Word in the history of the incarnation.[12]

This understanding of parable as the place where God reveals himself

in the word of the man Jesus has its attractions. It could for example,

be fruitfully combined with the similar but entirely unrelated idears of

I.M. Crombie.[13] The suggestion is not however without its own problems;

10. cf. esp. Gott u. Wort, and 'Jesus and Faith' from 'Word and Faith'
    201ff, also pp. 305ff, 'Word of God and hermeneutics'.

11. cf. Studies of the historical Jesus, and his 'Hermeneutik'. cf. too
    Gadamer, Wahrheit u. Methode op. cit p. 397f, and J. Fangmeier,
    'Ernst Fuchs' in Theologische Studien, Heft 80.

12. E. Jüngel, Paulus und Jesus, esp. pp. 135ff.

13. cf. I.M. Crombie in 'New Essays' ed. Flew and McIntyre pp. 109ff.

still there is a special hermeneutic of parable, when this category is
applied outside the parables of Jesus himself. It might be said that
the events themselves in the history of Israel and of Jesus in particular
(though not necessarily the concept 'incarnation' which is just as
vulnerable as any other concept), events in which Geschehen includes
Sprachgeschehen (in preference to Sprachereignis) provide the hinge of
discourse. If so, then no special hermeneutic is possible, just as all
analogies break down in reference to Christ. Even if it were to be
argued that God had chosen some special means of self communication, e.g.
the parable, in the time of Jesus of Nazareth, we would not then be
entitled automatically to extrapolate the concept of parable as the
universal category for language about God, though it might be an important
indicator among others. Even in the case of scripture, we may have to
look for other complementary ways to understanding.

It may be possible to conceive of different ways in which different
types of scriptural discourse may be understood. In scripture itself,
as far as it is witness to the history of Israel and of Jesus, the
history of God's involvement with men is brought to articulation. All
the various types of language, including that of parable, are models for
the articulation of the relationship. The word is itself one model which
always has to be related to the activity of man Jesus of Nazareth,
together with his death and resurrection. This model is also qualified
by being understood, for a great part of the tradition of the Church, in
terms of the doctrine of the Trinity, understood differently at different
times in what would in classical terms be called an essential and not

simply an economic frame of reference.[14]

The nature of the biblical models, though not the mode of their later application, is determined by the results of historico-critical method.

Such an understanding would avoid the hinging of the whole process upon the special hermeneutic of parable as in Jungel's model, in which the word becomes the Word in a Sprachereignis through the text itself, while still taking up and carrying further the concern of both Barth and Bultmann in the context of scripture.

An historical illustration, admittedly not created for the same purpose, can be seen in that Hilary's use of scripture. For certain purposes he employs an epitomising use of scripture in which all is understood as pointing to the incarnation of God in Jesus. For specific areas of exegesis he used other methods of interpretation including the use of typology, the rhetorical categories, symbolic of titles, numbers etc. We noted that in Hilary, the freedom to use all sorts of different interpretations for special purposes is grounded in the value of the incarnation itself. So, understanding the incarnation in the history of the Trinity, it may be possible to make use of different structures for different purposes in the interpretation of scripture, in which God reveals himself in the history of Jesus Christ through the Holy Spirit.

But the problems are very far from solved. In more recent discussion it is not the difference but the similarities between Barth and Bultmann which have rendered them equally unacceptable to their critics.

14. For an imaginative, if not entirely convincing restatement of the doctrine of the Trinity, in this case an interpretation of Barth's doctrine, cf. E. Jüngel, Gottes Sein ist im Werden.

For Moltmann in his 'Theology of Hope' the main weakness of the dialectical theology was its failure to carry through consistently the programme of eschatological reference which it proclaimed. God for Barth and Bultmann is present, in the context of scripture and elsewhere. But the basic scripture category is hope, promise, the new. Scripture is to be understood in the category of promise, and the presence of God is a hope to be fulfilled at the coming of the kingdom, for which we are now to work in the world. The basic difficulty is that the many other accents in the Bible, the given pluralism, and not least the witness to what has been accomplished by Jesus, the importance of the past as past, have disappeared in Moltmann's reconstruction.[15] Neither eschatology nor any other concept will provide a single 'key' to the Bible or to theology.

Pannenberg's attitude to the Bible and to the dialectical theology is more radical. (Indeed it is not for nothing that Barth remarked in one of his last seminars that he would gladly stretch out his hand 'under the table' to protect Bultmann from Pannenberg!) For Pannenberg, 'Die Auflösung der Lehre von der Schrift bildet die Grundlagenkrise der modernen evangelischen Theologie'.[16] Until in the late middle ages the authority of the Church was asserted to be higher than that of scripture and the charge was rebutted, the position of scripture was not a matter of serious controversy. Luther's teaching was a substantiation of the rebuttal. But the principle of sola scriptura meant later that all theological work had to be grounded in historico-critical exegesis, and this led to the modern crisis.[17]

15. Moltmann's later position in 'The Crucified God', is more subtle.
16. Pannenberg, Grundfragen systematischer Theologie, 13.
17. ibid. pp.13ff.

'Die Sache' der Schrift, die Luther in Sinne hatte, namlich Person

und Geschichte Jesu, ist für unser historisches Bewusstsein nicht mehr

in den Texten selber zu finden, sondern muss hinter ihnen erschlossen

werden....Dieser Situation kann die Theologie nur gerecht werden, wenn

es gelingt, das neuzeitliche Denken in den Zusammenhang der christlichen

Überlieferungsgeschichte einzuholen...durch einen Entwurf der beide

(Situationen) verbindenden Geschichte sowohl bewährt, als auch aufgehoben

werden.[18]

In fact (GS 130) 'Mit einer Mythisierung der allerdings ursprünglich

mythischen Rede vom Worte Gottes und mit einer nackten Gehorsamsforderung

an den mit der behaupteten Autorität des Gotteswortes bedrohten Hörer

allein genügt man der theologischen Aufgabe jedenfalls auf die Dauer

nicht.[19]

So much for a theology of the Word of God, from Hilary to Moltmann,

and the use of the Bible that has followed it. There is no doubt that

Pannenberg has provided important insights into weaknesses in the dialect-

ical theology,which can be welcomed without qualification.[20] At the same

time it is clear that his own proposals for an alternative, are in several

respects as problematic as the proposals which he wishes to replace. It

is not clear that 'history' can or should provide us with anything other

than history, and it appears unreasonable to be asked to identify this

with the gospel of the New Testament witness.[21]

18. ibid. 15ff.
19. ibid. 130.
20. The present is nothing without the future and the past. It is easy
     for dialectical theology to slide into a 'verbalism' in which the
     reality of salvation in Jesus is lost in an almost Gnostic pre-
     occupation with 'Word'.
21. cf, too the critique by G. Klein. 'Theologie des Wortes Gottes und die
     Hypothese der Universalgeschichte' Munich, 1964 (Kaiser).

In the Anglo-Saxon world further objections have been raised, and
certainly cannot be disregarded in a search for solutions to common
problems. Here the kerugmatic element in the theology of the Word has
been regarded as a legacy of the radical historical scepticism of
Kierkegaard, while the account of a divine encounter with man in the self
revelation of God in Jesus Christ is considered unacceptable in Barth
and Bultmann alike, the one in objectivising of knowledge of God in
revelation, the other in subjectivising of the same. The Bible's role
is seen as that of providing the earliest historical information about
Jesus; in the context of the narration of this information the church
lives and worship, faith is created and seeks a new understanding of
itself in the reinterpretation of biblical imagery and in the employment
of new images through the thought forms available at any given time. In
particular, developments in analytical philosophy raise new and pressing
questions for talk about God. If all is seen in terms of kerugma and
confrontation, grace alone, to the extent that grace becomes an
epistemological principle for the theologian, how is it possible to
specify truth conditions for the faith itself.[22]

In traditional Roman Catholicism, as in traditional Liberal Protest-
antism, authority is placed in a variegated complex of sources of
Christian truth as understood today, in which scripture is only one

22. Representative of this approach, in different forms, are Dietrich
    Ritschl (Memory and Hope), Van Harvey (The Historian and the
    Believer) and D.M. MacKinnon (cf. Borderlands of Theology, esp. pp.
    55-89).

element.[23]   In the orthodox tradition, authority is placed in scripture

as guided by the general ecumenical councils, scripture being the guide

of tradition and tradition the protector of scripture.[24]   In part at

least of the Anglican tradition, a historical approach to scripture

critical or precritical, combined with a parallel frame of theological

reference in philosophical theology, finds the Continental emphasis on

the key function of scripture as the place of the self revelation of

God obscure.[25]

Unless we take the view that the tradition with which we happen to

be most familiar possesses the truth and that others are simply blind,

we shall seek not simply to advocate a more palatable variation of our

own traditional approaches, but to make suggestions which provide a real

basis for a step forward in common discussion, fully aware that a

harmonising compromise will be rightly unacceptable on all sides.   There

is unlikely to be a single 'answer' valid for all time.

Some debate has been aroused by the so-called 'recovery of the Bible'

of the second Vatican council.

For it seemed clear that despite the high density of scriptural

quotation and reference, much of the theological argument was built up,

not from the biblical witness, but from theological systems entirely

---

23.   For an able Catholic presentation of the traditional position in
      its modern phase cf. J.R. Geiselmann, 'Tradition, Scripture and the
      Church' in 'Christianity Divided' (Sheed and Ward) pp. 39ff.

24.   cf. P.N. Trembelas, Dogmatics, 1.19f.

25.   cf. esp. the comparatively limited role of biblical exegesis and
      biblical concepts in the 'Soundings' symposium.

independent of the Bible, the whole then being illustrated by biblical imagery of a largely decorative nature.[26]

It is clear that agreement in understanding the interpretation of scripture and its role in theology is bound up with the understanding of the theological task as a whole. In both spheres, different intellectual traditions will doubtless long continue to make different interpretations. Constructive dispute is always preferable to artificial harmonisation. In practice, somewhat as acts of intercommunion take place without full concurrence in the understanding of these, so different traditions may make use of studies both in the interpretation of scripture and in theology in which scripture plays different roles.

Yet all truth in Christ is one, and so the inter-relations of these differences must be made clear, and the divergences made precise. In this search, the value of patristic study as part of the whole Christian tradition could lie in showing that progress is made only by taking these differences seriously and thinking them through, yet at the same time pointing in a common witness to a common Lord.

26.   cf,the constitution 'Dei Verbum' (Ed. Semmelroth and Zerwick, Stuttgart 1966). (The document stresses the central role of scripture in Christ through the scriptures (paras. 1-7) and the whole is documented at every point by scriptural references. On the other hand the section on the tradition of the Church (paras. 7ff) may be read to suggest that the relationship scripture/tradition has in no way altered since the Council of Trent and is not intended to do so. I am indebted to a seminar of Karl Barth for stimulating my interest in this area.

b)   Conclusion

One of the most significant features of recent work on the Bible is
the increasing awareness that the biblical witness to God's dealings
with men is human testimony and reflects all the incompleteness and
distortion of human reports. There is no need for a uniform method of
interpretation of this collection of various materials, nor is this
possible. The fact for example of Jesus having used the form of the
parable does not give this form any 'final' character. Jesus himself
did not limit himself to this form (cf, the Sermon on the Mount). It
might indeed be thought that after the Resurrection the freedom of
Christians means that they are able to use forms of discourse others
than those of the Bible and imagery beyond the limits of biblical imagery,
provided that they try to be faithful to the central message of salvation.
The nature of the condition of faithfulness takes us immediately beyond
the purely hermeneutical issue. Again, though Christians may ultimately
understand the Bible, and indeed all else in their lives, in relation to
God in Christ, - and this is of prime importance - the Bible clearly need
not be understood in terms of any sort of fixed analogical correspondence
to that centre. However one may interpret the theological relationship
between faith's understanding of God and the text of the scriptures, the
problem is clearly related intimately to the wider issue of the use of
human language in the doing of theology in general. That is to say, the
problem of the role of the Bible in theology embraces much more than
the technical hermeneutical issue.
Lack of awareness of the ramifications of the problem may be thought
to be one of the main difficulties inherent in the recent Continental

186

discussion. For from it being the case that all theology can be reduced
to hermeneutics, it appears that the hermeneutical issues themselves,
apart from the initial work of biblical 'introduction', can only be
worked out in conjunction with the decisions taken on the understanding
of the theological task as a whole. These decisions involve the choice
of metaphysical frameworks, not necessarily in traditional form which
are not readily subsumed under the general term 'hermeneutics' without
confusion. A further modification of the discussion arises from the
need to distinguish the epistemological and metaphysical issues from the
substantive issues of theology. These of course have to be related to
each other, but may need to be treated separately in the progress of the
enquiry. But further discussion of this area would lead us well beyond
the limits of the present exercise. A glance at the de facto state of
theological use of the Bible is not without interest in this connection.

Despite the universal acknowledgement of the importance of scripture,
De facto scripture's role in theology today is no longer what it once was.
This is no doubt connected with a change, an entirely salutary change,
in the understanding of the authority of the Bible: an authoritative
witness is not an object of blind obedience, but has the role of guidance,
of assistance in illumination. It is not there to close but to open
doors, not to delimit but to open up the truth of God.

The changing role of the Bible in theology today can scarcely be
underestimated. Apart from the special case of theologies which use
biblical symbolism in great measure for their own purposes in the manner
of (say Tillich), the swift demise of the unlamented 'Biblical Theology'
of the fifties and the turn to philosophical theology has made systematic
theologians wary of using the Bible explicitly at all. The Bible is to

be seen ultimately and as a whole, as pointing in witness to God in Jesus Christ, but beyond this we venture no further into detail.

Most theologians today would agree that the deposition of the Bible from its former role of an oracle of inerrancy was entirely for the good of theology, and even that the heyday of Biblical Theology in its post war manifestation included such that was obscurantist, arrogant and plain wrong. Some see many advantages in the new dispensation. Christopher Evans has said of the modern theologian 'He has to learn to live with incompleteness and inconclusiveness, and to forge ahead regardless.' The 'curse of the Canon' should be abandoned now that the reasons for its particular composition are seen to be inadequate. One may go further and say that though the interpretation of scripture may help us to understand the early Church, it can not help us to understand ourselves; our times and our questions are simply not theirs, though our questions may be partly influenced by traditions from the past. The OT and NT contain what we judge, on the basis of our life in society which includes the Christian tradition, to be theological errors. The words of Jesus are only one piece of data for the theological task of speaking of God: scripture is part of tradition, no more and no less important as the past in general is important to the understanding of the present and future.

27. C.F. Evans. Is Holy Scripture Christian? passim.cf. too the articles by D.E. Nineham in BJRL 1969 lii. 178-99, D.A. Templeton, in Modern Churchman, April 1974, R. Morgan in Religious Studies Dec. 1974, and M.F. Wiles in 'What about the New Testament?' S.C.M. 1975. Also H. Frei in The Christian Scholar (1966) 49/4 263ff, and now D.H. Kelsey's excellent 'The Uses of Scripture in Recent Theology', S.C.M. 1976.

The argument that the key to the understanding of scripture is given by the Church has of course a respectable tradition much wider than its classic formulation by J. H. Newman, and in structure is very similar to the argument from the key in the Christian in community, the whole of history, and so on. Certainly it is clear that a biblical passage may gain a new central importance for a Christian community in a given historical situation (what one may call, the mutual illumination of text and context). For example, in a situation of Apartheid the text 'In Christ there is neither Jew or Greek' may become of central importance in pointing to the impact of the Gospel in that setting, while such an apparently central text as 'The just shall live by faith' may be safely intoned ten times a day without any impact on the scene. For Jesus himself certain passages of the OT clearly gained in given situations crucial importance for his understanding of his mission. Barth's Romerbrief was written during and made its great impact upon the basis of the Great War.

But on the other hand, e.g. the Arab-Israeli conflict and the Nazi regime enabled people to interpret the text in context and justify inhuman treatment of the Jews, and indeed, of the Arabs. God may reveal different aspects of his truth to men in the context of scripture at different times in different ways. But the context also provides ample opportunity for human distortion of scripture. Judgement may and must be made, yet remains provisional. A whole Church may be wrong, and the acts of a few may be right. The most perverse activities may be and have been justified by reference to the incarnation in the context of scripture: this one might call the hermeneutics of the Grand Inquisitor.

The text then or the context, which is to be? Clearly there is no
simple solution. The history of theology is full of beautifully simple
solutions, and I venture to say that every last one of them is an over-
simplification. The gospel message may be simple: the message of the
reconciling love of God for all men in Jesus Christ. But as the working
out of reconciling love in the infinite complexity and diversity of
humanity is far from straightforward, so the understanding of God, for
whom to be is to love, often in the context of hate, is complex beyond
all imagining.

It appears that neither scripture without tradition nor tradition
without scripture is sufficient. But, it may be said, scripture is
itself part of tradition, and so we may appeal to a greater tradition of
the gospel, including scripture, Christian history and literature, the
community in which we live, and our private individual judgement. In
this case the way we do theology will depend on which parts of the complex
we stress most. Even if it is denied that there can be definite norms
and criteria about such matters, de facto variations in consciousness of
the priorities of these various factors will affect the way in which we
tackle the theological enterprise. Granted the lack of any metaphysical
distinction between scripture and tradition, it becomes all the more
important to ask which elements in the biblical data are indispensable
to the theological enterprise (i.e. would change the nature of that
enterprise if omitted) and in which ways.

Briefly listed, these elements appear to me to include the following:
1.   Certain basic historical data, involving the people of Israel, the
     life words and fate of Jesus, and the early Christian communities.

2. Certain basic theological affirmations, referring to what have been described as 'relational centres' of the Bible, including the love of God, Jesus as the Christ, the kingdom of God, the death and resurrection of Jesus C hrist, the presence of God. The understanding of God's salvation through Jesus Christ remains the central task of Christian theology.

3. The early Christian communities not only shaped the data concerning Jesus, deciding what for them constituted the essential Jesus, but they were themselves influenced by the historical events in which Jesus was involved - also by specific theological affirmations which he made and which were made by the communities themselves on the basis of their experience and reflection upon recent events.

4. In a similar way, it is not enough for the contemporary Christian communities today to decide what for them constitutes the essential gospel: unless they themselves are influenced decisively by external criteria, even where, inevitable, interpreted criteria - including the specific style of Jesus life and acts, - then the claims of Christian faith become insuperably difficult to justify.

5. If we can and do speak of some parts of the Church's tradition as inadequate or one sided in witness to the gospel, then we must operate and in fact continue to operate with some sort of scriptural norm.

6. Christian communities may hope to act under the guidance of the Holy Spirit, but they cannot identify their decisions with those of the Spirit. These decisions reflect the provisionality of the present as present, as well as its eschatological limitation.

7. The dimension of the future is important; it is grounded not simply
    on the biblical categories of eschatology but on the hope of more
    illumination through the Holy Spirit which is a central aspect of
    the gospel.

8. The authoritative witness of the Bible is above all an affirmation
    of faith. The much stressed dangers surrounding the theological
    use of the category of faith should not disguise the fact that faith
    is central to the understanding of every aspect of the gospel.
    Faith is not a substitute for the weighing and analysis of all the
    factors involved in understanding of scripture, but it is an
    indispensable part of the framework, the remainder of which may be
    necessary but is never sufficient. Without faith the present is
    meaningless, and a theology which relies too heavily on the past
    and future without present is at best a rather precarious
    proposition.

9. The problems of the authority of scripture and tradition are
    inextricable related and cannot be completely separated. But it is
    important that their mutual relationships should be carefully
    analysed. As in technology, making the wrong connections can reduce
    the whole to futility.

10. It is on the basis of this record of historical events and
    theological affirmations that the Bible seems indispensable. This
    leaves us free to affirm of course that some of the data within the
    canon may be quite useless to us. We may say too that we are able
    to make use of the biblical narratives as focal points only with
    the aid of the intellectual tradition and the experience of the
    communities in which we live (and most of us live simultaneously in

several overlapping community traditions - cultural relativity does
not entail complete cultural relativism. It is from these
theological focal points that we interpret and evaluate the
remainder of the biblical data. It is also with a view to deepening
further these foci that we continue to regard the Bible as an
important element in the ongoing theological enterprise.

So much then for a brief account of what remains indispensable.
But it may be objected that I have said little of the role of faith
beyond the assertion that it belongs to the total picture, and almost
nothing at all of the Word of God, that central concept of much
hermeneutics. In this last section I would like to say a little more on
these points.

Faith, which is the appropriate human response to the proclamation
of the gospel, arises within the life of the Christian community and is
sustained by that life. Its focus or centre is God and it is intensified
or deepened by reflection, within the life of the community, upon the
date of historical events and theological affirmations to be found in
the Bible. Without the biblical data the focus loses clarity and becomes
a matter of arbitrary speculation only around these data can authentic
faith flourish: hence we may affirm with the Reformers sola scripture,
sola fide, but this never in the sense of solitaria scriptura, solitaria
fide.

But what of the Word which has been supposed to bring its own
conviction in the context of say preaching? Has it gone completely?
Perhaps not quite gone.

It may be affirmed that through the indirect witness of the biblical
data faith comes to a knowledge of God through his own Son Jesus Christ.
The way in which this knowledge is understood will depend on the confessional and cultural background and imagination of the individual, but
the picture will be affected in important respects by the biblical data:
how these data are brought to life for the individual may be seen as the
work of the Holy Spirit.

The characteristic indirectness of the communication, means that
the details cannot be pressed too far or uniformly throughout. The
manner of God's communication of his word, the way in which it is
perceived, is not to be found as a hermeneutic structure in scripture
(as was thought in much of the hermeneutic tradition) but is indeed given
ad modum recipientis, through a complex structure of devotional tradition,
persuasion by argument, experience of the world etc.

One may be grasped by the power of the Gospel, one may say all that
Barth and Bultmann wishes to say about the awareness of the Love of God
in contrast to the unloving nature of man including oneself - but
different people will be struck in different ways by different though
related facets of the gospel. Neither the given nor the way of receiving
the given is uniform.

It is then for the individual to relate various focal points to the
whole structure of faith. The historical Jesus is indeed a central
element of the Gospel. But this centre has then to be related to the
risen Christ to God the Father and to the Holy Spirit. We may speak of
Jesus communicating himself as a word-event (Sprachereignis) - but this
event must then be unpacked in terms of its place in a living and ongoing
process of the reorientation of existence and at the same time a

process of exploration of faith.

The parables, as Jesus' self explanation and at the same time
explanation of the Kingdom of God, may be seen as typical of this process
of the communication of the gospel. At the same time, the gospel is not
concerned entirely with explanation - even in parables: there is a
fundamental unintelligibility about the crucifixion itself which simply
belongs to it.

In the NT Christ may be seen as the hinge of discourse between God
and man - but this is not so in the OT - here God speaks directly,
according to the OT writers: a further problem for attempts to produce
a uniform hermeneutical model for interpreting scripture.

In brief it seems to me that the ideas of scripture as self-
interpreting, or of revelation as self-authenticating, despite their
honourable tradition in theology are in no sense an exact or authoritative
explanation of the communication between God and man.

In speaking of centres and foci of the biblical narrative I take it
that not all parts of the canon, which is in itself a concept with the
roughest edges, as we all know, are to be taken to be on the same level
as data for theology. Selections must be and are made. Further Jesus
himself modified considerably various central emphases of the OT, and we
too must see which of the foci has the most relevant cutting edge in the
various context in which our life in society is lived out. And of course,
we can only do this because of the work that has gone into the history
of interpretation in the past. We may reject previous interpretations,
in part or as a whole, but without them we would not be in a position to
see what we do see: and we know that what we do is itself at best only a
minor contribution to a continuing process.

It has been said that the basic reason why we have to dispense with scripture is that the main purpose of much hermeneutics past and present - of understanding ourselves, our world and our questions today with the aid of an interpretation of the biblical narrative, has failed, because our questions are simply not the questions of the past, and that is that. We may concede that the Bible will not answer our questions fully - pace many of its modern interpreters. But it does provide a part of the framework - for Christians an indispensable part of the framework - on the basis of which we may go on to work out contemporary Christian answers to contemporary questions.

In conclusion I should perhaps try to offer at least one specific example of how the use of scripture seen in the manner described above as one indispensable element in theological enterprise, might begin to work out in practical terms. One focal point in the biblical material which has long seemed to me to be a fruitful source of new theological exploration is the love of God.

The God of the Old Testament is always with his people, loving them and being concerned for them in all their fortunes and misfortunes. [28] This facet of the OT picture would not of course automatically strike the reader of the text immediately. It arises on the basis of acquaintance with a long theological tradition of interpretation. But given that primary orientation, which first arose in the tradition through Christian reflection on the texts, I may then hope to discover more about the nature of God's love through further reflection on the texts.

28. I have discussed further the role of the Old Testament in Christian Theology in MC. April 1973 238pp.

196

It would be idle to see the scene as a closed context of reader and text, however. All our human experience, whether at first hand or through literature, report, etc, will be of service in helping us to recognise God's love for what it is. This is not to say of course that God's love may not transcend all our experience and expectation, enlarging the horizon of our understanding by leading us from the more to the less familiar.

That God is love is then a far from simple, uncomplicated and self evident state of affairs. Use of the theme will not lead to certain theological progress, as readers aware of the diffuse and sentimental quality of much writing on the subject will be only too well aware. Love may be seen as a programmatic term, like say History in the work of Pannenberg, with all the ambiguities which that involves, which is used to bring into shape and focus the purposes of God's activity and the character of God. Love is a term which we import in our search for understanding and reaction. It raises epistemological and metaphysical issues when applied to talk of the transcendent, personal God of the classical Christian tradition, and its content is partly defined by our creative activity in selecting some things and not others things in the biblical narrative and in all our experience, direct and indirect, for ourconcentrated reflection. But its content as a substantive issue of theological study is defined also, and most importantly, by the detailed particularity of the historical, and (and this is clearly not the same thing) the transhistorical activity of God. The choice of love rather than say hate or indifference as the most appropriate term for under-standing the nature and activity of God remains of course a matter of personal preference.

The supreme ground for a theological assertion of the centrality of the love of God has always been the NT record of God's self-giving in the sacrifice of his Son and in Jesus's self-giving for God and mankind. Again however it is not obvious that love is more central than other key words like justice and forgiveness in the NT, and it does not appear that the early Church immediately thought in terms of the love of God as the controlling category. The choice is made for present theological purposes for example in order to stress the action of God in the NT as involving a unity of love between Father and Son, including all that has been traditionally said of unity of being, with all that this implies for the structure of creation and redemption.

To explore the implications of such a radical application of the theme of the love of God would take on into highly technical discussions involving every area of theology and theological methodology and content, going far beyond the biblical imagery. I have deliberately eschewed throughout this study explicit treatment of the vast but everywhere related issue of the theological implications of the modern philosophical critique of traditional metaphysical frameworks. That is a study in itself. But I have tried to take account of the issues raised, esp. on p.189ff. cf. my forthcoming Theology of the Love of God.

But the biblical record remains an indispensable piece of data if the exercise is not to degenerate into mere truism or uncontrolled speculation. This, it seems to me, is a danger to which all central theological concepts are prone as soon as they are abstracted from the partially mysterious but partly sharply clear picture of the biblical tradition, mysterious because the transcendent is involved, sharply clear in the reality of the crucifixion of its central figure.

198

The particular sort of self-giving in which God is involved in interpreted in the NT and in the later areas of tradition in different and to some extent conflicting ways. Some parts of the picture continue to be the focus of attention, the public ministry of Jesus, the Pauline interpretation of his life, death and resurrection, the Johannine reflection on Christology and discipleship. To be God appears from these narratives, to involve among other things giving oneself in such a way as to enable mankind to give itself without restraint, destroying alienation from within, (This is the opposite of self giving which thrusts itself upon the recipient in such a way as to create   alienation). God's self giving involved him in Jesus' death. But this itself would simply compound the tragic futility of life. I think it essential to see the resurrection as an important part of the divine self-giving, though resurrection without self-giving would involve the worst sort of triumphalism. God's love is first and foremost an effective love, good news rather than a pathetically beautiful but tragic failure.

I am only too well aware that this example raises a host of unanswered questions. The object was not however to discuss in extenso the love of God, but to show briefly how the sort of interpretation of scripture and use of scripture in theology discussed in these pages might begin to look in practice. I hope I have been able to offer some sort of indication that the use of biblical material in theology is not only capable of critical revision but also of extensive constructive development.

BIBLIOGRAPHY

Ackroyd, P.R. and Evans, C.F.:   Cambridge History of the Bible, Vol.I,
                                 Cambridge, 1970.

Adler, M.:   Studien zu Philo v. Alexandrien, Breslau, 1929.

Aleith, - Hoffmann E.:   Paulusverstandis in der alten Kirche. BZNW,
                         Berlin 1937.

Altaner, B.:   Kleine Patristische Schriften, Berlin 1966 (incl. Alt-
               lateinische Übersetzungen von Schriften des Athanasius v.
               Alexandrien Byz. Zeitschr. 41, 1941)

Amsler, S.:   L'Ancient Testament dans L'Eglise. Neuchatel, 1960.

Arbusow, L.:   Colores Rhetorici. Gottingen, 1948.

Aristoboulos,: der Thorausleger: Ed. Walter, TU 86 Berlin, 1964.

Arsfahl, G.:   Vergleich und Metaphor bei Quintilian, Stuttgart, 1932.

Asconius Pedianus.:   Commentarii ed. C. Ciamatano, Amsterdam, 1967.

Asconius: Ed. Th. Stangl. 1912.

Ashby, G.W.:   Theodoret of Cyrrhus as exegete of the Old Testament,
               Rhodes Univ., S.A. 1972.

Atberger, L.:   Geschichte der altchristlichen Eschatologie, Freiburg,
                1896.

Auerbach, E.: Figura. Archivum Romanicum XII 1938, 436-89.

Auerbach, E.:   Literatursprache u. Publikum in der lateinischen
                Spätantike u. im Mittelalter.

Bachelet Le: art. Hilaire in DTC VI.2 Paris, 1947.

Baltzer, J.:   Die Theologie des HI. Hilarius v. Poitiers, Rottweil,
               1879.

Bardenhewer, O.:   Geschichte der altchristlichen Literatur, Freiburg,
                   1912.

Bardenhewer, O.:   Des Hl. Hippolytus Kommentar zum Danielbuch, Freiburg,
                   1877.

Bardy, G.:   La culture Grecque dans l'Occident Chretien au IV Siècle
             RSR 29.1. 1939. 5-59.

Bardy, G.:   Un humaniste Chretien St. H. de Poitiers, RHEF 27 1941. 5.25.

Bardy, G.:   Paul de Samosata, Bruges, 1923.

Bardy, G.:   La question des langues dans l'Eglise ancienne. Paris, 1948.

Bardy, G.:   Traducteurs et Adapteurs au IV Siecle RSR 30 1940 257-306.

Barr, J.:   Old and New in Interpretation, London, 1966.

Barr, J.:   St. Jerome and the sounds of Hebrew. JSS 1967. 1-37.

Barr, J.:   The Bible in the Modern World. London, 1973.

Barth, Carola,:   Die interpretation des NT in der valentinischen Gnosis. TU 37.3. Berlin 1914.

Barwick, K.:   De Iunio Filargiri Vergilii interprete. Leipzig, 1908.

Beck, A.:   Römisches Recht bei Tertullian u. Cyprian. Halle 1930. (Schriften der Konigsberger Gelehrtenges. G-W KI. 7.2)

Beck, A.:   Die Trinitatslehre des H.v. Poitiers. Mainz, 1903.

Benoit, A.:   St. Irenee. Paris, 1960.

Benrath, G.:   Wyclif's Bibelkommentar. ARG 36, Berlin, 1966.

Benz, E.:   Marius Victorinus. Stuttgart, 1933.

Betti, E.:   Allgemeine Auslegungslehre. Tubingen, 1967.

Betti, E.:   Die Hermeneutik als allgemeine Methodik der Geistes-wissenschaften. Tübingen, 1962.

Beumer, J.:   Hilarius v. Poitiers, eine Vertreter der christlichen Gnosis. Theol. Quartalschrift 132 (1952) 170-92.

Bigelmair, A.:   Zeno v. Verona. Munster, 1904.

Bigg, C.:   Christian Platonists of Alexandria. Oxford, 1913 [2]

Bjorndalen, A.:   Metodiske Benerkninge til Sporsmalet etter allegorier i det gamle Testamente TTK 1966, 146f, Oslo.

Bochenski, I.:   Ancient Formal Logic. Amsterdam, 1951.

Bochenski, I.:   History of Formal Logic. Notre Dame, 1961.

Boethius: Commentary on Porphyrius. CSEL, 1906.

Bonassieux: Les evangiles synoptiques de St. Hilaire. Lyons, 1906 (cf Julicher in TLZ 1907)

Bonwetsch, (G) N.:   Die Theologie v. Methodius v. Olympus.   Berlin 1903.

Bonwetsch, N.:   Die Theologie des Irenaeus.   Gütersloh, 1925.

Borchardt, C.F.A.:   Hilary of Poitier's role in the Arian Struggle.
The Hague 1966.

Bornocque: Les Declamations et les declamateurs d'apres Seneque le Pere,
Lille, 1902.

Bousset, W.:   Judisch-christlicher Schulbetrieb in Alexandria u. Rom.
FRLANT NF6, Göttingen, 1915.

Brehier, E.:   Etudes de philosophie antique. pp. 97-130.
(From 'Histoire de la philosophie, Paris, 1960)

Brisson, J.:   Hilaire de Poitiers Traite des Mysteres.   SC19 Paris 1947.

Brown, R.:   Parable and allegory reconsidered, Nov. Test. 5, 1962, 36-45.

Brox, N.:   Offenbarung, Gnosis u. Gnostisches Mystos bei Irenaeus v.
Lyon, Salzburg, 1966.

Bruce, A.B.:   The Humiliation of Christ[5]   Edinburgh, 1914.

Buffiere: Les Mythes d'Homere et La pensee grecque.   Paris, 1956.

Bultmann, R.:   Der Stil der Paulinischen Predigt u. die Kynisch-Stoiscen
Diatribe. Göttingen, 1910.

Bultmann, R.:   Ursprung u. Sinn der Typologie als hermeneutischer
Methode TLZ 1950 205f.

Burghardt, W.:   On Early Christian Exegesis, Theol. Studies XI 1950
78-116.

Buttell, M.:   The Rhetoric of St. H. of Poitiers, CUA Patr. Stud. 38
(1933).

Cadiou, R: Dictionnaires antiques dans l'oeuvre d'Origen, Rev. Et. Grec.
XLV.281f.

Chadwick, H.:   Art. Hilaire of Poitiers, in RGG3.

Childs, B.:   Biblical Theology in Crisis.   Philadelphia 1970.

Ciceronis orationum Scholasticae: ed. Stangl.   Leipzig, 1912.

Comeau, M.:   St. Augustin, Exegete du quatrieme Evangile.   Paris 1930.

Cornutus: ed. Lang Teubner, Leipzig, 1881.

Coulange, L.: Metamorphose du consubstantiel, Athanase et Hilaire.
RHLR 8, 1922. 169-214.

D'Ales, A.: La Theologie de St. Cyprien. Paris, 1922.

D'Ales, A.: La Theologie de Hippolyte. Paris 1906.

D'Ales, A.: La Theologie de Tertullian. Paris, 1905.

Danielou, J.: Message evangelique et culture hellenistique.

Den Boer, W.: De Allegoreses in het Werk van Clemens Alexandrinus.
Leiden, 1940.

Didymi Chalcenteri opera: Ed. Diels/Schubart. Berlin, 1904.

Dilthey, W.: Die Entstehung der Hermeneutik. GS V. 1924 317f.

Dobschutz, E. von: Vom vierfachen Schriftsinn. Harnack Ehrung Leipzig,
1921.

Doignon, J.: Hilaire de Poitiers avant l'Exile. Paris, 1971.

Duchrow, U.: Sprachverständnis u. biblisches Hören bei Augustin.
Tubingen, 1965.

Diestel, L.: Geschichte der AT in der Christlichen Kirche, Jena, 1869.

Dudden, F. Holmes: Ambrose I, II. Oxford, 1935.

Ebeling, G.: Evangelische Evangelienauslegung. Munich, 1942.
(Darmstadt, 1962)

Ebeling, G.: Die Anfänge v. Luther's Hermeneutik, ZThK. 1951. 172f.

Elliger, K.: Studien zum Habakuk-Kommentar vom Toten Meer. Tubingen,
1953.

Emmenberger, J.: The Functions of faith and reason in the theology of
St. Hilary of Poitiers. CUA Washington, 1947.

(ed) Etudes Augustiniennes. Hilaire et son Temps. Paris, 1969. Hilaire
de Poitiers 368-   1968.

Engelbrecht, A.: Zur Sprache des H v. Poitiers u. seine Zeitgnossen WS,
1927 135-61.

Epitome,: Art in RAC 5. also Arts. Evangelium, Exegese, Lesungen in
RAC.

Erbse, H.: Beitrage zur Überlieferung der Ilias scholien, Zetemata 24
1960.

Faider, P.:   Repertoire des Editions des scholies et commentaires
                d'auteurs latins, Paris, 1931.

Favre, R.:   La communication des idiomes dans les oeuvres de St. Hilaire
                de Poitiers Gregorianum 17. 1936. 481-514.

Feder, A.:   Studien zu Hilarius v. Poitiers
                    I SBW 164.2 Wien 1910.
                   II SBW 165.5   1911.
                  III SBW 169.5   1912.

Feder, A.:   Epilegomena zu Hil. Pict. I II WS 1919 51-60, 167-81.

Feder, A.:   Kulturgeschichtliches in den Werken des hl. HvP. Stimmen
                aus Maria Laach 81, 1911 30-45.

Fierro, A.:   Sobre la gloria en san Hilario, Anal. Greg. 144. Rome, 1964.

Fischer, B.:   Die Psalmenfrömmigkeit der Martyrkirche, Freiburg, 1949.

Flessemann van Leer, E.:   Scripture and Tradition in the Early Church.
                           Leiden, 1955.

Forster, W.:   Von Valentin zu Heracleon, BZNW 7 Giessen, 1926.

Fonck, L.:   Le parable del signore nel evangelo Roma, 1924[3].

Förster, T.:   Zur Theologie des Hilarius. Th. St. u. Krits. 61. 1888.
                645-686.

Fuhrmann, M.:   Das systematische Lehrbuch, Göttingen, 1960.

Funaioli, E.:   Esegesi virgiliana antica. Milan, 1930.

Galtier, P.:   St. Hilaire de Poitiers. Paris, 1960.

Gariglio, A.:   il commento al salmo 118 in s. Ambroglio e in s. Ilario
                (Atti della accademia delle scienze di Torino C12 90
                (1955156) 56 356-70.)

Gastaldi, N.:   Hilario de Poitiers, exegeta sel Salterio. Paris, 1968.

Geffken, J.:   Die Entstehung u. Wesen des griechischen Kommentars,
                Hermes 67 (1932). 397-412.

Georgi: Die antike Vergilkritik. Philologus. Suppl. 9 212-39.

Giamberdini, G.:   De divinitate verbi doctrina s. Hil. Pict. 1. Cairo,
                   1951.

Goffinet, E.:   Kritisch-filologisch element in de psalmen-commentaar van de h. Hilarius van Poitiers. Rev. Belg. de Pholol. et d hist. 1960 130-44.

Goetz, K.:   Geschichte der Cyprianischen Literatur bis zu der Zeit der ersten erhaltenen Handschriften. Diss Marburg, 1890. Basel 1891.

Goppelt, L.:   Typos, Berlin, 1939.

Gräfenhan, R.:   Geschichte der Klassischen Philologie I-IV. Bonn, 1843ff.

Grant, R.:   Historical criticism in the ancient church, JR 1945, 25.183-97.

Greer, R.:   Captain of our Salvation. Tübingen, 1973.

Griffe, E.:   La Gaule chretiene a l'epoque Romaine I. Paris, 1947.

Grillmeier, A.:   Christ in Christian Tradition. London, 1975[2].

Grabmann, M.:   Die Geschichte der scholastischen Methode. Herder, Freiburg, 1909.

Gronau, K.:   Poseidonius u. die judisch-christliche Genesis-exegese. Berlin, 1914.

Gudeman, A.:   Grundriss der Geschichte der klassischen Philologie, 1907.

Haarhof, T.:   Schools of Gaul. Oxford, 1920.

Hackemann, L.:   Servius and his sources in the commentary on the Georgics. Columbia N.Y., 1940.

Hadot, P.:   Typus: Stoicisme et monarchianisme au IV Siecle. RthAM 18. 1951, 177-87.

Hagendahl, H.:   Methods of citation in post classical prose. Eranos. 45, 1947, 114-28.

Hahn, T.:   Tyconiusstudien, Leipzig, 1911.

Halm, C.:   Rhetorici Latini minores. Lipsiae, 1863.

Hamel, A.:   Kirche bei Hippolytus von Rom. Gütersloh, 1951.

Hanson, R.:   Allegory and Event. London, 1959.

Hanson, R.:   Notes on Tertullian's use of scripture, JTS NS12, 1961, 273-9.

Harl, M.:   Origene. Paris, 1952.

Harnack, A.:   Der kirchengeschichtliche Ertrag des exegetischen Arbeit des Origenes. TU 42, 1919.

Harnack, A.:   Marcion: Das Evangelium vom fremden Gott. Berlin, 1924[2].

Hitchcock, F.:   Irenaeus of Lugdunum. Cambridge, 1914.

Heinisch, P.:   Der Einfluss Philos auf die Aelteste Christliche Exegese. Munster, 1908.

Heinrici, G.:   Die valentinische Gnosis u. die heilige Schrift. Berlin, 1871.

Hermaniuk, M.:   Le parabole evangelique. Louvain, 1947.

Herrera, S.:   Irenee de Lyon Exegete. These. Paris, 1920.

Hoffman, M.:   Der Dialog bei den christlichen schriftstellern der ersten vier Jahrhunderten. Diss, Heidelberg, 1960.

Hoh, J.:   Die Lehre des hl. Irenaeus uber das NT. Munster, 1918.

Holl, A.:   Augustin's Bergpredigtexegese. Herder, Wien, 1960.

Holmes, T.S.:   The Origin and Development of the Christian Church in Gaul during the first Six Centuries of the Christian Era. London, 1911.

Huber, G.:   Das Sein u. das Absolute: Studien zur Geschichte der ontologischen Problematik in der Spätantiken Philosophie. Basel, 1955.

Holte, R.:   'Spermatikos Logos', Studia Theologica 14, 1960.

Hyldahl, N.:   "Hegesippus Hypommenata", Studia Theologica 8 1960 14. 70-113.

Ivanka, E.v.:   Plato Christianus. Einsiedeln, 1964.

Jannssens, Y.:   Heracleon, Commentaire sur l'evangile selon S. Jean, 72(1-2) 1959, 101-157.

Jeanotte, H.:   Le Psaultier de D. Hilaire, Paris, 1917.

Jones, J.:   Allegorical interpretation in Servius. Class. Jour. 56 1961. 217-26.

Jordan, H.:   Geschichte der altchristlichen Literatur. Leipzig, 1911.

Jullian, C.:   Histoire de la Gaule VI VII. Paris, 1926.

Jungmann, J.:   Missarum Sollemnia I. 1949.

Jolles, R.:   Einfache Formen.   Halle, 1956[2].

Jüngel, E.:   Paulus u. Jesus.   Tübingen, 1967[3].

Kannengiesser, C.:   art. Hilaire de Poitiers. Dict de Spir. VII/1. 446f.

Karpp, H.:   Schrift u. Geist bei Tertullian.   Gütersloh, 1958.

Kayser, W.:   Das Sprachliche Kunstwerk.   Bern u. Munchen, 1963.

Kelly, J.N.O.:   Early Christian Doctrines.   London, 1965[3].

Kihn, H.:   Theodore v. Mopsuestia u. Junilius Africanus als Exegeten. 1880.

Kinnavey, R.:   The Vocabulary of St. Hilary of Poitiers.   CUA Patr. Stud. 47 (1935).

Klostermann, E.:   Formen der exegetischen Arbeit des Origenes. ThLZ, Oct, 1947. 203f.

Klostermann, E.:   Zur Überlieferung der Matthaeuserklarung des Origenes. TU47.2, 1931.

Klotz, A.:   Valerius Maximus u. die Exempla, SBAW, 1942.

Kneale, W. and M.:   The Development of Logic.   Oxford, 1962.

Koch, H.:   Cyprianische Untersuchungen AKG 4.   Bonn, 1926.

Koeble, A.:   De Hypomnematis Graecis I II.   Berlin, 1842f.

Koffmann, B.G.:   Geschichte der Kirchenlatein.   Breslau, 1879.

Köppen, K.:   Die Auslegung der Versuchungsgeschichte unter besonderer Rucksichtung der alten Kirche.   Tübingen, 1961.

Keil, H.:   Grammatici Latini V.   Lipsiae, 1857.

Kornhardt, H.:   Exemplum: eime bedeutungsgeschichtliche Studie. Diss. Phil. Gottingen, 1936.

Krause, G.:   Studien zu Luthers Auslegung der klienen Propheten BHT 22 Tübingen, 1962.

Kronasser, H.:   Handbuch der Semasiologie.   Heidelberg, 1952.

v. Kubler,:   ed. Gaius Institutes.   1935[7].

Kutter, H.:   Clemens Alexandrinus u. das NT.   Giessen, 1897.

Labriolle, P. de: St. Ambroise et l'exegese allegorique.Annales de
                    phil. chretienne, IV 5 1908. 591-603.

Lammert, F.:   Bursian's Jahrbuch 251 for 1936 107f, on Latin grammarians.

Lausberg, H.:   Handbuch der literatischen Rhetorik. Munich, 1960.

Leisegang, H.:   Die Gnosis. Stuttgart, 1955.

Lietzmann, H.:   art. Hilarius in PWK VIII. Stuttgart, 1913.

Lindemann, H.:   Des hl. Hilarius v. Poitiers Liber Mysteriorum.
                 Munster, 1905.

Loewenich, W. v.:   Das Johannesverständnis in zweiten Jahrhundert,
                    BZNW 13. Giessen, 1932.

Löffler, P.:   Die Trinitatslehre des Bischofs Hilarius v. Poitiers
               zeischen Ost u. Westen, ev. theol. diss. Bonn, 1959.

Löffler, P.:   Die Trinitatslehre des Bischofs HvP, ZKG 71, 1960. 26-36.

Long, A.G.:   (ed) Problems in Stoicism. London, 1971.

Loofs, F.:   Art Hilarius in PRE³. Leipzig, 1900.

Lorenz, R.:   arts, on Augustine in ZKG 1952, 1956, 1964 and ThR 1959
              1-75.

Lubac, H. de: Exegese Medievale. I. Aubier, Paris, 1959.

Ludwich, A.:   Aristarchs homerische Textkritik. Leipzig, 1884.5.

Lundstrom, S.:   Studien zur lateinischen Irenaeusubersetzungen, Lund,
                 1943.

Lundstrom, S.:   Neue Studien zur Lat. Iren, Ubers. Lunds Universitets
                 Arsskrift NF 44, (1948).

Lundstrom, S.:   ibid, NF 51.91955. Ubersetzungstechnische Untersuchungen
                 auf den Gebiet der Christlichen Latinität.

Lyttkens, H.:   The Analogy between God and the World. Uppsal. Univ.
                Arsskrift 1953.

Maas, F.:   Von der Ursprung der rabbinischen Schriftauslegung. ZThK 52
            (1955) 129-61.

Macrobius: cf. Stahl: Macrobius' commentary on the Dream of Scipio.
             N.Y. 1952.

Maier, J.:   Die Texte vom Toten Meer. Basel, 1960.

Malunowicz, L.:   De Voce sacramenti apud St. Hil. Pict. Lublin, 1956.

Mann, M.:   The clausulae of St. Hilary of Poitiers, CUA Patr. Stud. 48, 1936.

Maries, L.:   Etudes preliminaires a l'etude de Diodore de Tarse sur les psaumes. Paris, 1933.

Marinone, N.:   Elio Donato Macrobio e Servio commentatori di Vergillio. Vercelli, 1946.

Martinez Sierra, A.:   Arian exegesis on St. Hil. In Pss. Miscelanea Comillas 41.293-376 and 42.43-153, 1964.

Mates, B.:   Stoic Logic. University of California Press, Berkeley, 1961^2.

Meijering, E.P.:   Orthodoxy and Platonism in Athanasius, Synthesis or Antithesis? Leiden, 1968.

Meridier, L.:   La seconde sophistique dans l'oeuvre de Gregoire de Nysse. Paris, 1906.

Merlan, P.:   From Platonism to Neoplatonism. The Hague, 1960.

Molland, E.:   The Conception of the Gospel in Alexandrian Theology. Oslo, 1938.

Mondesart, C.:   Essai sur Clement D'Alexandrie. Paris, 1944.

Monnard, C.:   De Gallorum orationum ingenio, rhetoribus et historicis, romanorum tempore. Bonnae, 1848.

Morrica, U.   Storia della Letteratura latina christiana, I-III Torino, 1923-34.

Neoplatonism: Recherches sur la tradition platonicienne, Entretiens sur l'antiquite classique III. Geneve, 1955. (Courcelle, Marrou, Waszink) Fond. Hardt.

Neumann, K.J.:   Hippolytus v. Rom. Teubner. Leipzig, 1902.

Norden, E.:   Die antike Kunstprosa. Teubner. Leipzig, 1898.

Oepke, A.:   Das Neue Gottesvolk. Gütersloh, 1951.

Olympiodori: Philosophi in Platonic Phaidonem commentaria. ed. Norwin. Leipzig, 1913.

Overbeck, F.:   Uber die Anfänge der patristischen Literatur. 1882.

Pannenberg, W.:   Analogie u. Offenbarung, Diss. Habil, Heidelberg, 1958.

Pannenberg, W.: Grundfragen systematischer Theologie. Göttingen. 1968.

Penna, A.: Principi e carattere dell Esegesis di S Gerolamo. Roma, 1950.

Pelikan, J.: Development of Christian Doctrine I. Yale, 1969.

Pepin, J.: Mythe et allegorie. Paris, 1958. (rev. by I. Opelt in JAC 1962 165f).

Pepin, J.: Le challenge Homere/Moise aux premieres Siecles Chretiens. RSR, 1955 29.105-22.

Petre, H.: L'exemplum chez Tertullian. Dijon, 1940.

Peter, H.: Die geschichtliche Literatur uber die romische Kaiserzeit I II, Leipzig, 1897.

Peter, H.: Wahrheit u. Kunst. Geschichtschreibung u. Plagiat im klassischen altertum. Leipzig, 1911.

Pirot, J.: Paraboles et allegories evangeliques. Paris, 1949.

Pollard, T.: The exegesis of scripture and the arian controversy. BJRL 41-2 1959 414-29.

Prigent, P.: Justin et l'ancient Testmant. Paris, 1964.

Probus: apud Hagen, Appendix Serviana, 1902.

Quaquarelli, A.: La retorica antica al bivio. Roma, 1956.

Qillacq, J.: Quomodo lingua latina uaus est St. Hilarius. Paris, 1903.

Redepenning, E.: Origenes I,II. Bonn, 1846.

Reinkens, J.: Hilarius v. Poitiers. Schaffhausen, 1864.

Reuss, E.: History of the Sacred Scriptures of the New Testament. Edinburgh, 1884.

Reuss, J.: Matthaeuskommentare der griechischen Kirche. Berlin, 1959.

Reveillard: Cyprian: L'oraison dominicale. Paris, 1964.

Richard, M.: Asterius. Oslo, 1956.

Roche, J.: Die homerische Textkritik im Altertum, 1866.

Roger, M.: l'enseignement des lettres classiques d'Ausone a Alcuin.

Rosenmüller: Historia interpretationis libr. sacr. Lipsiae, 1807.

Sagnard, F.:   La Gnose valentinienne et la temoignage de Saint Irenee.
Paris, 1947.

Schanz-Hosius: Romische Literaturgeschichte art. Hilarius.
(IV 1.277f) etc.

Schelkle, K.:   Paulus, Lehrer der Väter. Düsseldorf, 1956.

Schelkle, K.:   Wort u. Schrift. Düsseldorf, 1966.

Simon, R.:   Histoire critique du vieux testament. Paris, 1680.

Simon, R.:   Histoire critique des principeaux commentateurs du mouveau
testament. Rotterdam, 1693.

Simonetti, M₀: Note sul commento di Ilario di Poitiers, Vet. Chr. I,
Bari, 1964.

Simonetti, M.:   Ilario e novatiano. Riv. de cult. class. e. med. VIIe.
1905, 1034-47.

Schellauf, F.:   Rationem afferendi locos litterarum divinarum quam in
tractatibus super psalmos sequi videtur St. Hil.
Graz, 1898.

Schneider, H.:   Kultur u. Denken der alten Agypter. Leipzig, 1907.

Schoeps, H.:   Theologie u. Geschichte des Judenchristentums. Mohr,
Tübingen, 1949.

Schrockh, J.M₀: Historia Religionis et Ecclesiae Christianae, (45 vols)
1768-1812.

Schulz, F.:   History of Roman Legal Science. Oxford, 1946.

Schwartz, E₀: Zu Clemens tis he sozomenos ploutos? Hermes 38.1 1903.

Schwartz, E.:   Zwei Predigten Hippolyts. SBAW ph. hist. cl. 1936, 75f.

Seibel, W.:   Fleisch u. Geist bei den hl. Ambrosius. München, 1959.

Siegfried, G.:   Philo v. Alexandrien. Jena, 1875.

Simonetti, M.:   Eracleone e Origene Vet Chr 3 (1966) 3.76.

Smulders, P.:   La doctrine trinitaire de s, H de P₀ Anal. Greg. 32
Rome, 1944.

Soden, H.v.:   Mysterium u. Sacramentum in den ersten Jahrhunderten der
Kirch, BZNW, 12(1911) 1-7.

Souter, A.:   Text and Canon of the New Testament. London, 1913.

Spicq, P.:   L'exegese latine au moyen age. Paris, 1944.

Spanneut, M.:   Le stoicisme des Peres de l'eglise. Lille, 1957.

Stein, E.:   Die allegorische Exegese des Philo von Alexandria BZN 51
                 Giessen, 1929.

Steinthal, H.:   Geschichte der Sprachwissenschaft bei den Griechen u.
                 Romern I,II. Berlin, 1890.

Strauss, G.:   Schriftgebrauch, Schriftauslegung u. Schriftbeweis bei
                 Augustin. Tübingen, 1959.

Schindler, A.:   Wort u. Analogie in Augustin's Trinitatslehre.
                 Tübingen, 1965.

Stroux, J.:   Zum allegorischen Deutung Vergils, Philologus, 86,1931 363f.

Stuhlmacher, P.L.:   Gottes Gerechtigkeit bei Paulus FRIANT 87 1965.

Suringar, W.:   Historia critica scholastorum latinorum. Lugduni
                 Batavorum, 1834.

Süsemihl, F.:   Geschichte der griechischen Literatur in der
                 alexandrinerzeit I II Leipzig, 1891-2.

Steinmann, J.:   S. Jerome. Paris, 1958.

Tate, J.:   On the history of allegorism. Class. Quart. 28(1934) 105-114.

Thomas, R.:   Essai sur Servius. Paris, 1879.

Thyen, H.:   Der Stil der judisch-hellenistischen Homilie. Gottingen, 1955.

Travis, A.:   De Serv. carm. verg. interp. 1940.

Überweg, E. Praechter, Kl: Die Geschichte der Philosophie Die philosophie
                 des Altertums. Berlin, 1909.

Uptrup, K.M. zu: Zur Hermeneutik des Ambrosiaster, Diss. Heidelberg,
                 1950.

Vaccari, A.:   La theoria nella scuola esegetica di anticcha. Biblica, I
                 1920 1.36.

Violard, E.:   Etude sur le commentaire d'Hippolyte sur le livre de
                 Daniel. Paris, 1903.

Vischer, L.:   Basilius der Grosse. Basel, 1953.

Völker, C.:   Quellen zur Geschichte des christlichen Gnosis. Tübingen,
                 1932.

212

Volkmann, R.:   Die Rhetorik der Greichen u. Romer. Berlin, 1872.

Watson, E.:   St. Hilary of Poitiers, Select Works ANF IX Oxford, 1899.

Wehrli, F.:   Zur Geschichte der allegorischen Deutung Homers in Altertum.
Leipzig, 1928.

Weinstock, S.:   Die platonischen Homerkritik Philologus, 82. 1927 121f.

Welter, J.:   L'exemplum dans la litt. religieuse et didactique du moyen
age. Paris, 1927.

Wendland, P.:   Die hellenistische Kultur in ihren Beziehungen zu
Judentum u. Christentum. Tübingen, 1912.

Werbeck, W.:   Jacobus Perez von Valencia: Untersuchungen zu seinem
Psalmenkommentar. BHTh. Tübingen,1969.

Werkner, J.:   Der Paulinismus des Irenaeus TU6.2.

Wieacker, F.:   Textstufen klassischer Juristen. Göttingen, 1960.

Wiles, M.:   The Making of Christian Doctrine. Cambridge, 1967.

Wille, W.:   Studium zum Matthauskommentar des Hilarius von Poitiers.
Diss. Hamburg, 1969.

Wilmart, A.:   L'Odysee du MS de s. Pietro qui referme les oeuvres de s.
Hil. Festschr. for E.K. Rand 293-305.

Windisch,H.:   Das Evangelium des Basileides ZNW 7(1906) 236-46.

Winter, K.:   Bibliographie zur antiken Bildersprache. Heidelberg, 1964.

Wlosok, A.:   Laktanz u. die philosophische Gnosis. Heidelberg, 1960.

Wohlenberg,:   Ein alter lateinischer Kommentar uber die vier Evangelien.
Festschr. fur Th. Zahn. 1909.

Wolf, E.:   Augustin u. das lateinische Neuplatonismus. Theol. Blätter 12
(1933) 300-8.

Wunderer, C.:   Polybiusforschung. Teubner, Leipzig, 1909.

Zeller, E.:   Stoics, Epicureans and Sceptics. London, 1892.3

Zimmermann, G.:   Die hermeneutischen Prinzipien Tertullians Diss. phil.
Leipzig, 1937.

Zingerle, A.:   Griech-Lat Worterklärung aus dem Hilarianischen Pskomm.
(Commentationes Wolfflinianae. 213-8)

Zingerle, A.:   Textual studies in WS 1889 314-23, and in Kleine Phil.
Abhandl. Innsbruck I 1871, ii 1877, iii 1882 iv 1887
75-89 (Die lateinischen Bibelcitate bei St. Hil. Pict.)

Zuntz, G.:   Die Aristophanes Scholien der Papyri:
Byzantion 13 (1938) 631-90.
Byzantion 14 (1939) 545-652.

Select Index